National Institute of Economic and Social Research
Policy Studies Institute
Royal Institute of International Affairs

Joint Studies in Public Policy 11

THE FUTURE OF
BRITISH DEFENCE POLICY

National Institute of Economic and Social Research
Policy Studies Institute
Royal Institute of International Affairs

Joint Studies in Public Policy

STEERING COMMITTEE

National Institute of Economic and Social Research
Policy Studies Institute
Royal Institute of International Affairs

Joint Studies in Public Policy 11

THE FUTURE OF
BRITISH DEFENCE POLICY

Edited by
JOHN ROPER

Gower

Published by
Gower Publishing Company Limited,
Gower House,
Croft Road,
Aldershot,
Hants GU11 3HR,
England

and

Gower Publishing Company,
Old Post Road,
Brookfield,
Vermont 05036,
U.S.A.

Acknowledgement
The Steering Committee gratefully acknowledges the support of the Economic and Social Research Council which financed the conference and the research and editorial work involved in the preparation of this book.

British Library Cataloguing in Publication Data

The Future of British defence policy. — (Joint studies in public policy; 11)
    1. Great Britain — Military policy
    I. Roper, John   II. Series
    355'.033541   UA647

ISBN 0 566 00922 6

Printed in Great Britain at the University Press, Cambridge

Contents

Contributors and Participants

General Sir Hugh Beach, St George's House, Windsor Castle
Ken Booth, Department of International Politics, University College of Wales
Malcolm Chalmers, School of Peace Studies, University of Bradford
Michael Clarke, Department of Politics, University of Newcastle (Brookings Institution)
Keith Hartley, Institute for Research in the Social Sciences, University of York
Brigadier Kenneth Hunt, Visiting Professor, University of Surrey
Farooq Hussain, Director of Studies, Royal United Services Institute
M.A.S. Joyce, National Institute of Economic and Social Research
D.L.I. Kirkpatrick, Ministry of Defence (Procurement Executive)
Robbin Laird, Center for Naval Analysis, Virginia, USA
Malcolm Levitt, National Institute of Economic and Social Research
Sir Leo Pliatzky, HM Treasury, 1950-77
John Roper, Editor, *International Affairs*, Royal Institute of International Affairs
R.P. Smith, Department of Economics, Birkbeck College, University of London
William Wallace, Director of Studies, Royal Institute of International Affairs
Phil Williams, Research Fellow, Royal Institute of International Affairs

Other Participants

Sir John Aiken	David Nicholls
Colonel Jonathan Alford	J.R. Sargent
Bridget Bloom	Graham Sharp
Admiral Sir James Eberle (chair)	J.M. Stewart
Professor Lawrence Freedman	Peter Stratmann
Pierre Lellouche	John Weston
Roger Morgan	Ivan Wilson
Pauline Neville-Jones	

Foreword
James Eberle

The papers in this volume were prepared for one of the series of conferences on Joint Studies in Public Policy sponsored by the National Institute of Economic and Social Research, the Policy Studies Institute and the Royal Institute of International Affairs. The papers formed the basis for a conference which was held in Chatham House from 12 to 13 December 1984 under my chairmanship. The comments which appear at the end of most chapters are those of participants in the conference who had been asked to introduce discussions on particular papers. All the papers and comments, which were circulated in advance to the participants, have been revised in the light of the conference exchanges and appear together with an introduction and final report of the proceedings.

The theme of the conference is one of increasing interest and importance in Britain. Our discussion was aimed at examining possible alternative strategies to meet Britain's security needs. We examined alternatives against the background of the national political debate, of our relationship with allies in both North America and Western Europe, and of the likely future economic climate. We did not expect to reach new, specific and agreed solutions to the policy and resource dilemmas which face defence planners. Indeed, our discussion again and again highlighted the practical constraints which are imposed upon any significant change in British defence policy by the realities of international political relationships. However, I believe that the opportunity for free, uninhibited and informed discussion within a group of participants of widely different backgrounds was a valuable experience for all who took part. We hope that others, by reading this publication, will be able to share in that experience and so contribute more to the continuing debate.

I should like, on behalf of the three Institutes concerned, to thank the Economic and Social Research Council for providing resources to support the series of JSPP Conferences.

1 Introduction
John Roper

There was little debate over defence policy in Britain in the 1970s. That has certainly not been the case in the first half of the 1980s, during which defence has played a major part in the General Election of 1983, and it is unlikely to be the case for the remainder of the decade. The substantial policy differences between the political parties on defence issues and the budgetary constraints which lie ahead both suggest a continuing active debate on defence.

There are four factors that combine to make the present a particularly apposite moment for a new study on the future of defence policy. First, the broad consensus on defence issues which existed between the political parties in the postwar period has clearly ended. The Labour Party's policies on defence would, if introduced, mean a radical change not only in Britain's own defence policy but also in the relations with its allies, especially with the United States. Second, the Conservative government has made it clear that the period of rapidly increasing resources for defence is coming to an end and that after the current financial year there will be no further increase in resources for defence. Third, the reawakening of interest in European Defence Cooperation suggests that we may be seeing a change in the relative importance for the United Kingdom of its relations with the United States and with its European allies. Finally, there is at present within NATO a wider examination of the 'conceptual military framework' for the next twenty years; questions of the relative roles of conventional and nuclear weapons are thus under renewed consideration.

As will be seen from the papers in this book, the defence debate takes place in a variety of frameworks. This derives from the nature of British defence policy, and the varying assumptions about what can be changed. For over thirty-five years, the main focus of British defence policy has been Britain's membership of the North Atlantic Alliance. Many of the current proposals for changes in British defence policy are thus in effect proposals that Britain should attempt to persuade its NATO allies to change collective policies. Short of leaving NATO, which is advocated in Britain by virtually no one, changes to NATO policies take place by agreement among all its members, and this will

1

inevitably take time. However, as was pointed out in the conference discussion, there are now parallel debates on defence policy, particularly on its nuclear component, taking place in many of NATO's member nations.

There are certain aspects of British defence policy which are primarily of national significance, although, when they consume resources which might otherwise be available for NATO missions, the distinction is not complete. These are in particular Britain's strategic nuclear forces and its capability for military activities outside the NATO area. It might appear that decisions on these could take place on a purely national basis, but it became clear during the conference that they would also provoke varying reactions from Britain's allies.

The first two papers, by Phil Williams and Ken Booth, together with the comments by Malcolm Chalmers, Hugh Beach and Ken Hunt, set out the structure of the British debate. Phil Williams outlines the case for continuing with the existing strategy and shows that it represents a set of insurance policies, against various eventualities, which contain both Alliance and national components. He also suggests that the effectiveness of British defence expenditure must be judged not only in terms of deterring potential adversaries but also in terms of persuading the United States that Europeans are making an adequate contribution to their own defence. Ken Booth and Malcolm Chalmers, in challenging the basis of current defence policy and suggesting changes, do so against the background of their lack of belief in the robustness of nuclear deterrence. Ken Booth argues that if there is a risk of failure of nuclear deterrence, one should move to a position of enhanced conventional deterrence which would permit the adoption of a strategy of 'no first use' of nuclear weapons.

Ken Hunt and Hugh Beach both challenge this approach and suggest that even if one could persuade the rest of NATO to move to a 'no first use' strategy on the Central Front in Europe, it would be very difficult to find either the finance for new equipment or the manpower that would enable the Alliance to rely on a purely conventional defence. New technological developments can improve the effectiveness of non-nuclear defence, but even if resources for them can be found, they will take a considerable time to install. Ken Hunt, towards the end of his comment, points to the potential conflict in the struggle for limited resources between the plans to replace Britain's strategic nuclear force with submarines capable of deploying the Trident II missile and the maintenance of effective British conventional contributions to NATO. If the opportunity cost of Trident becomes too great in terms of the loss of effectiveness of Britain's conventional forces, then other options for maintaining a nuclear capability must be examined again.

The second group of papers, by Mike Clarke and William Wallace, and the comment by Robbin Laird, place the British debate and proposals for change in British defence policy into the context of our relations with our principal allies. Britain, the conference was told, has been very successful in making sure that people in Washington do not think of a separate British defence policy. In the same way Pierre Lellouche expressed the view that no one in Europe pays much attention to British defence policy, because everyone takes its continuity for granted. It was clear that this will not necessarily continue to be the case. Mike Clarke, in discussing American attitudes, shows the difficulty a Labour government would have in presenting its non-nuclear defence policy to Washington. A reluctance to share the risks of nuclear deterrence would be seen as a form of 'creeping neutralism'.

On the other hand, financial burden-sharing could prove a more immediate issue with the present government's decision to abandon the NATO commitment to 3 per cent annual growth in defence expenditure after 1985/6. Congress is still very unhappy with what it perceives as the failure of the Europeans to contribute adequately to their own defence. Britain has been able to claim until now that it has lived up to the NATO goals, but in future it will be listed by Congress as one of those that is failing to meet the target. Britain has already received insufficient credit for the seven fat years of 1978/9 to 1985/6, when it increased the resources available for defence by 25 per cent in real terms and expenditure on equipment increased by almost 50 per cent, and it is now liable to be criticized for its failure to maintain this remarkable rate of growth.

William Wallace in his paper looks at defence as one component in Britain's relations with its European allies. In this respect, there are important links between defence policy and industrial policy. A decision by a British government not to participate in the joint project for a Future European Combat Aircraft would be seen by many of our European partners as being as harmful as a decision not to proceed with the Trident programme. West European allies of Britain would also be concerned if radical changes in British policy were to have an impact on transatlantic security relationships. An attempt by a Labour government to remove American nuclear bases would have very considerable spill-over effects. In the view of Pierre Lellouche, it would push France back to a purely national defence policy and it would create a precedent for pressures to remove American nuclear bases from other European countries.

There are a whole range of opinions in European countries on the British decision to maintain its strategic nuclear forces as a top priority by going ahead with the Trident programme. William Wallace in his paper suggests that, outside France, Britain's European partners would be concerned if that were to lead to cuts in other parts of Britain's defence programme. France, on the other hand, would be very seriously affected by a decision to cancel Trident, which would leave it as the only West European country with its own strategic nuclear capability.

The third group of papers moves the focus of discussion away from the world of international politics and strategy to that of political economy: the economic pressures on resources for defence and the most efficient means of using those resources. Malcolm Levitt and Michael Joyce, Ron Smith and Keith Hartley in their papers, and Leo Pliatzky, David Kirkpatrick and Farooq Hussain in their comments, show that defence policy from the bottom up is the outcome of a vast number of individual decisions involving a range of national considerations relating to domestic politics.

Malcolm Levitt and Michael Joyce document the growth in defence expenditure and the prospects for its future growth in the light of government statements. If the government keeps to its objective of preventing any further growth in public spending as a whole, it is difficult to see how the share going to defence can be allowed to rise any further, given its existing size and the competing claims of other programmes. In a period when there is unlikely to be any further increase in inputs, they suggest it is necessary to examine what more can be done to improve the efficiency with which the inputs are used. As Leo Pliatzky points out in his comment, resources in real terms may not be maintained at the present level if inflation runs ahead of the government's forecast.

Against the background of such a rigorous restriction on the resources available for defence, Ron Smith's paper examines the various proposals that have been made to reduce costs, including less complex weapons, more competition in defence procurement, international collaboration and improved productivity. While all of these have advantages, their full benefit could only be obtained if the Ministry of Defence were prepared to sacrifice some of the various objectives which at present they are trying to achieve simultaneously. As Leo Pliatzky told the conference, government, in defence policy as elsewhere, is about the management of dilemmas. There is no single overriding objective and, as David Kirkpatrick points out in his comment, the existence of multiple goals, including maintaining employment in defence industries and a productive capacity in high-technology defence industries, makes it more difficult to arrive at low-cost solutions. David Kirkpatrick goes on to suggest that there are a series of vicious circles: more use of advanced technology leads to rising unit costs, which lead to shorter production runs and less opportunity for economies of scale, which in turn put greater pressure on defence costs.

In the final paper, Keith Hartley considers the implications for Britain of a shift in NATO towards a more integrated policy for defence procurement. Drawing primarily on examples from the aircraft industry, he argues that Britain pays a significant premium for maintaining a domestic industry. There may be good political reasons for choosing weapon systems made in Britain, but there should be more accurate assessments of the additional costs that this involves. The present government is committed to increasing competition in defence procurement, but it is not clear how far this applies to international competition. Farooq Hussain in his comment looks particularly at the problems of international collaboration in the area of research and development. The precedents for collaboration within NATO are not altogether happy, and the addition of an international level of decision-making to the highly complex national decision-making process will not in itself solve the problem.

It is clear that the dilemmas facing Britain in its decisions relating to defence economics are as difficult as those in the world of international relations and strategy. The papers in this volume do not claim to provide the answers to any of them, but it is hoped that their presentation here will clarify and assist the future debate.

Part I Options and Reactions

2 Meeting Alliance and National Needs
Phil Williams

Critics of British defence policy enjoy a relatively easy target. The policy has evolved through a series of incremental and disjointed changes in which considerations of status have often seemed to loom as large as the question of security itself. Furthermore, the opportunity costs of high defence spending appear particularly onerous in the light of the intangible nature of the benefits and the very real sacrifices that have to be made in other areas of public expenditure such as health, education and welfare. Devoting fewer resources to defence would make it possible to develop a more caring, healthier and better-educated society.

The allocation of resources within defence is also open to criticism. For some commentators, the main target is Britain's strategic nuclear capability; for others, it is the naval forces; for yet a third group of critics, it is the deployment of British forces in the Federal Republic of Germany as a symbol of the continental commitment. As well as demands for limited, albeit significant, changes within the existing force structure, there are also calls for more fundamental reappraisals. Even within the unilateral nuclear disarmament movement, the range of criticism extends from those who are concerned primarily with the moral implications of the possession and possible use of nuclear weapons to those whose opposition is not to strategic nuclear forces as such, but to the acquisition of the Trident system with its unprecedented cost and a capability vastly superior to that of Polaris. This particular debate has been sharpened considerably by the broader controversy in Europe and the United States over NATO strategy. The arguments for 'no first use' of nuclear weapons, as well as the more modest demands that the Alliance move towards 'delayed first use', have entered into the British debate and strengthened the position of those critics who see the Trident decision as a diversion of funds away from conventional forces.

Against all this, it can be argued that current British defence policy represents, as much by accident as by design, a series of hedges against a variety of political and military contingencies, both in Europe and elsewhere. The policy can be understood as a prudent compromise between immediate preoccupations and challenges to British security which might arise in the medium or long term. It also strikes an appropriate balance between national considerations and Alliance concerns and is therefore a sustained and impressive attempt to manage a continuing dilemma. As Peter Nailor has argued, the best mix of defence capabilities from a purely national standpoint may not be particularly helpful in contributing to a best mix for the Alliance as a whole, whereas the alternative of restricting British defence policy to a role within overall Alliance strategy could leave defence forces which, from a national point of view, are unbalanced.[1] This dilemma is made more acute by the continuing uncertainty over the future of the Atlantic Alliance and the American commitment to the security of Western Europe. The 1980s have been a period of considerable turmoil in European–American relations, and the disagreements over the nature of the Soviet threat and how it can best be managed seem likely to continue in the future. In these circumstances, Britain's dual policy of being a good ally, while providing capabilities which would contribute significantly to British security in the absence of the Alliance framework, seems the best way of coping with the perennial problem of balancing Alliance needs against purely national requirements. It is also a sensible precaution: the familiar, relatively stable, and even rather comfortable framework within which British defence policy has been formulated since the creation of the Atlantic Alliance can no longer be taken for granted. Consequently, a policy which contributes explicitly to the maintenance of that framework while planning implicitly for its demise has much to recommend it. Yet it is also a policy which is difficult to justify in public; and an official rationale in these terms would perhaps help to create the very contingency that the more immediate part of the policy is designed to prevent.

The implications of this are twofold. First, British defence policy would seem to have a degree of subtlety that is not always fully appreciated by critics who demand fundamental changes in either posture or provision. We might have arrived where we are for many of the wrong reasons, but the current position has a powerful rationale. Second, major changes would seriously disrupt the delicate compromises and balances contained within the existing posture. Indeed, further increases in defence expenditure may be necessary beyond 1986, if the major roles and missions which the United Kingdom currently undertakes are to be maintained in the future. These roles and missions are indispensable elements in a prudent approach that is designed to forestall or contain a variety of contingencies which would otherwise seriously jeopardize British security.

It is not sufficient, however, simply to extol the advantages of current defence policy in these rather general terms. The case for the policy adopted by the Conservative government and its predecessors has to withstand more detailed scrutiny and more specific criticisms. The latter fall into three broad categories. The first concerns the overall level of resources allocated to defence; the second challenges the desirability of modernizing the strategic deterrent force; and the third revolves around the most appropriate priorities for spending in conventional capabilities. Each of these issues must now be examined.

How much is enough?

One of the criticisms that is often levelled at the Thatcher government is that it devotes an inordinate share of public expenditure to defence. Since Mrs Thatcher's arrival in office, defence spending has increased at a faster rate than expenditure on either the National Health Service or education. She has thereby halted and indeed reversed what had appeared to be a secular trend since the mid-1950s towards the relative downgrading of external security concerns in favour of domestic well-being. What makes this even more unpalatable to many of the critics is that on several indicators of comparative burden-sharing the British effort exceeds that of its European allies. In terms of percentage of GNP devoted to defence, as well as GNP per capita spent on defence, Britain is doing more than either France or the Federal Republic of Germany. Indeed, the UK's record in meeting the target, agreed upon in 1977, of a 3 per cent per annum real increase in defence budgets is better than that of most of the European allies.

This level of effort is sometimes criticized as symptomatic of Britain's obsession with status rather than security. Such accusations, however, are particularly ill-founded. British efforts to meet the agreed Alliance goals represent a realistic understanding of the nature of the American commitment to European security and the conditions which need to be met if that commitment is to be maintained. Being a good ally, bearing a fair share of the burden and living up to the 3 per cent pledge, all help to demonstrate to the United States that at least some of the European allies are serious about their own defence. To dismiss this as a symbolic rather than a substantive matter is to overlook the point that symbols are critically important in the American debate about European security. The failure of many other allies to live up to the 3 per cent pledge has provoked considerable frustration and discontent in the United States Congress, sentiments that in June 1984 led Senator Nunn, a strong supporter of NATO, to introduce legislation mandating American troop withdrawals from Europe unless the allies meet the 3 per cent goal or take other measures to improve the prospects for sustained conventional defence. Although the amendment was defeated, a compromise measure introduced by Senator Cohen, and passed overwhelmingly, means that the allies' performance in meeting force and expenditure goals will be subjected to increasingly close scrutiny.

Despite the improvements in infrastructure and ammunition stocks announced by NATO in December 1984, the burden-sharing issue seems likely to loom even larger in Alliance relations during the next two or three years. It has emerged against a background in which the focus of American policy seems to be moving away from Europe to other areas, a trend symbolized by the growth of US trade in the Pacific region and the security preoccupation with Central America. Concern about the Persian Gulf has introduced yet another dimension to America's global commitments.[2] In one sense, of course, there is nothing new about all this. The US has always been a Pacific as well as an Atlantic power. Nevertheless, there could well be a widening gap between America's commitments and its ability to meet them. In these circumstances, it is more important than ever that the Europeans are perceived as bearing a fair share of the burden, not least because this makes it easier for the advocates of the *status quo* to defend the deployment of 350,000 American personnel in Europe against those who believe that the United States should rely less on forward deployments of ground forces and much more on the flexibility offered by maritime supremacy. The willingness of the British government to make the necessary sacrifices may reflect a more acute awareness in the UK than elsewhere in Europe that the American commitment of ground troops at existing levels can no longer be taken for granted. There is an attempt underway to change the emphasis in the burden-sharing debate from budgetary inputs to military outputs. Yet such a change will not take place immediately. The 3 per cent acts as both target and litmus test, and has a simplicity which makes it attractive to many congressmen. In this connection, it is as well that the British government has agreed to maintain the 3 per cent increase until March 1986 and somewhat unfortunate that the commitment is not being extended beyond this date.

Although such arguments might appeal to committed Atlanticists, some critics of the government's defence policy find the close links with the United States not so much a source of security as a source of danger and insecurity. Europe is seen as a potential battleground for the superpowers, a fate which is best avoided through disengagement from what is essentially a Soviet–American conflict. This kind of argument, though, has two fundamental flaws. The first is that Europe is unable to disengage from at least one of the superpowers. As Lawrence Freedman has argued, the Soviet Union is a European power by virtue of geography, the United States only by invitation.[3]

Any disengagement, therefore, would be asymmetrical, and would leave the West Europeans facing the preponderant power of the Soviet Union. It is not necessary to believe that Moscow is particularly malevolent or aggressive to foresee potential dangers and instabilities in such an outcome. The second flaw is that laying many of the problems of peace and security in Europe at the door of the United States is profoundly ahistorical. The American commitment to Western Europe has helped to impose a degree of stability on the Continent that had previously been lacking. As Joseph Joffe has argued, 'By protecting Western Europe against others, the United States also protected the half-continent against itself. And by paving the way from international anarchy to security community, the United States not only defused ancient rivalries, but also built the indispensable foundation for future cooperation'.[4] In the absence of the United States, however, such cooperation might prove difficult to sustain. As Joffe once again has argued, the withdrawal of the US security commitment to Western Europe might leave the Federal Republic of Germany in a situation in which it sees no alternative other than the acquisition of nuclear weapons. Yet moves in this direction would frighten not only the Soviet Union but also France, and could well spark off a resurgence of historical rivalries.[5]

All this might seem far removed from the question of 'how much is enough?', but it is in fact closely related. The size of Britain's defence effort has at least as much to do with keeping the Americans in as it has with keeping the Russians out. Being a good ally has always been important for the UK, and is arguably becoming even more so, since the United States appears to be undertaking a gradual, but nonetheless very serious, reappraisal of its commitment to Western Europe. Therefore, scaling down the British defence effort so that it is on a par with the European allies would be a move in the wrong direction. It would be much more helpful if the allies tried to emulate the United Kingdom.

This kind of argument will satisfy neither those who feel that military effort has to be a direct function of the threat posed by the adversary, nor those critics who see defence spending as a wasteful diversion of resources away from domestic social welfare objectives. Yet it provides a pragmatic approach which recognizes not only the advantages of the existing security framework in Europe, but also the dangers and the financial costs of possible alternatives. Indeed, without American support, the Europeans would either have to spend much more on defence or accept a high degree of political subservience to the Soviet Union. In these circumstances, the current level of effort by Britain might appear grossly inadequate rather than unnecessarily extravagant.

In addition to those critics who believe that Britain is spending a disproportionate amount of its national wealth on defence, there are others who feel that defence has the right priority overall, but that the priorities within defence are awry. The main target here is the strategic modernization programme, which has united radical opponents of nuclear weapons with more pragmatic critics who are worried either about the opportunity costs of Trident or about its implications for arms control. The validity of their criticisms must now be examined.

Trident: wasteful luxury or security imperative?
The case for Trident divides into two parts. The first attempts to answer the question, 'Why does Britain need a strategic nuclear deterrent?'; the second concerns the advantages of the Trident system over possible alternatives.

The rationale for a British contribution to strategic nuclear deterrence rests upon what might be described as a mealy-mouthed Gaullism. The French have always been explicit about their unwillingness to rely on a security guarantee which requires the United States to commit suicide on behalf of its European allies in the event of Soviet aggression. Britain, in contrast, claims to have no doubt about the reliability of the United States and its willingness to 'help defend the integrity of its European allies by whatever means are necessary, without exception'.[6] Problems arise, however, because:

deterrence is a matter of perception, and perception by a potential adversary. The central consideration is what that adversary may believe, not what we or our allies believe; our deterrence has to influence possible calculations made by leaders whose attitudes and values may differ sharply from those of the West. The decision to use United States nuclear weapons in defence of Europe, with all the risk to the United States homeland this would entail, would be enormously grave. A Soviet leadership – perhaps much changed in character from today's, perhaps also operating amid the pressures of turbulent internal or external circumstances – might believe that it could impose its will on Europe by military force without becoming involved in strategic nuclear war with the United States. Modernized US nuclear forces in Europe help guard against any such misconception; but an independent capability fully under European control provides a key element of insurance.[7]

Underlying this somewhat bland and circumspect rationale for a second centre of decision-making, there is once again a clear understanding of the limits of the American commitment. That the United States, in present circumstances, is fully committed to the security of Europe is not in doubt. Nevertheless, there are inevitable doubts about what actions Washington would be prepared to take on Europe's behalf in the event of Soviet aggression. The superpowers, after all, would have a common interest in limiting hostilities, both geographically and in terms of the weapons used. Whether they would actually be able to keep the war non-nuclear and retain sanctuary status for their homelands is debatable; that they would have considerable incentive to do so is undeniable. The 'no first use' argument is an explicit manifestation of the aspiration of some Americans to ensure that a war fought for Europe is also fought exclusively *in* Europe. In these circumstances both British and French strategic nuclear forces are an important complicating factor. They increase the potential for escalation and make Soviet estimates of risk and benefit even more ambiguous. In some respects the British system may be even more significant than the French, because it is indistinguishable from American SLBMs.

It might be objected that this is simply a vague and diluted form of the old trigger argument, and that it is inconceivable to expect the United Kingdom to use its strategic nuclear capabilities unilaterally when the United States is witholding its own strategic arsenal. Such an argument cannot easily be dismissed. Certainly the constraints on the United Kingdom would be very considerable. Yet the very existence of Britain's strategic nuclear forces means that the adversary cannot rule out such a contingency, or the drastic consequences which might flow from it. As Thomas Schelling pointed out some years ago, and as Robert Jervis has recently reiterated, deterrence often rests upon threats that leave something to chance.[8] Imprecision may be a strategic and political asset rather than a doctrinal weakness. Although many analysts make confident predictions about the course of a future war in Europe, such confidence is spurious. The pace, scope, intensity and duration of hostilities can only be guessed at. Britain's strategic nuclear forces make the estimates even more complex and simultaneously underline for the adversary the costs of miscalculation.

If part of the rationale for a British contribution to NATO's nuclear deterrent stems from apprehension that America's commitment to Europe might be implemented in ways which lead to decoupling, there are also anxieties that, in the long term, Western Europe might be altogether abandoned by Washington. Prudence therefore demands that there be some indigenous nuclear capabilities in Western Europe. This is not to claim that the British and French strategic forces would provide the kernel of a European nuclear deterrent, or anything similarly ambitious. It is simply to suggest that separate national nuclear deterrent forces in Western Europe would make a particularly important contribution to European security in the absence of the US nuclear guarantee. In other words, although Britain's defence efforts are devoted in large part to ensuring the perpetuation of the US commitment, its nuclear policy is based partly on the premise that this may not succeed indefinitely. As already suggested, there are a number of trends in the United States which, at the very least, imply that Europe will be a less important element in America's security policy than it has been hitherto. There is something rather ironic, though, in the fact that Britain depends on Washington for the modernization of a strategic nuclear force whose underlying rationale is that Washington, in conditions of extremity and in the long term, is unlikely to prove wholly reliable as an ally.

In spite of this irony, the decision to opt for Trident has much to recommend it. Although the Trident system is sometimes described as a Rolls-Royce response to a problem that requires a Cortina, the analogy is both inappropriate and misleading. If Trident is to be compared to a motor vehicle, then perhaps the best comparison is with a Land-Rover, which has the virtues of durability, resilience and an ability to cope with rough terrain. Trident is a highly sophisticated system, but it will have to operate in a highly sophisticated environment in which defensive systems may well be much more effective than they are at present. As the Open Government Document on the acquisition of Trident noted, the replacement for Polaris will have to operate:

well into the second decade of the next century. To give high probability of this we need . . . a system which represents a big enough advance in capability to provide some margin to meet the greater operational demands which continuing efforts on the Soviet side must be expected to impose. Re-equipment providing only a small advance in capability could before long prove a false economy, and our experience with Chevaline . . . shows that mid-life improvement can be a heavy task.[9]

As well as these general considerations which argued in favour of Trident, the case was strengthened by the shortcomings of the various alternatives. Land-based missiles, for example, have a high degree of vulnerability, especially in a relatively small geographical area like the UK. Similarly, air-launched cruise missiles, which have advantages of flexibility and ease of command and control, would need to be more or less permanently airborne in order to attain anything like the degree of invulnerability associated with submarines. When past experience with Polaris was added to the assessment, the case for submarines as the launch platforms was overwhelming. Even so, there was still the option of equipping them with cruise, rather than ballistic missiles. This was rejected for several reasons. Cruise missiles were deemed to be potentially more vulnerable to Soviet defences than their ballistic counterparts. They also suffered from a shorter range and a longer firing-time (which would make the submarines vulnerable to counter-battery fire from land-based ballistic missiles).[10] The idea of modifying the hunter-killer submarines to enable them to launch cruise missiles through the torpedo tubes was also rejected, partly because it would impose on these submarines a second role which was incompatible with the existing operational tasks. As one government document put it, 'to hold back our SSN force for a strategic role would effectively make it impossible for it to fulfil its crucially important ASW function'.[11] Furthermore, because each cruise missile only carries one warhead, there would also be a requirement for a larger number of missiles and submarines than contemplated in the choice of Trident.

What made the Trident acquisition even more controversial was the decision to upgrade the missile from the C4 to the D5. The latter offered such improvements in accuracy, range and the number of warheads, that the government was forced to declare that the D5 would not endow the United Kingdom with a first-strike capability. Indeed, the main reason for choosing the D5 was that the United States had decided to phase out the C4 missiles through the 1990s in favour of the D5. It was therefore clearly the preferred option for the United Kingdom. As a government statement on the Trident programme explained, the D5 offered 'greater commonality with the United States' system through its projected service life. This would give us continued assurance of weapon system reliability without the large investment programme which would be required to provide an equivalent degree of assurance with a weapon system unique to the United Kingdom'.[12] In short, the Trident D5 was deemed the most reliable and cost-effective way of modernizing Britain's strategic nuclear capability.

Yet the decision has still been subjected to intense criticism, partly because of the increased cost involved, but also because of the increased potential capability in terms of warhead numbers. There is something rather ironic about the latter argument. In the past, critics of the Polaris force claimed that it was too small to be a significant addition to the formidable capabilities deployed by the United States. Trident is now under attack because it will overcome the limitations of the UK's current strategic nuclear force and add significantly to the overall strategic capability of the Western Alliance.

The more serious version of this argument, however, is that the acquisition of Trident (as well as the French strategic modernization) will end the 'period of West European strategic irrelevancy' and unnecessarily, but fatally, complicate the task of arms control in Europe.[13] The Soviet desire for 'equal security' with the United States and its nuclear allies already conflicts with the American insistence – stemming from the Jackson Amendment to SALT I – on equal ceilings between the two superpowers. The difficulties this poses may become more acute. Consequently, it is essential to include British and French forces in arms control negotiations before the modernization takes place. Such arguments, however, not only place too high a value on arms control, but implicitly assume that it is primarily France and Britain who will sabotage the prospects for agreement between the superpowers. The history of negotiations since the Carter administration deferred the ratification of SALT II suggests otherwise. Furthermore, despite the euphoria generated by the Shultz-Gromyko meeting in January 1985 and the decisions of the superpowers to resume negotiations, there are few grounds for optimism about the talks. Technological developments have blurred the traditional categorizations which facilitated arms control in the early 1970s, while the sheer complexities of the issues involved can hardly be overestimated. Asymmetries in the force structures of the two superpowers, the difficulty of finding acceptable trade-offs between strategic and intermediate or offensive and defensive systems, and the traditional stumbling block of verification do not augur well for the negotiations. When set against such formidable difficulties, the additional problems that might result from the modernization of British and French strategic nuclear forces appear less significant. It is not necessary to agree with the critique of arms control offered by conservative American analysts to see dangers in allowing arms control to inhibit programmes which, on other criteria, are deemed essential. This is not to argue that the British government should be oblivious to the arms control implications of its policies, or that it does not need to develop more positive and imaginative arms control proposals to accompany its defence efforts. It is simply to recognize that this is a lower priority than the modernization programme, which is essential if British security is to be guaranteed in the face of growing uncertainty about the future of the Atlantic Alliance.

The other main objection to the Trident programme comes from those who are concerned about the opportunity costs, and in particular the implications of the Trident programme for Britain's contribution to NATO's conventional forces. These critics include those whose opposition to Trident is based on anxieties about its cost-effectiveness when compared with possible alternatives, as well as those who believe that the United Kingdom should completely opt out of the strategic nuclear business. The first group consists of pragmatic critics opposed to Trident but willing to sanction cheaper nuclear alternatives; the second propounds what Ken Booth has described as a 'hard unilateralism'.[14] Such unilateralism is based not on emotional or moral distaste for nuclear weapons, but on a belief that such weapons can have no rational purpose. Where both sets of critics agree is in the contention that NATO must reduce its reliance on the threatened use of nuclear weapons. As part of an attempt to reconcile deterrence with the need for a rational strategy should deterrence fail, the Alliance, it is argued, must bolster conventional forces. Although not all the critics would go so far as to accept the 'no first use' recommendations of Bundy, Kennan, McNamara and Smith, even those who dissent from this proposal generally accept the need to move to a position of 'delayed first use'.[15] This requires an increase in conventional forces, but the implication of the Trident acquisition is that there may well have to be a decrease in the British contribution to NATO's conventional force goals – especially in view of the fact that defence spending is planned to increase far less during the second half of the 1980s than it did in the first.

The government has tended to play down the impact of the Trident acquisition on the UK's conventional forces, arguing that Trident will absorb only 3 per cent of the total defence budget during the period of its procurement, and 6 per cent of the equipment budget.[16] David Greenwood has argued very persuasively that such assessments are far too sanguine. During the peak years from 1988/9 through to 1992/3, for example, the Trident costs will represent just under 7.5 per cent of the defence budget and somewhere between 15 and 20 per cent of the procurement funds.[17] These arguments become even more potent as a result of the decline in the value of the pound against the dollar – a trend which, if it continues, will make the acquisition of parts from the US even more expensive. It is, however, possible to agree with Greenwood's analysis of the likely costs of Trident without necessarily concluding that the opportunity costs of the programme are prohibitive. The key issue is the strategic and political rationale rather than the costs. Even if Trident does cut into resources for conventional defence, this may be a price worth paying. For Greenwood, it is not. In his view, 'achieving a last line of defence by forgoing a first, second and third line' is not a sensible option.[18] The counter-argument, though, is that the benefits to deterrence in Europe from the British acquisition of Trident will more than outweigh the damage inflicted by the decrease in Britain's conventional capability. Ultimately, the issue centres on the respective contribution of nuclear and conventional weapons to the implementation of deterrence in Europe. There are two competing models. The first emphasizes the costs and risks for the aggressor, and argues that if these are sufficiently high, then question marks about credibility do not detract too much from the overall effectiveness of deterrence. The second approach suggests that what counts is a capacity for sustained defence which would very obviously deny victory to an aggressor. The debate of the last few years has nudged NATO slightly away from the former approach and towards the latter. Yet it is important not to go too far in this direction. Europe should not be made safe for conventional war, nor should the Soviet Union be encouraged to believe that the risks inherent in an attack upon Western Europe are anything other than wholly unacceptable. It is not necessary to believe that the Soviet Union is anxious to initiate aggression in Europe to recognize that there might be circumstances in which the allies will want to induce restraint in Moscow. For this purpose strategic nuclear weapons are almost certainly far superior to any alternative. Given a choice, Moscow would probably prefer the United Kingdom to abandon Trident, rather than simply cut conventional forces. This in itself suggests a need for caution. In a strict sense, conventional forces are the first line of defence, but this does not mean that they add more to deterrence. And the name of the game in Europe, first and foremost, is deterrence.

In other words, it is possible to accept Greenwood's argument that current projection of costs and expenditures make a budgetary squeeze inevitable in the latter half of the 1980s, without also accepting his conclusion that the abandonment of Trident is the most appropriate way of forestalling or containing such a development. It is neither the only, nor the best option. One way of avoiding, or at least ameliorating, the squeeze would be to extend the 3 per cent commitment. This, of course, has been ruled out; yet it does not necessarily follow that conventional forces should be increased and Trident abandoned.

One of the arguments for giving priority to conventional forces is that the United States is currently very anxious to reduce NATO's dependence on nuclear weapons. Certainly a reasonable investment in conventional defence is essential in order to make the risks of involvement in Europe acceptable to Washington. Consequently, a British decision to reduce its conventional capabilities would not be popular either with the administration or in Congress. Yet much the same could be said about the cancellation of Trident. Indeed, the impact of such a move would probably be even greater. Congressional dissatisfaction with Western Europe is as much a product of very general perceptions of European seriousness about security as it is a result of detailed scrutiny of European defence efforts. Abandoning Trident, with all the publicity this would generate, would be widely interpreted as yet further evidence of Europe's unwillingness to make sacrifices for its own security.

This might conceivably be avoided if the decision could be presented as part of a larger package of measures designed to strengthen conventional defence and deterrence in Europe. The demands of General Rogers, Senator Nunn and other Americans, that the Europeans strengthen their conventional contributions to the

Alliance, provide an opportunity for the United Kingdom to present a cancellation of Trident and a renewed commitment to non-nuclear forces as a positive reorientation of its defence efforts, rather than a negative response to economic stringency and continued resource allocation problems. Ironically, it is only a future Labour government which is likely to make such a decision on Trident, and it would probably do so as part of a broader shift in British policy. The result of this would be the disruption, if not the destruction, of the very. Alliance framework which makes such a cancellation a reasonable proposition. If the Labour Party's statement on defence issued in the summer of 1984 is to be taken seriously, cancellation of Trident would be accompanied by the eviction of US nuclear bases, nuclear-armed aircraft and the recently deployed cruise missiles.[19] The impact on the Alliance would be traumatic. In particular, the reversal of policy on cruise missiles would almost certainly have a knock-on effect on the smaller Alliance members, and might possibly lead to an unravelling of the whole implementation programme. This would in turn have far-reaching implications for Atlantic cooperation, not least because it would disrupt what, with one or two exceptions, has hitherto been a reasonably smooth implementation of the 1979 deployment decision. The United States might even conclude that what one American ambassador described as 'a battle for the soul of Europe' had been lost.[20]

In short, such measures by a future government would confirm, perhaps irrevocably, American perceptions of Western Europe as pacifist, neutralist, ungrateful, anti-American and no longer worth defending. The damage would almost certainly be far more severe than after de Gaulle's decision in 1966 to take France out of NATO and NATO out of France. The General's action could be explained in terms of idiosyncrasy. Furthermore, it was mitigated by the concern of the other Europeans to ensure continued American cooperation and commitment. It is far from certain that in the mid- and late 1980s these mitigating circumstances would be present: whereas de Gaulle's behaviour was accepted as an aberration, the decision of a future Labour government to implement the Party's current plans would be interpreted in Washington as part of a wider European pattern. The shock would be all the more profound because Britain, unlike France, has traditionally been a good ally. In other words, cancellation of Trident with a renewed commitment to conventional forces is one thing; the Labour Party programme is quite another. There is an inherent contradiction in the Party's proposals. The notion of staying in NATO while carrying out these other measures takes no account of the damage that such policies would inflict on the Alliance. It is not inconceivable that there would no longer be a NATO – at least in its present form – for Britain to remain within.

In circumstances where the United States is already reappraising the value of the alliance with Western Europe, the adoption by the United Kingdom of a defence policy which was both anti-nuclear and anti-American would be liable to provoke an American disengagement. On the other hand, it could be argued that a substantial loosening of ties with Europe and, ultimately, a withdrawal of the US security guarantee, is inevitable anyway. If it is assumed, for example, that current trends in NATO are potentially irreversible and that Atlantic tensions will worsen rather than abate, then a weakening of the US commitment to Western Europe becomes a possibility that must be taken very seriously by defence planners. Yet this argues for a more nationalistic approach: rather than shape its defence efforts to fit in with Alliance priorities, the United Kingdom should adopt policies and maintain a national order of battle which have a validity and coherence that goes beyond the NATO framework. The implication of this is that the long-term case for Trident is particularly powerful. If the United States withdraws its nuclear umbrella from Western Europe, then indigenous European nuclear forces will take on an unprecedented importance. Without them, the risks for Moscow of aggression against Western Europe could, under some circumstances, begin to look tolerable. The corollary of this, though, is *not* that conventional forces are insignificant. On the contrary, the major conventional roles currently undertaken by the UK are of immense significance. The rationale for these roles must now be examined.

British conventional forces

The United Kingdom's conventional forces fulfil four major functions. As well as defence of the British homeland, Britain contributes to forward defence on the European mainland; British maritime forces make a major contribution to the naval presence in the North East Atlantic, where their presence would facilitate reinforcement and resupply during hostilities; and Britain also maintains a limited capacity for operations outside the NATO area. All these roles are related to some extent to the Atlantic Alliance. Both the continental commitment and the maritime forces in the North East Atlantic are exclusively within the NATO framework. The defence of the homeland is also related to Alliance contingency planning: the United Kingdom would act as a vital staging post for reinforcement and resupply from the United States, and would have to take measures to ensure that the flow of men and material could continue with as little disruption as possible from Soviet air attack. (It might also be worth noting, in passing, that the UK's possession of a strategic nuclear capability could also serve to inhibit Soviet attacks on the homeland, thereby bolstering Britain's role as a staging post.) Out-of-area roles are less clearly within the NATO framework. Britain has its own commitments to the Falklands and several other remnants of the Empire, but the ability to deploy forces beyond the European theatre has become an increasingly important issue within NATO. The United States has made it clear that Alliance members, though not the Alliance itself, have an important contribution to make towards dealing with security threats from outside Europe. Washington is prepared to take the major responsibility for this, but some support from the allies is deemed essential. As well as compensating for American forces diverted elsewhere, the Europeans are expected to facilitate such deployments wherever this is feasible. And participation is welcomed. Although participation is possible for very few of the European allies other than Britain and France, what gives it a symbolic importance beyond any substantive effort involved is the fact that it feeds back into the burden-sharing debate. The more the Europeans appear to be supporting the United States outside the NATO area, the more disposed the United States will be to maintain its military presence in Europe at fairly high levels. The less support that is provided, the more resentment there will be in Washington. Contributing to out-of-area deployment is not strictly a contribution to NATO, but in effect it may contribute significantly to the cohesion and well-being of the Alliance. Considerable political benefits can be obtained from limited military investments.

More costly and more important are the direct contributions Britain makes to the Alliance order of battle in the North East Atlantic and in the Federal Republic. The significance of both roles has been underlined by the discussions about reducing dependence on nuclear weapons in NATO. In the event of aggression, the land and air forces in the Federal Republic would have a major role to play in attempting to halt the Warsaw Pact incursion as close to the intra-German border as possible, and in delaying the time when NATO might feel it has no alternative other than to resort to the use of nuclear weapons. Furthermore, by having forces *in situ* capable of responding immediately to aggression, the Alliance becomes slightly less dependent on political warning-time. While the British forces in the Federal Republic contribute significantly to NATO's capacity to respond to a sudden attack and make it less likely that the Soviet Union could win a short war, the maritime forces are an important component in a long war. Without reinforcement and resupply from the United States, NATO would be unable to sustain hostilities for very long. The initial Pact advance might be thwarted, but this would merely postpone the time when a decision would have to be made on whether to use nuclear weapons or surrender. Here again, different elements in the

British forces complement each other in militarily significant ways.

Consequently, in the event of another round of budgetary stringency (whether or not it is precipitated by Trident), there would be no easy choices for the United Kingdom. Defence of the homeland has long been neglected and could not sensibly be pared down – especially when there is increasing emphasis on conventional sustainability and delayed use of nuclear weapons. The out-of-area contribution is politically important and, apart from the Falklands, not particularly expensive. In Europe, both the land/air and maritime contributions appear to be militarily indispensable. They are also important, politically, as part of the continuing attempt to minimize the dangers for the United States of its commitment to Western Europe, and as a demonstration that Europe does not take the threat to its security lightly.

If the United Kingdom finds it impossible to continue funding all these capabilities within current financial projections, it would have several alternatives. One would be to accept the need for further increases in the defence budget of around 3 per cent. In terms of both military strategy and Alliance cohesion, this would be the optimum course. Now that it has been ruled out, there will be an increasing emphasis on minimizing administrative costs and on improving efficiency. That this will be sufficient to avert another defence review seems unlikely – even if it is not officially described as a review. In these circumstances, the least damaging alternative would be to revert to the stance adopted in the second half of the 1970s, when the government's approach was to 'inflict equal misery' and engage in cutbacks across the board. This might be more acceptable to the Alliance than major reductions in the forces deployed either in the Federal Republic or in the North East Atlantic. That it would be more sensible in military terms, however, is perhaps questionable. As Greenwood has pointed out, there are dangers in attempting to maintain existing roles and missions if this means spreading resources so thinly that these roles and missions cannot be implemented effectively. The alternative is to establish a clearer set of priorities among them.[21]

Should the government attempt to do this, the RAF, with its prominent position in the equipment budget, could prove more vulnerable than it has been for some time. The European Combat Aircraft – earmarked by the UK as a replacement for the Jaguar – might well be an early casualty of budgetary stringency, especially in view of the doubts about the effectiveness of future generations of manned aircraft. Procurement of the army's main battle tank could also be stretched out. Should changes in patterns of provisions prove insufficient to ease budgetary pressures, however, the government might be forced to consider more drastic changes. If so, the issue could come down once again to the maritime contribution versus the continental commitment. This was the issue John Nott confronted when planning *The Way Forward* in the early 1980s.[22] His response was to cut the size of the surface navy. Under the impetus of the Falklands, rather than the urgings of the navy lobby, there has been a substantial retreat from the scale of reductions that was envisaged. Yet it can be argued that, if cuts do have to be made in one of Britain's two major conventional roles, the priorities established by Mr Nott should be reimposed. The case for regarding forces in the Federal Republic rather than maritime capabilities as sacrosanct is predominantly political. Although a partial American withdrawal from Western Europe might be inevitable, the United Kingdom should do nothing to hasten it. A reduction of British forces in Federal Germany could have precisely this effect. The UK's land and air forces on the Continent have an importance in terms of political symbolism that goes far beyond their military strength. Evidence of weakening British resolve to maintain its continental commitment can only encourage and strengthen the proponents of US troop reductions in Europe. Naval forces do not have the same symbolic importance.

Against this, it could be argued that what appears to be the lesser evil in the short term may be severely debilitating in the long term. A paring down of the navy might be defensible as the price of maintaining BAOR and RAF Germany and, by extension, the American military presence in Europe. If, however, US retrenchment goes ahead anyway, such a course might appear to be a serious mistake, since it would deprive Western Europe of the maritime capabilities necessary to deal with extra-European contingencies. On the other hand, if US forces are withdrawn from the Continent, the significance of the British contribution to the defence of the Central Front will be enhanced rather than diminished. Furthermore, even if the United States disentangles itself from direct participation in European defence, it can hardly opt out of the superpower competition for power and influence elsewhere. If Washington does in fact reject the alliance approach, it will be in favour of a unilateralist strategy based on maritime supremacy rather than a reversion to isolationism. One result of this would be to render European maritime forces irrelevant to most contingencies outside what is currently the NATO area, thereby going far to confirm the long-term wisdom of the emphasis on the continental commitment.

Nevertheless, it must be emphasized that a cut in maritime capabilities is not an attractive option. The chief point in its favour is that it would be slightly less damaging than the main alternative. It would also enable the United Kingdom to maintain a semblance of balance between short-term and long-term considerations, and between national and Alliance priorities. Yet it also has to be acknowledged that, if the United Kingdom really wants to ensure that its dual-track policy of keeping the United States committed to Europe, while simultaneously being prepared for its possible departure, is to remain effective, then the government will have to spend more on defence than it now regards as acceptable. Without such expenditure, the delicate equilibrium which British defence policy maintains seems likely to be undermined. The precise implications of this are uncertain; that they will be significant is not in doubt.

Notes

1. P. Nailor, 'Choices in Defence Policy' (unpublished paper).
2. For a fuller discussion, see P. Williams, *US Troops in Europe*, Chatham House Paper 25 (London: Routledge and Kegan Paul, 1984), especially pp. 29-35.
3. L. Freedman, 'Europe Between The Superpowers', in G. Segal, E. Moreton, L. Freedman and J. Baylis, *Nuclear War and Nuclear Peace* (London: Macmillan, 1983), p. 115.
4. J. Joffe, 'Europe's American Pacifier', *Foreign Policy*, No. 54 (Spring 1984), pp. 64-82 at pp. 68-9.
5. *Ibid.*, p. 75.
6. *The Future United Kingdom Strategic Nuclear Deterrent Force*, Defence Open Government Document 80/23 (July 1980), p. 3.
7. *Ibid.*
8. T.C. Schelling, *Arms and Influence* (New Haven and London: Yale University Press, 1967), and R. Jervis, *The Illogic of American Nuclear Strategy* (Ithaca and London: Cornell University Press, 1984).
9. *The Future United Kingdom Strategic Nuclear Deterrent*, pp. 8-9.
10. *Ibid.*, p. 15.
11. *The United Kingdom Trident Programme*, Defence Open Government Document 82/1 (March 1982), p. 4. SSN: submarine(s), nuclear (i.e. nuclear-powered); ASW: anti-submarine warfare.
12. *Ibid.*, p.5.
13. G.M. Seignious II and J.P. Yates, 'Europe's Nuclear Superpowers', *Foreign Policy*, No. 55 (Summer 1984), p. 40.
14. K. Booth, 'Unilateralism: a Clausewitzian Reform?', in N. Blake and K. Pole (eds.), *Dangers of Deterrence: Philosophers on Nuclear Strategy* (London: Routledge & Kegan Paul, 1983); see p. 57 in particular.
15. A good overview of the 'no first use' debate, as well as some of the major contributions, can be found in F. Blackaby, J. Goldblat and S. Lodgaard (eds.), *No First Use* (London: Taylor & Francis for SIPRI, 1984).
16. *Statement on the Defence Estimates 1984*, I, Cmnd. 9227-1 (London: HMSO, 1984), p. 25.
17. See D. Greenwood, *Trident: The Budgetary Impact* (Centre for Defence Studies, University of Aberdeen, April 1984).
18. Quoted in Seignious and Yates, op. cit., p. 5.
19. *Defence and Security for Britain*, Statement to Annual Conference 1984 by the National Executive Committee (London: Labour Party, 1984).
20. For elaboration of this, see P. Williams, 'The United States Commitment to

Western Europe: Strategic Ambiguity and Political Disintegration?', *International Affairs*, Vol. 59 (Spring 1983), No. 2.

21. The need for clearer priorities is a continuing theme in the writings of David Greenwood.

22. *The United Kingdom Defence Programme: The Way Forward*, Cmnd. 8288 (London: HMSO, 1981).

Comment on Chapter 2
Malcolm Chalmers

A new policy needed

The last five years have seen increased tension between the super-powers and an acceleration in the arms race. The United States is now devoting massive resources to the acquisition of capabilities for nuclear 'warfighting' and Third World intervention. If Soviet leaders attempt to match this effort, the world could be in for a very uncomfortable period in the next decade.

In this situation, present government policy, as outlined in Phil Williams's paper, is increasingly perceived as inadequate by large sections of the British public. People no longer believe that nuclear war can indefinitely be avoided. The probability of any one crisis getting out of control may be small, but there is no longer general confidence that, one day, someone will not miscalculate. And any temporary return to conditions of détente would be undermined by the momentum of the arms race.

In constructing a defence policy that responds to these concerns, deterrence is no longer enough. Nations cannot base their security indefinitely on irrational threats – 'threats that leave something to chance'. The need to *deter* the Soviet Union from military aggression must now be supplemented by the requirement that we *reassure* them that our own intentions are purely defensive. Only in this way can we provide a foundation for long-term mutual security.

Two proposals which address this concern now attract widespread support within NATO member states: a bilateral nuclear weapons freeze and a policy of 'no first use'. The main objective of a freeze would be to halt the development of the new generation of highly destabilizing counterforce nuclear weaponry. There is already a grotesque level of overkill on both sides, making the concept of nuclear superiority quite meaningless. Yet current developments in strategic nuclear weaponry can only be understood as logical in military terms if they are intended to provide first strike capabilities. A freeze on such developments would reassure both superpowers that the other no longer clung to the illusion that such a capability was in fact attainable.

The adoption of a 'no first use' policy would also reassure the Soviet

Union – and Western public opinion – that NATO no longer believes that nuclear war can be fought and won. It would increase the chances for successful negotiations to establish nuclear-weapon-free zones, and perhaps also facilitate a process of wider disengagement in Europe. Together with a bilateral freeze on strategic arsenals, it would be a major step towards a policy of minimum deterrence.

Britain's role in NATO
In the attempt to win US and NATO agreement for such a policy, independent British moves could be decisive. Were Britain to renounce its independent nuclear force, remove US nuclear bases and support a 'no first use' policy for NATO, the political impact would be considerable. It could not fail to provoke a vigorous public debate throughout the Alliance. Such a debate would be an extremely healthy development. Moreover, provided Britain stressed its continued commitment to NATO membership, it might also be able to mobilize considerable support for its ideas from other European member states. Some of the smaller nations – Denmark, Holland, Greece, Norway – are already unhappy with current NATO strategy. Now that the West German Social Democratic Party is committed to a defence policy that has much in common with Liberal and Labour proposals in Britain, even the Federal Republic might be won over by a disarmament-oriented government in London.

The biggest question mark would be over the US response. In attempting to predict that response, one must start with the recognition that the United States sustains a large military presence in Europe because it believes it to be in its own interests to do so. Naturally it wants European countries to spend more on defence and share the burdens of the Alliance. Moreover, it is clear that it would be likely to oppose British proposals for a non-nuclear defence policy. It is not, however, likely to withdraw its commitment to Europe in exasperation if it does not have everything its own way. Though a shift in American defence priorities away from Europe is possible, perhaps even likely, Europe is too important to US global strategy for complete withdrawal to be seriously considered.

It is also important to remember that proposals for reducing reliance on nuclear weapons have considerable support in the United States. A bilateral weapons freeze is supported by the Democratic Party and a majority of the American public, and 'no first use' has traditionally been more popular in the US than in Europe. It is reasonable to suppose that proposals by Britain and the Federal Republic of Germany for a rethink of NATO policy would find sympathetic, as well as hostile, audiences in the American debate. Indeed it may be in their impact on that debate that independent moves by European members of NATO could have their most important effect.

Britain's conventional forces

If the US commitment to Europe is more robust than Phil Williams suggests, Britain may also have more room for manoeuvre on the conventional side. Provided that Britain remains committed to NATO, there may be considerable scope for a more independent determination of priorities. It is by no means clear, for example, why Britain benefits from retaining a capability for supporting the US outside the NATO area. Phil Williams argues that the US would welcome a European out-of-area contribution, and that it would be prudent for Britain and France to oblige. Yet it does not appear that the United States is reluctant to undertake a global policing role. With the 'Vietnam syndrome' wearing off, quite the opposite may now be true. If there is a case for a European out-of-area capability, it rests instead on its potential for restraining an American administration that is prone to viewing every conflict in the Third World as inspired by the Soviet Union. There is little evidence that political and economic measures could not fulfil this restraining function more effectively. Nor is it entirely convincing to argue that Britain's current level of defence spending is needed to maintain the US commitment to NATO. That commitment is considerably stronger than some interpretations of congressional opinion would suggest. The *size* of the US military presence may be sensitive, to some extent, to trends in the European allies' defence spending, but the US commitment to such a presence is not seriously in doubt.

There is, however, a stronger argument for maintaining Britain's non-nuclear contribution to NATO. In order to sustain support for a 'no first use' policy, NATO must maintain adequate military capabilities to deter conventional attack. Such a capability may not require large increases in conventional defence spending, but, for political as well as military reasons, it probably does require that the level of spending is not substantially reduced.

Conclusion

Phil Williams correctly identifies the importance of symbolic and political factors in the determination of British defence policy, and the necessity of formulating that policy in the light of likely reactions by other NATO members. His defence of current policy, however, appears to require a further assumption: that the risks of nuclear war occurring (if current trends continue) are negligible. If one were to assume, on the other hand, that the probability of nuclear war is significantly greater than zero, and may be increasing, the conclusions one draws will be radically different. Alternative defence policies would then be seen as necessary and urgent. And the potential political repercussions of independent British initiatives may become an incentive for, and added attraction of, such action rather than an argument against it.

3   The Case for Non-nuclear Defence
Ken Booth

In Britain in the early 1980s, 'Ban the Bomb' was transformed from a slogan on the banners of peace marchers into a strategy – or rather a set of strategies – going under the label of 'alternative defence'.[1] While it would be very premature to say that an alternative, non-nuclear defence policy for Britain is an idea whose time has come, politically, there is reason to think that it is an idea whose time may be coming. Attitudes are shifting. Of particular note has been the steady increase in the number of 'authorities' critical of major aspects of existing nuclear policy.[2] One major political party, Labour, endorses non-nuclear defence, while two others, the Liberals and the SDP, reject major aspects of Conservative policy. The consensus of the last thirty years on British defence policy has cracked, and neither the General Election of 1983 nor the deployment of cruise missiles has killed the issue, as government spokesmen claim. There is still a debate to be won. The years 1987-92 will be critical.

What is wrong with what we have?
In the opinion of its supporters, Britain's nuclear defence policy has been a remarkable success. They argue that it has helped to keep the peace in Europe for a generation, that it has given Britain status in the world, and that it has been relatively cheap. In short, it has worked, and at an acceptable cost: so why change a winner? According to the critics, the reasons for changing Britain's nuclear defence policy are numerous:[3]

– It is immoral to threaten and/or use weapons of mass destruction. The use of nuclear weapons would violate the 'just war' principles of proportionality and discrimination; and it is wrong to threaten that which it would be grossly immoral to do.

– If nuclear deterrence were to fail, the consequences for Britain would be catastrophic almost beyond imagination. At worst, it would mean the onset of 'nuclear winter'; at best, the massacre of millions. In either case, a small overcrowded country such as Britain is peculiarly vulnerable to the effects of nuclear war.

– The so-called independent British deterrent is not credible. The only – last-resort – scenario in which it might be employed is again almost unimaginable, and any decision to use it would be tantamount to a British leader deciding to commit national suicide.

– NATO's strategy of flexible response, in which Britain's defence efforts are intimately enmeshed, is incredible, inflexible, escalatory and dangerous.

– Nuclear deterrence is becoming increasingly unstable because of doctrinal and weapons innovations.

– Since any nuclear war might quickly become uncontrolled, and since 'nuclear winter', might be the outcome of firing even a fraction of existing arsenals, nuclear disarmament is imperative. In spite of this, the British government plans to increase its nuclear capability, not reduce it.

– The British government's actual nuclear behaviour under-mines its declared commitment to non-proliferation. The arguments used to justify Trident strengthen the hands of those in near-nuclear countries who want their governments to take the nuclear option.

– Britain's existing nuclear posture requires a very close relationship with the United States. This weakens our vaunted independence and entails the unacceptable risk that Britain might be dragged into a war between the superpowers.

– The Soviet military threat to Western Europe has been greatly exaggerated, in terms of both intention and capability. Nuclear deterrence, as it has been practised, exacerbates conflict and undermines the possibility of long-term stable relations.

– With its existing posture, Britain is a priority nuclear target for the Soviet Union.

– Nuclear weapons are an extravagance for Britain. They consume scarce economic and scientific resources.

– The possession of nuclear weapons has not brought Britain international prestige. They have not won for us a seat at the top table in international diplomacy.

– Not only is the independent deterrent incredible as a weapon of last resort, it is useless in lesser contingencies. British strategy and diplomacy have gained nothing from the country's possession of nuclear weapons.

– Finally, we do not in fact know whether British nuclear policy has contributed to maintaining stability in Europe. We cannot know whether or not our nuclear strategy has worked, because we cannot know if it has deterred the Soviet leaders from testing it. Certainly nuclear deterrence has not failed in the sense that no territory in Western Europe has fallen to the Soviet Union since

1945. But at what cost? The megalogic of nuclear deterrence has institutionalized the cold war and stimulated a process of competitive weapons innovation which ultimately represents a greater threat to the countries in the East-West confrontation than they do to each other.

Such criticisms of existing nuclear policy as those listed above are argued in varying combinations and with different emphases by those in the anti-nuclear movement. However, before elaborating the case for a shift to a non-nuclear defence, three major points arising out of these criticisms deserve special attention.

1. *We need to think more carefully about the operational dimension of strategy.* Despite the widely perceived need to strengthen NATO's conventional military capabilities, the Alliance's posture remains heavily pro-nuclear. This is a matter of considerable concern, since the risks of nuclear war appear somewhat greater in the future than they have been in the recent past.[4] The risks are small, but even a small risk is worrying, given the dreadful consequences. If nuclear deterrence does someday break down, we will leave the realm of strategic thinking and tumble headlong into a nightmare. It is imperative therefore that Britain should make a bigger contribution not only to reducing the risk of war, but also to raising the nuclear threshold and contributing to a more rational war-fighting and war-terminating strategy than present arrangements allow. A shift to a more robust conventional defence will help this. Providing, as we do now, the wherewithal to threaten the destruction of the nation in order to save it does not represent the optimum allocation of Britain's scarce defence resources. It detracts from our ability to help remedy the weaknesses of NATO's existing operational strategy.

2. *The possession of nuclear weapons gives Britain a power of indiscriminate mass destruction which it is neither right nor prudent to threaten to use, let alone actually use.* By the 1990s, with Trident and Tornado, Britain will be able to destroy 724 strategic targets in the Soviet Union.[5] It is wrong that we are preparing, even in retaliation, to engage in a massacre of Russian people which is too inhuman for decent imaginations to contemplate. But nuclear deterrence numbs the imagination. To make it work, it has to be made 'credible', and this requires elaborate preparations – strengthening thought processes as well as hardware – to ensure that the adversary believes that retaliation will take place if it is deemed necessary. The British community is therefore colluding in a strategy whose implementation would stand shamefully alongside the worst war crimes in recorded history. There is no likely issue between Britain and the Soviet Union which could justify it. Not only would it be a crime, it would also be

the height of stupidity. A kamikaze nuclear attack on Soviet cities by Britain, as a last ditch effort to throw back a Soviet offensive, would provoke such massive retaliation that it would turn the clock of British history back to the Dark Ages.

3. *The infrastructure of nuclear deterrence since the late 1940s has institutionalized the cold war.* Conflicts of interest exist, and will continue to exist, between the Soviet Union and Western countries, but there is no objective reason why war should be the outcome. However, the cold war framework of relations militates against the development of long-term coexistence between East and West. Rational suspicions, worst-case forecasting, inertia, vested interests, and simple sovietology have led to a dangerous militarization of our thinking about the Soviet Union. US governments have acted as if the military balance, particularly its nuclear component, was the only serious determinant in US–Soviet relations, and as if war was a not unlikely end-product of the confrontation.[6] East-West relations have been trapped in a vicious circle of over-militarized policies and perceptions, continuous weapons innovation, and the infrastructure and dynamics of nuclear deterrence. Together, these have produced strategic stability of a sort, but at the cost of any hopes of positive peace. If there is no move away from the ideology of nuclear deterrence, stability will have to rest indefinitely on the strategic rationality of the nuclear powers, the non-invention of weaponry which can tempt people to think that a nuclear war might be won, and not a little good luck through all the crises and conflicts with which international politics will inevitably be strewn. It will be a dangerous stability.

Nuclear weapons are impressive deterrents. Their effects are so obvious that they impose a novel degree of caution. But even if they have 'worked' in the recent past, it does not necessarily follow that it is sensible for Britain to pursue a policy of independent nuclear deterrence for the foreseeable future. It is well to remember that the battlefields of strategic history are monuments to the attempts of nations to give yesterday's answers to tomorrow's questions. The fears and reactions of the late 1940s were understandable and justified, on the part of both Western and Soviet leaders, but it is now clear that the cold war paradigm is anachronistic as well as dangerous. Nevertheless, there are powerful forces that make change difficult, not least the suspicions and dogmas which exist in Soviet strategic culture. We must take all this into account, but not always let it prevent us from acting when we might improve matters. There is room for manoeuvre in East-West relations.

What are the characteristics of a non-nuclear defence?
It is one thing to criticize existing policy: it is another matter altogether to replace it with something generally agreed to be better. However, the anti-nuclear critics have been busy, and the menu of non-nuclear strategies is now lengthy. Not surprisingly, there are differences of opinion among the critics over the best mix of ingredients in their policies. Non-nuclear strategies are also susceptible to the ambiguities, inconsistencies, and fudging which bedevil any defence policy. The non-nuclear defence policy which will be proposed below takes the best from various approaches, and offers some ideas of its own. It consists of three main elements, one of which is unilateral, and two multilateral.

1. From nuclear to non-nuclear forces
A complete unilateral move to conventional forces has been at the heart of the revived anti-nuclear campaign since the late 1970s. It is argued that all nuclear weapons in Britain's arsenal should be scrapped, and dual-capable systems should be converted to conventional use only. The money freed from Trident and other nuclear systems would be used to strengthen Britain's conventional forces.

In order to fulfil the requirements of such a change in policy, it would be logical to reintroduce conscription. This should help to raise the nuclear threshold; increase the allies' ability to contain limited Warsaw Pact aggressions; reduce dependence on warning-time; add to Britain's manpower reserves; strengthen territorial defence at home; and send political signals to both adversaries and allies that Britain is serious about defence.[7] Conscription would not be a revolutionary step: all our West European allies have national service. They also spend less, per capita, on defence. Initially the costs of converting to national service would be high, but they should be regarded as a small price to pay for freeing us of the nuclear burden.

2. From flexible response to defensive deterrence
When it was adopted in 1967, flexible response was intended to improve NATO strategy: it was supposed to be a climb-down from massive retaliation; to offer more rational options; to raise the nuclear threshold; and to provide the possibility for graduated reactions to aggressive moves. The promise has not been fulfilled, and the strategy has recently provoked much criticism, even from former supporters.

NATO has always believed that conventional forces were necessary, but only as a phase in a nuclear-based defence. It would be preferable for NATO to change the balance of its strategy entirely, and move from its pro-nuclear doctrine of flexible response to one of defensive deterrence based on conventional forces. Defensive deterrence means 'having the capacity to inflict heavy losses on any invading force, but at most only a limited capacity to mount offensive operations in the opponent's territory'.[8] Several studies have attempted to translate defensive deterrence into military reality.[9] Tactical and other problems abound, as they do with flexible response, but the aim is to create a capability to wear down and frustrate the offence. It is widely believed that developments in weaponry, including some aspects of 'emerging technology', have been aiding the defence, and this good news is further supported by the fact that the NATO allies are technologically superior, can put more men in the field, and are economically stronger than the Warsaw Pact. It seems likely that we shall see the progressive vulnerability of the tanks and aircraft on which any massive offensive into Western Europe would rely. Thus the prospect of any quick victory in Europe is decreasing. Robust conventional forces should thereby constitute a credible defensive deterrent. Yugoslavia's conventional deterrent has apparently worked, so why should not a stronger one, put into operation by the more powerful members of NATO?

The guardians of NATO's traditional doctrines and threat assessments are not ready to contemplate a speedy or complete shift away from dependence on nuclear weapons. Nevertheless, there are straws in the wind. Recent years have seen a much greater willingness on the part of senior commanders to give the Alliance a stronger conventional emphasis; the desirability of removing at least some if not all battlefield nuclear weapons has been widely recognized; the defence spokesmen of the NATO allies have been somewhat less prone than formerly to give crude assessments of the Soviet military threat; and the unease with flexible response has grown. But there is still very far to go: the supporters of non-nuclear defence must accept that overcoming entrenched interests and addictive behaviour will be difficult.

The initial step away from pro-nuclear flexible response should be the adoption of a 'no first use' strategy. This should be pressed more for what it would do to our own addiction than for what it might signal to the Russians. After this, US theatre nuclear weapons should be withdrawn, followed by the withdrawal and preferably destruction of all battlefield nuclear weapons. The latter would be easier if suitable reforms had already been put in hand in conventional defence efforts. By the end of the process, NATO strategy would have become decoupled from US nuclear strategy. It is inconceivable that the United States itself would renounce nuclear weapons; the aim of its allies should therefore be to encourage it to maintain its nuclear forces simply to deter direct nuclear attacks on its homeland.

Conventional deterrence would neither be cheap nor easy to

achieve. And if it failed, and war broke out in Europe – even a conventional war – the destruction would be terrible. If this is recognized by friend and adversary alike, conventional forces will become an effective deterrent. But conventional deterrence is not an escape from the burdens of international politics. However much change there has been in the Soviet Union, it remains a superpower, with all the domineering attitudes that implies.

3. From an Atlanticist to a European NATO

Some supporters of a non-nuclear strategy for Britain entirely reject the North Atlantic Alliance. In their opinion it merely perpetuates an international order which fosters arms competition, the maintenance of tension, the cultivation of suspicion, and the continuation, in the name of stability, of the repression of nations and human rights. Nevertheless, a significant proportion of non-nuclear supporters, including the Labour Party, do at least conditionally accept continued British membership, albeit as a disagreeable necessity.

While the criticisms of NATO just mentioned have some validity, NATO also has a positive side. Furthermore, realistic reformers accept that we have to begin from where we are, and that for the foreseeable future Europe has no alternative but to live with the results of World War II and under the shadow of the superpowers. Even were NATO to be disbanded overnight, Soviet interests and power in East Europe would remain. In such circumstances, Western defence should remain collective. Britain should therefore continue to reaffirm its commitment to the security of the group of liberal-democratic states in Western Europe: the West will be stronger collectively than individually; as a major middle power, Britain has a responsibility to help the security of smaller European states; a divided Western Europe would be more likely to defer to a militant Soviet Union than if its states were able to act together; an integrated alliance offers the prospect of rationalizing defence efforts; NATO gives the Federal Republic of Germany a role and a limitation; NATO helps set a framework for the discussion of détente, arms control, and confidence- and security-building measures; for Britain it is prudent that forward defence lies as far east as possible; NATO helps to keep the United States in Europe, which lessens the risks of a Soviet attack or nuclear blackmail; and a coherent alliance helps to draw those sharp lines which are useful for deterrent purposes.

For all these reasons, it is desirable that Britain should remain committed to the North Atlantic Treaty. The question immediately arises, however, whether a non-nuclear Britain could indefinitely remain a member of an integrated military alliance if it proves impossible to persuade the allies to begin to shift in a non-nuclear direction. The answer must be no, but it would not be wise, at the outset of Britain's attempt to encourage a denuclearization of the Alliance, to lay down an ultimatum, since that would reduce diplomatic flexibility. Parallel with the attempt to denuclearize NATO strategy, Britain should continue the process, begun in 1984, to give more explicit recognition to the separate interests of the European and American sectors of the Alliance.

Once serious arguments had begun about the relative merits of nuclear versus non-nuclear strategies, there would inevitably be problems in Britain's relations with the United States, and a change in the character of the strategic coupling between the United States and Western Europe. It can be assumed that the present occupants of the White House would not approve of denuclearization: it would not match their image of what constitutes 'walking tall'. No progress can be expected at the governmental level until at least 1988, since the present occupants of Downing Street are not likely to put the Reagan White House to the test. But the possibilities may be much more open after the next set of General Elections. A good deal would then depend upon how well a new British government presented the proposed changes. It would have to demonstrate to its US ally that it was serious about defence, by actions as well as words; that it was committed at least conditionally to NATO; that it was taking practical steps to prevent proliferation; and that it was attempting to bring about reforms in Western defence which would reduce the risk of the United States being dragged into a nuclear war for the sake of Europe. These would be words and actions which many Americans would welcome.

The isolationism of the United States between the Wars and the excessive commitment of US governments to Europe since the cold war were both aberrations in US–European relations. A more appropriate and mature long-term relationship will avoid both these extremes. Continued US military commitment with nuclear decoupling would seem to represent the sensible military dimension of such a relationship. Those in the West whose minds are dominated by the fears and habits of the cold war relationship, characterized by US dominance and West European deference, might find it difficult to contemplate such a change. They want things to stay the same. But this is unrealistic. Can NATO in the decades ahead, with all the changes likely to take place within and between the allies, survive an effort to stay the same?

The three shifts in strategy just outlined represent the major features of an alternative, non-nuclear defence for Britain. It consists of hard unilateralism, a robust conventional defence effort, and a refusal to throw out the NATO baby with the dirty nuclear bathwater. The majority of British public opinion – those who think about the subject and the many who do not – still strongly favours a posture of independent deterrence and a nuclear-based NATO strategy. It is therefore necessary to address their fears and worries.

What are the weaknesses of a non-nuclear defence policy for Britain?

The critics of change, like the critics of the *status quo*, package their arguments in different ways and give them different emphases. But there are five familiar criticisms:

1. It would be hypocritical for a non-nuclear Britain to remain within NATO

Bernard Williams, a moral philosopher sympathetic to the unilateralist cause, has argued that moral arguments are best kept out of the nuclear debate. However, the arguments of Anthony Kenny and others, that moral arguments cannot be excluded, is stronger.[10] But to say this is not to condone moralizing, for we should all recognize that people have honestly come to different conclusions about moral questions in international politics. It is incumbent upon a liberal democracy to agonize about the acceptability or unacceptability of various means, and about what constitutes defensible or indefensible goals. Indeed, such moral issues are of more importance than defence economics. The actual boundaries of our defence spending are established by what we want to afford as a community, not by what we can afford; and what we want to afford is affected by our sense of right and wrong, of what we believe should be defended and how. Because of the importance of moral considerations, and the peace movement's particular sensitivity to them, the charge that it would be hypocritical for a non-nuclear Britain to hide under the umbrella of somebody else's nuclear weapons is a serious one. There are various counter-arguments:

Nuclear pacifists have a role in alliances. Within states we accept the right of individuals to be pacifists. They sometimes attract hostile criticism, on the ground that they are not good citizens – being 'free riders' on the security provided by others – but liberal societies recognize and accept that they have a particular vision which we would not want to lose. By analogy, in an alliance, we should be willing to accept the idea of states which are nuclear pacifists. Even though a nuclear pacifist state will receive some protection from the deterrent effect of nuclear weapons, that state cannot be criticized for being hypocritical if it tries to shift the alliance away from its nuclear policies; if it does not profess standards contrary to its behaviour; or if it shows itself serious about its responsibilities towards common defence in other ways.

There is no escape from the nuclear balance. On first sight, the morally consistent line for a non-nuclear Britain would be to pull out of NATO immediately, since not to do so would involve relying on others for the nuclear protection one has renounced oneself. But moral consistency is sometimes the hobgoblin of small minds. The fact is that neutral Sweden and Switzerland receive some deterrent cover from the central nuclear balance, and so inevitably would a non-nuclear Britain. States cannot become hermits. However, nobody in Britain berates Sweden or Switzerland for being hypocritical, although their security is affected by the nuclear exertions of other countries, especially the United States; and nobody attacks these two countries for not taking up the nuclear option. It should therefore be apparent that it would be morally justifiable for Britain to remain committed to the North Atlantic Treaty, as a nuclear pacifist state, and attempt to change the behaviour of its allies. The 'moral lead' argument in favour of British nuclear disarmament has always made most sense in relation to our allies, and opting out of Western defence would be likely to minimize Britain's influence in this respect.

Morality is contextual. It is always easier for individuals to have absolutist principles than it is for governments. For the latter, moral principles and *raison d'état* knock sparks off each other, and the traditional moral guideline has been the idea of the lesser evil. In contemplating the lesser evil, in any specific set of circumstances, the size, location, and power of the state concerned will be significant. What is acceptable or justifiable behaviour for a small country under the shadow of a hostile great power is likely to be very different from what is thought acceptable or justifiable behaviour for a great power. There is a case for arguing that there is one set of principles for the weak, and one for the strong. Thus it was justifiable for Denmark to surrender to Nazi Germany without fighting to the bitter end. This would not have been justifiable for Britain, which had no choice. Similarly, US governments have little choice, realistically speaking, but to keep nuclear weapons as long as the Soviet Union and other states have them. What else could they realistically do? British nuclear disarmers have to deal with states as they are, and it is inconceivable that the most powerful states will renounce them. It is right that Britain gets rid of its nuclear weapons, but British nuclear disarmers must accept that US governments will keep them. This should not be a cause for moralizing or rejecting relations with the United States, but a challenge to work for a safer world.

The critics are themselves inconsistent and hypocritical. Those defenders of present policy who argue that it is Britain's duty to share the nuclear burden with the United States, and that it would be hypocritical for a non-nuclear Britain to shelter under America's umbrella, do not carry their love for consistency and burden-sharing into practice. If burden-sharing and moral consistency were such a priority, these critics should loudly denounce all our allies who fail to take their proper share in nuclear deterrence. Indeed, Britain should presumably help them to acquire nuclear status, in order to share moral burdens more equitably and extend deterrence more credibly. For some reason, this has not been done. Furthermore, criticism of the anti-nuclear movement on the grounds of hypocrisy does not come well from governments which demand non-proliferation, but which themselves proliferate; which impose sanctions against some countries where martial law is declared, but not others; which condemn the human rights violations of selected governments, but not all; which denounce terrorism, but which allow their own agents to practise it; and which denounce nuclear war as unthinkable yet practise nuclear strategies which have nuclear war-fighting as an integral element. In the British defence debate the label 'multilateralist' has understandably become synonymous with hypocrisy: the label is a cloak to cover the maintenance of *status quo* thinking and further escalations of nuclear arms competition.

2. The renunciation of nuclear weapons by Britain would make nuclear war more likely
If Britain ceased to be a nuclear power, and successfully encouraged its allies to follow, supporters of the *status quo* argue that NATO would be shattered in the short term, and in the longer term the West would be opened up to nuclear blackmail. A power vacuum would be created which could tempt Soviet strength. In short, the road to nuclear disarmament, though paved with good intentions, would lead to international instability and so, perhaps, to the abyss of nuclear war.

The reasoning behind this argument is clear, but the validity of the conclusions is not. Pro-nuclear strategists cannot satisfactorily forecast that nuclear renunciation will lead to nuclear war with any more authority than they can guarantee that nuclear deterrence will continue to 'work', through all the forthcoming decades of technological change, international crises, the growth and decline of states, and the rise and fall of crazy leaders and regimes. No policy can be free of the risks of nuclear war or, it now seems, of its wintry consequences. Indeed, now that the stability of nuclear deterrence has been eroded by the shift to highly accurate weapons and the adoption of war-fighting doctrines, the Alternative Defence Commission is justified in arguing that the burden of proof in this business of risk assessment ought to rest with those who seek to maintain peace indefinitely by means of the mutual threat of genocide.[11] What confidence can we have, through thick and thin, in good seasons and bad, that international affairs will always be attended by rationality and good luck?

Nobody can guarantee the future, but for reasons advanced in the final part of this paper, there is reason to believe that a denuclearization of Western strategy (of which Britain's nuclear renunciation would be an essential part) will be more conducive to a long-term and stable peace than the heavily pro-nuclear strategies and heavily militarized thinking of today. The incantation of nuclear deterrers, who say that any departure from what we have is likely to trigger off the catastrophe it was designed to prevent, has been described by the Alternative Defence Commission as a form of intellectual blackmail whose aim is to paralyse strategic thinking outside the orthodox and official framework.[12] This blackmail has been resisted, and the response has been the idea of conventional deterrence, which would be robust enough to maintain the irrationality of war – any war – between the major industrialized powers.

3. *British nuclear disarmament would weaken, if not shatter, NATO*

A central element of the argument that British nuclear disarmament would make war more likely is the view that such a step would lead to a collapse of NATO, and thus end the stability which has characterized Europe since the late 1940s.

It must be admitted that NATO's demise might be hastened by an ex-nuclear Britain, but it need not, for it is not certain what the long-term allied reaction would be to a British decision to renounce nuclear weapons. While a poll of allied governments at the present time would almost certainly indicate disapproval of British nuclear disarmament, the extent to which this disapproval was positive support for Britain's independent nuclear deterrent or fear that nuclear disarmament would be a signal that Britain was simply opting out of European defence would not be clear. Furthermore, disapproval now does not necessarily mean that the allies would not adjust to the new reality were it ever to come about. The eventual outcome would very much depend upon when the change took place, who was in power at home and abroad, and the state of inter-allied relations at the time.

Although the Labour Party has delivered to President Reagan a decisive message on defence – 'you ain't seen nothin' yet' – the administration has not so far become excited about the prospect. The possible defence policy of a possible Labour government in Britain was not a priority in the minds of the Reagan administration through the prolonged succession struggle which eventually led to the (electoral) coup of November 1984. It is unlikely to be a priority in

Reagan's second term. American administrators have heard unilateralist noises before from Labour, when in opposition. That having been said, it is apparent that the idea of British nuclear disarmament *per se* has been unpopular in Washington, since it is believed to represent another example of West European reluctance to share the burdens of defence. But for the moment, the administration does not feel it has to do anything; it is a problem which time might solve.

One of the biggest problems involved in speculating about NATO's future is the difficulty of generalizing about 'American' views on anything. Who knows what 'Americans' will think? Which 'Americans'? Given the uncertainties, it would be foolish to allow British policy to be vetoed by anything as unpredictable as 'American' thinking about an issue which is several years ahead, when the United States and the state of international politics might be quite different. There are, however, some encouraging signs. A recent nation-wide opinion poll in the United States showed that American public opinion does not have nightmares about the Soviet nuclear threat; is concerned about nuclear proliferation; does want to curb the escalation of nuclear arsenals; is committed to defending Europe; and does want to shift towards a conventional emphasis in NATO strategy.[13] If a future administration reflected such attitudes, it would at least be somewhat sympathetic to the change of direction proposed by non-nuclear advocates in Britain. If the poll was accurate, it suggests the important conclusion that on nuclear matters the silent, as opposed to the moral, majority in America is significantly to the left of the President.

What adds to the difficulty of speculating about future US opinion is the fact that much would depend on how any change in British policy was packaged and handled. A Britain committed to NATO and making exertions for defence should not attract complaints from a sensible United States: the latter might have lost a nuclear ally, but it would be gaining a robust defensive friend. Furthermore, the force of any US opposition to Britain would be ameliorated if a stronger West European identity in defence had been established. In such circumstances Britain would be seen merely as 'one of the Europeans', rather than as the one with whom the United States had a 'special relationship'. If all went well, the United States could live with a non-nuclear Britain within NATO; but if the change were handled badly – with crude diplomacy and a failure to reinforce words with acts – then the United States would undoubtedly see British nuclear disarmament in terms of the defection of an old and major ally.

The problem has so far been presented in terms of the risks to the American connection, but the disadvantages of this connection must also be brought into the equation. The dangers of being drawn into the US global confrontation with the Soviet Union were referred to earlier: disagreements have occurred between Europeans and the White House over US policy towards the Middle East, Central America and the Soviet Union in particular. US administration spokesmen have sometimes criticized West Europeans for drifting towards neutralism and pacifism, but Ronald Reagan has done more to encourage West European neutralism than any beguiling words from the Politburo.

NATO would not necessarily 'shatter' (Michael Heseltine's word) if Britain announced a policy of unilateral nuclear disarmament: it would face a crisis. But what is wrong with a crisis? Crises clarify. They are moments of opportunity as well as danger. NATO, for example, emerged stronger as a result of the French crisis of the mid-1960s. Skilful crisis management might achieve the same again. Even if NATO did lose some cohesion, unity at any price should not be the objective of our Alliance policy, any more than strength at any price should be the objective of military policy. What matters is that one's interests are being furthered. Means are too often confused with ends in foreign affairs.

British security interests are not likely to be furthered if we always defer to the United States in the name of Alliance unity. It may be, at some point down the line, that it becomes clear that NATO will never bend from its pro-nuclear stance. At that point, it would be necessary for a non-nuclear British government to follow the French line, and announce its intention of leaving the integrated military organization. This would be a difficult step, but one which might have to be contemplated, after full consultation and with maximum collaboration with the allies.

Those in Britain who worry – though not very publicly – that British nuclear disarmament represents slippage *vis-à-vis* France in the international status league table, also worry – more publicly – that if Britain dropped out of the game, the Federal Republic of Germany might gain a few places by going nuclear itself. The likelihood of Federal Germany going nuclear, it is argued, will grow considerably if British nuclear disarmament led to the collapse of NATO. The reasons why states decide to go nuclear are a complex mixture of strategic and political consideration. Whether the Federal Republic of Germany would take such a decision – following British nuclear disarmament and/or a collapse of NATO – would depend on many factors, notably the general state of European security at the time and West German confidence in US guarantees. But British supporters of nuclear deterrence, who use the threat of West German nuclear weapons as an argument against British nuclear disarmament, do not have a strong case in terms of their own theory. If, as deterrence supporters constantly reiterate, nuclear states will not attack other nuclear states, then what is better than the major industrial power in Central Europe going nuclear?

To British nuclear disarmers, the problem of Federal Germany and nuclear weapons presents itself in a rather different form, at least in the short run. Disarmers are frequently confronted by the argument that the Federal Republic does not want conventional deterrence; its geopolitical position is such that it must place absolute reliance on nuclear deterrence. The argument has some force. However, the likely opposition of the Federal Republic to a decisive shift from a nuclear strategy by NATO should not be allowed to dictate allied strategy. Britain should not allow Federal Germany's preferences for the risks of nuclear war to those of conventional war to dictate its own security policy.

The reaction of the smaller members of NATO to a British decision to scrap nuclear weapons would again partly depend on the way Britain packaged its policy. It may well be that the governments in power would disapprove of such an action on Britain's part, since it would leave the United States as the only nuclear power in NATO, and because it might be seen as yet further evidence of Britain's opting out of European affairs. Among the signals, however, that Britain might send to its smaller allies in the years ahead, it is likely that a run-down of our conventional forces, as recommended by some, would have far more serious consequences than a nuclear renunciation. A large reduction of forces in BAOR would increase the difficulties some allies have been having in maintaining their defence efforts.[14] So, from the signalling point of view, it is clear that Britain has alternatives other than nuclear weapons if it wishes to show it is serious about defence, anxious to encourage the allies, and committed to European affairs. Unfortunately, while the Labour Party's defence proposals point in the right direction on nuclear issues, the Party's attitudes to Europe and credibility in defence matters leave much to be desired, in the opinion both of West Europeans and British voters.

Over the years, NATO has become overblown. It has been such a success, in a world where alliances are normally characterized by impermanence, that it has ceased to represent the bulk of the solution to our security problems and instead has become part of the problem. NATO has institutionalized an image of the threat (inflated), how it should be met (heavily pro-nuclear), and how the response should be organized (with a tightly integrated alliance under US leadership). All these need to be downgraded, without undermining the general framework.

The aim, within a few years, should be to encourage the United States to freeze its own nuclear programmes and adopt a more sensible attitude to the Soviet Union; to encourage NATO to adopt a 'no first use' strategy; and to seek the withdrawal of all nuclear weapons (theatre and battlefield) from Western Europe. At the end of the process, NATO's strategy will have been decoupled from US nuclear weapons. The United States will maintain its nuclear forces simply for the purpose of deterring direct attacks on the US homeland. The future is there to be shaped, not passively accepted: Britain should be seeking to create a new reality, and not simply adjusting to powerful images of the old.

4. Nuclear disarmament would severely weaken Britain in the event of war

Not only would nuclear disarmament make war more likely, the critics argue, it would also disastrously weaken NATO in the event of war. Who would want to command conventional forces against a nuclear enemy? It goes without saying that there are obvious dangers for any non-nuclear state involved in a war against a nuclear power. Some of the restraints which exist under mutual deterrence would go, including the possibility of intra-war deterrence; but, equally, some of the dangers of escalation would also be missing. The dropping of the atomic bombs on Japan in 1945 is brought forward by the critics to clinch the argument, but against this is the fact that nuclear powers have fought non-nuclear adversaries in several wars since 1945, but have restricted themselves to conventional weapons. In the case of a future European war, in which a nuclear Soviet Union might be involved against a non-nuclear NATO, the Soviet Union would still have to take residual US nuclear power into account. And the Soviet commitment to 'no first use' indicates concern about escalation, in addition to a desire for favourable propaganda. A Soviet Union contemplating attacking a non-nuclear Western Europe would also have other problems to reckon with, notably that of trying to control yet more territory, when it is already overcommitted. As a non-nuclear country, Britain would be less of a prime target, and there would be no sense in lunatic destruction by the Soviet Union, if it were to destroy what it presumably wished to control (although limited nuclear strikes might do the job it required).

Clearly, there is no hiding from the problem of nuclear coercion in war, but history gives some comfort, as does the widespread opinion that the actual risk of any European war is very low. In the view of all serious analysts of the Soviet Union, the prospect of a Soviet attack against Western Europe is extremely remote. Soviet leaders know the risks, they know the cost of empire, and they know the problems they face in making even their own country work. But there will always be some risk, since superpowers will behave like superpowers.

While recognizing the dangers facing a non-nuclear defence strategy in war, its supporters argue that the risk is worth taking to help create a safer world and relieve us of the burden of nuclear weapons. Even defeat in such circumstances would be preferable to a 'victory' in a general nuclear war. Fighting against a nuclear enemy would involve great risks and difficult choices, but would they be less than the perils of trying to fight a limited nuclear war? Nobody would like to command conventional forces against a nuclear enemy, but who would relish opposing a nuclear enemy with nuclear weapons? Once any war in Europe begins, the choices are terrifying.

The critics of non-nuclear defence sometimes argue that nuclear powers would not even have to use their weapons against a non-nuclear enemy: the threat (nuclear blackmail) would be sufficient to bring about victory. The two most likely situations in which nuclear blackmail would be used against Britain would be as follows: first, if British troops still resisting Soviet forces on the Continent refused to surrender; and second, in order to get Britain to surrender if Soviet troops had actually reached the Channel.[15] The temptation of nuclear blackmail in such circumstances cannot be ignored; but in wars in other continents since 1945, nuclear temptations have been resisted, or have not worked. And would the United States – could it – ever allow the Soviet Union to get away with nuclear blackmail in Europe? Furthermore, would a Britain with an ultimate nuclear deterrent be much better off, with its troops falling back before Soviet forces on the Continent? Would a British government use its nuclear weapons, whatever it had said in advance? It is likely that a blooded and bloodied Soviet leadership which had coldly decided to risk aggression would not be deterred from threatening or invading a nuclear-armed Britain before or just following a nuclear-age Dunkirk.

Counter-strategies for non-nuclear states against the threat or use of nuclear weapons are few.[16] Civil defence, territorial defence, civilian resistance and continued non-nuclear resistance would all be of limited use against a determined nuclear enemy. In such circumstances, the threat of being able to inflict unacceptable damage in retaliation is the most intimidating deterrent. The threat of nuclear blackmail in war will therefore remain a major problem for advocates of non-nuclear strategies. In the end, it is simply a risk which will be accepted in order to lessen other risks. But is this risk greater or more likely than that which nuclear strategists would face if confronted by a collapse of their conventional forces, or by the first use of nuclear weapons by the other side?

5. *Nuclear disarmament would expose Britain to the serious risk of nuclear blackmail*

The most frequent argument against British nuclear disarmament, and reliance on conventional or non-retaliatory deterrence, is that a non-nuclear Britain would be exposing itself to the threat of nuclear blackmail. War would not be necessary for a nuclear adversary; with a nuclear monopoly, it could get its way by coercion. A nuclear monopoly might tempt an ambitious state to behave more aggressively than it would under conditions of mutual nuclear threat.

The issue of nuclear blackmail is undoubtedly important, and this is recognized by those who are sympathetic to nuclear disarmament.[17] However, the risk of blackmail is accepted as preferable to the risks and burdens of independent nuclear deterrence and flexible response. But how much risk of nuclear blackmail would there be? This is a subject where there is a good deal of assertion, but not much analysis. Closer inspection usually reveals that there is less to the idea that nuclear disarmament would lead to nuclear blackmail than meets the eye.

Nuclear blackmail is an ambiguous bogy. Before we can say much about the risk of nuclear blackmail, we must know more clearly what it is, how it works, and whether it has been effective in the past. Relatively little work has been done to clarify these matters. What has been done, interestingly, has tended to confirm that the idea of nuclear blackmail is ambiguous in theory and uncertain in practice.[18] Until matters are further clarified, nuclear blackmail will remain at least as much a bogy as a real strategic problem. The phobia about nuclear blackmail and Finlandization is a symptom of the nuclear hypochondria of the powerful and of those who believe they should be more powerful. Furthermore, the concept of nuclear blackmail is also compounded by semantic difficulties. What we call nuclear blackmail is not analogous to real blackmail, and it is often difficult to draw a precise distinction between nuclear blackmail and nuclear deterrence.[19]

Nuclear blackmail is likely to be rare. We need not expect an outbreak of Soviet attempts to coerce non-nuclear European countries in future, especially if the NATO framework is maintained. NATO would immediately confront the Soviet Union with the nuclear power of the United States, and Soviet leaders can have few illusions about the importance to the United States of not allowing its superpower adversary to 'get away with blackmail'. Unless one takes a mechanistic view of Soviet behaviour, it is not self-evident that British nuclear disarmament, or even the denuclearization of NATO strategy, would necessarily result in Soviet nuclear aggressiveness.

Not only would nuclear blackmail be rare, it is also likely

declining asset. The more unused it remains, and the more often non-nuclear states stand up to nuclear states (and even fight them when the occasion arises), the more difficult it will be for nuclear powers to make credible coercive nuclear threats. Nuclear blackmail is a strategy which has atrophied since its birth.

Nuclear blackmail is a one-shot strategy. One of the biggest constraints on nuclear blackmail will be self-imposed. This is because nuclear powers understand that if they attempt blatant nuclear intimidation against a non-nuclear power, and if it proves successful, then the result will be the biggest rush to nuclear proliferation since the atomic bomb was invented.

As matters stand, most non-nuclear states are relatively satisfied with their security arrangements. Their worries are about the conventional threat from neighbours rather than nuclear blackmail. This attitude would change profoundly if, instead of its present uncertain history, nuclear blackmail were suddenly seen to work. Were the Soviet Union, sometime in the future, to attempt to intimidate some neighbour or adversary with nuclear threats, then that country (and many others) might well feel the need to go nuclear or at least attempt to find shelter under the umbrella of the United States. Neither of these outcomes would be desirable for the Soviet Union. It has long been clear that the Soviet Union has even more to fear from nuclear proliferation than has the United States, since the next enemy for most near-nuclear powers, after some regional power, is the Soviet Union. Some authority for this idea was given by Leonid Brezhnev, shortly before his death. In a conversation with a Western visitor he said, 'You must remember that every nuclear weapon in the world is either in the Soviet Union or aimed at the Soviet Union.'[20]

Because it is in the interests of the United States, as well as the Soviet Union, to stem proliferation, a rational United States would not only refrain from proliferation itself, but would also attempt to offer protection to those who might be challenged by the Soviet Union. The possible use and the utility of nuclear blackmail are easily exaggerated. The superpowers have been adversary partners in controlling nuclear proliferation; they should also be partners in resisting the temptation to be blackmailers.

Nuclear blackmail is neither easy nor cost-free. In peacetime there are strong political constraints operating on a state not to employ nuclear blackmail, and it is significant that the historical record of nuclear blackmail has not been impressive. There are no strong grounds for potential blackmailers to believe that they will be able to achieve their objectives successfully. Basing his conclusions on his study of supposed cases of nuclear coercion – Iran, Korea, the Middle East and so on – McGeorge Bundy has challenged the view that nuclear weapons are useful in times of peace for political coercion.[21] It is difficult to think of the gains which Moscow might hope to achieve as a result of using nuclear blackmail against a non-nuclear Britain, in so far as it would risk provoking the acquisition of nuclear weapons by all those states which are suspicious of the Soviet Union.

Blackmail can be resisted. If nuclear blackmail were to take place against a nation without a nuclear retaliatory capability, the latter could take one or a combination of counteractions, but what could be done in practice would be very dependent on the scenario. Sometimes a threat could be ignored; at others a threatener's bluff could be called; and on occasions it might be sensible to defer. There is a similar range of options for those states with minimal nuclear deterrents when they have to face nuclear giants.

A strong-willed government will not easily bend before nuclear blackmail, since it will understand the potential costs for the threatener, as well as for itself. A non-nuclear Britain would continue to receive some residual nuclear protection from the United States, even if the two countries were no longer formally allied – a situation not recommended in this paper. Soviet leaders are not likely to believe that Washington would allow them to coerce into submission a country with which the United States has always had a special relationship. And on issues less than coercion into submission, are Soviet nuclear threats likely to be credible? As it is, the reason why Britain has not been subject to blatant nuclear blackmail may not have been due to its independent nuclear power, but rather to the US nuclear umbrella.

This brief discussion has indicated some of the problems associated with the idea of nuclear blackmail. It is, admittedly, a risk facing non-nuclear powers, but all strategies involve some risk or another. It is therefore sensible to choose the risk whose consequences are less catastrophic, the one which does not entail our participation in a strategy based on the threat of a crime against humanity, and the one which – if things go wrong – still entails some hope of a continuation of politics.

Some would argue that those who support a non-nuclear strategy for Britain have already succumbed to implicit nuclear blackmail. That is, the simple presence of Soviet nuclear weapons has frightened a significant proportion of the British population into advocating nuclear disarmament. This may be so for some individuals, but it is not generally the case. For the most part – and increasingly so – opponents of British nuclear weapons are also supporters of a robust defence policy. It is the fear of nuclear war and the implications of the arms race, not a fear of the Soviet Union as such, which has produced a determination to try to do something towards reshaping the European security system.

Given that the idea of nuclear blackmail is ambiguous, the mechanisms uncertain, the risks remote, the likelihood incalculable, the counteractions various, and the dangers exaggerated, we should therefore conclude that this dimension of the problem, though important, is not sufficiently so to prevent Britain moving towards nuclear disarmament or pressing for the denuclearization of NATO. By doing the latter, we would be doing our limited best to help create the conditions for reciprocal security in Europe.

Conclusion: reciprocal security in Europe

The search for national security has a habit of being self-defeating. The interplay between national mistrust, the action–reaction phenomenon and the dynamics of weapons innovation, can produce greater national strength, but not necessarily greater national security. When one country attempts to increase its security against another by accumulating military power, the insecurity of the targeted country grows. Neither national nor international security is enhanced if major powers feel edgy and vulnerable. The insecure in any society are not the easiest to handle. Because we have the destructive power to wipe out the Soviet Union as an effective industrial society, and they have the destructive power to wipe out us, and because neither of us has a guaranteed defensive capability in sight, *national* security is ultimately impossible. There is only reciprocal security.

Reciprocal behaviour means a relationship in which something is given by each of two parties; there is mutual and conscious interaction in a particular direction. Between individuals there may be reciprocal friendship, and between countries there may be reciprocal trade. Reciprocity should also be the objective in the security policies of the major powers, since national security is impossible. Reciprocity implies the mutual exchange of privileges and, in the late twentieth century, the greatest privilege which nations can exchange is that of security – the fundamental right to exist, independently, and free of the risk of genocide or domination. The achievement of such a goal should place the denuclearization of East-West relations at the top of the agenda of European security problems.

Obviously, reciprocal security is easier said than done. It is a long-term process in which we can expect failures as well as successes, but its tendency will be towards positive East-West peace. At the beginning, Britain's 'moral' lead in nuclear disarmament should be directed towards persuading its allies of the desirability of reform. That in itself will be difficult enough. We must first encourage our allies to begin a process of reducing the arms competition, the paranoia, the institutions of confrontation and the militarization of thinking which grew so rationally out of the pressures and perceptions of the late 1940s. Having persuaded our allies, we must hope that some day the Soviet Union will reciprocate. We must take the first step. The West has the power and the liberal instincts, and, of all Western powers, Britain has most room for manoeuvre in the initial stages.

Reciprocity is not an alien idea in strategic life. Both the theory and practice of Mutual Assured Destruction and of arms control involve the idea of formal or tacit agreements between adversaries – the mutual exchange of privileges. Such agreements need to be made much more explicit, and in order to achieve this, several shifts in attitude must be made. First, nuclear deterrence must be taken away from the centre of our thinking about security. Second, we must appreciate that our security does not rise in direct proportion to the growth of Soviet insecurity. Third, we must give much more attention to the development of confidence-building measures in our relationship with the Soviet Union; these deserve more attention than 'war-fighting' options or even traditional arms control. Fourth, in developing a relationship of reciprocal security with the Soviet Union, we must be willing to undertake unilateral as well as multilateral actions. We must have the nerve to take some risks, and anticipate failures as well as successes, just as we do at present with our more negative conception of security. Finally, in order to take such steps, British opinion-formers and voters in general need to know much more about the Soviet Union. It is a remarkable fact that the gap is extremely wide between almost all Western specialists on the Soviet Union and Western decision-makers. Soviet specialists are far more relaxed, as a whole, about Soviet strategic intentions and capabilities. However, power lies in the hands of the stale sovietology of the hard-liners, who merely feed the militarized attitudes and institutions of the cold war.

The Soviet Union might not reciprocate as far or as fast as we would like. We might have to be patient and accept that it can only go at its own pace. Even so, it is evident to many that the Soviet Union is a more reasonable and normal country in its foreign policy behaviour than Western official propaganda allows. Even if the Soviet Union did not reciprocate, we would scarcely be any worse off. The fact is that we have a margin of safety and that the likelihood of a coldly calculated war being launched by the Soviet Union is grossly exaggerated. If nuclear war were to occur, the chances are that it would not be the result of a sober calculation by the Politburo. A Soviet decision to attack would be 'contingent' rather than 'intrinsic'.[22] Scenarios can be envisaged in which an edgy leadership, which in normal circumstances would entirely eschew the nuclear option, might be pressed to decide the opposite: 'it's now or never'; 'we've no choice'; 'we can't back down'. Fear rather than ambition will be the spur to the next European war. Reciprocal security seeks to minimize the occasions when any leader might persuade himself, or herself, that firing nuclear weapons makes sense. There is little reason to suppose that Soviet leaders want war in Europe or would even participate in one, except in extreme conditions. We must therefore de-emphasize the prospect of war with the Soviet Union, in words and action, and certainly reject the eschatological beliefs of Ronald Reagan and others about Armageddon.[23] It is worth remembering that Soviet leaders gave up the idea of the 'fatalistic inevitability' of war between the two blocs thirty years ago.

In the period since 1945, our relations with the Soviet Union have sometimes been better, sometimes worse; but they have lacked a constructive long-term strategy. The détente policy of Nixon and Kissinger in the early 1970s was a breakthrough, but their own country's need for instant gratification, even in diplomacy, prevented the consistency which is essential for a successful 'Western philosophy of coexistence'.[24] We cannot expect to change the nature of the relationship with the Soviet Union overnight. Although some of the requirements for reciprocal security fly in the face of traditional Soviet strategic culture, change is possible in the Soviet Union. It has already occurred in such well-established ideas as the inevitability of war, war as a continuation of politics and the value of strategic superiority. Change will be a slow process, and in the meantime the Soviet Union will remain a problem because of its power, ideology and interests. Reciprocal security might not work, but have we any choice but to try, when the alternatives are either preparing to fight the Russians, or hanging on with nuclear deterrence until that unthinkable combination of events occurs, when Murphy takes revenge on the almost absolute confidence of the nuclear deterrers?

The process of reciprocal security must start in Europe, because we must begin from where we are; because Europe is the most heavily armed continent; and because the Soviet Union has us targeted. But Europe cannot remain a stable ship of peace if the seas all around are stormy. We have a strategic interest as well as a moral duty to try to resolve crises and reduce the risk of great-power intervention, which may lead, though not inevitably, to escalation.

The periods of greatest danger since World War II have not been when the Soviet Union has felt relatively comfortable (the late 1950s or the early 1970s), but rather when the United States has been aggressively strong and the Soviet Union has felt pushed into a corner and afraid that time might be running out (the late 1940s, the early

1960s and the early 1980s). It is not true, as White House spokesmen have claimed, that the resurgence of US military power under Reagan has made for a safer world. Indeed, the opposite is the case. The Reagan resurgence has merely exacerbated suspicions, set back arms control by many years, and strengthened Soviet determination to proceed with arms acquisition programmes. Reciprocal security requires that the intimidatory character of the nuclear stand-off be balanced by forms of reassurance. A shift to defensive deterrence by Britain would be a step in the right direction.

Notes

1. The most comprehensive presentation of the case is *Defence without the Bomb. The Report of the Alternative Defence Commission* (London: Taylor & Francis Ltd., 1983); the most important, since it puts the power of a major party behind the idea, is *Defence & Security for Britain* (The Labour Party: Statement to Annual Conference 1984 by the National Executive Committee).
2. Of the growing number of former public servants who have criticized current nuclear strategy, the best known in Britain is Field Marshal Lord Carver; see his *A Policy for Peace* (London: Faber, 1982). Note also General Michael N. Harbottle *et al.*, *The Arms Race to Armageddon: Generals Challenge US/NATO Strategy* (Leamington Spa: Berg, 1984); and Gwyn Prins (ed.), *The Choice: Nuclear Weapons Versus Security* (London: Chatto & Windus, 1984).
3. See, *inter alia*, *The Report of the Alternative Defence Commission*, op.cit.; Nigel Blake and Kay Pole (eds.), *Dangers of Deterrence: Philosophers on Nuclear Strategy* (London: Routledge & Kegan Paul, 1983) and *Objections To Nuclear Defence: Philosophers On Deterrence* (London: Routledge & Kegan Paul, 1984); Jeff McMahan, *British Nuclear Weapons: For and Against* (London: Junction Books, 1981); Robert Neild, *How To Make Up Your Mind About The Bomb* (London: André Deutsch, 1981); Prins, op.cit.; and Gwyn Prins (ed.), *Defended To Death* (Harmondsworth: Penguin Books, 1983).
4. Ken Booth, 'Unilateralism: A Clausewitzian Reform?', in Blake and Pole (eds.), *Dangers of Deterrence*, pp.42-6.
5. *The Economist*, 18 September 1982, p.31.
6. These arguments have been advanced with most clarity, and authority, by George F. Kennan, the dean of American Soviet specialists. See his *The Nuclear Delusion: Soviet–American Relations In The Atomic Age* (London: Hamish Hamilton, 1984).
7. This is elaborated in Ken Booth, 'Strategy and Conscription', in John Baylis (ed.), *Alternative Approaches To British Defence Policy* (London: The Macmillan Press, 1983), pp.154-90.
8. *Report of the Alternative Defence Commission*, op.cit., p.9.
9. *Report of the Alternative Defence Commission;* F. Barnaby and E. Boeker, 'Defence Without Offence: Non-Nuclear Defence for Europe', *Peace Studies Paper No.8* (Bradford: Bradford University School of Peace Studies, and London: Housmans, 1982); D. Fernback and L. Mackay (eds.), *Nuclear Free Defence* (London: Heretic Books, 1983); M. Kaldor and D. Smith (eds.), *Disarming Europe* (London: Merlin Press, 1982); D. Smith, 'Non-Nuclear Military Options for Britain', *Peace Studies Paper No.6* (Bradford: Bradford University School of Peace Studies, and London: Housmans, 1981); and Prins, *The Choice*, op.cit.
10. Bernard Williams, 'Morality, Scepticism and the Nuclear Arms Race', in Blake and Pole, *Objections To Nuclear Defence*, pp.99-114; Anthony Kenny, 'Better Dead than Red', *ibid.*, pp.12-27. The case for the moral dimension is most comprehensively put by Michael Walzer, *Just and Unjust Wars: A Moral Argument with Historical Illustrations* (Harmondsworth: Penguin, 1980).

11.   *Report of the Alternative Defence Commission*, p.46.
12.   *Ibid.*
13.   The poll was conducted by Abt Associates of Cambridge, Massachusetts: reported in *New Society*, 25 October 1984.
14.   On the question of British troops in Federal Germany, for example, a senator in the Belgian parliament, General Robert Close, declared in 1982: 'If the British go, the Belgians go.' Quoted by Frederick Bonnart, 'Troops are needed to maintain credibility', *The Times*, 14 December 1982.
15.   McMahan, *British Nuclear Weapons*, p.41.
16.   *Ibid.*, pp.137-8.
17.   *Ibid.*
18.   *Ibid.*, pp.40-7, 83-5, 137-8, 140-3, 145-6; see also McMahan, 'Nuclear blackmail', in Blake and Pole, *Dangers of Deterrence*, pp.84-111, and McGeorge Bundy, 'The unimpressive record of atomic diplomacy', in Prins (ed.), *Defended To Death*, pp.42-54.
19.   McMahan, *British Nuclear Weapons*, p.41.
20.   Quoted by Freeman Dyson, *Weapons and Hope* (New York: Harper & Row, 1984), p.284.
21.   Bundy, op.cit.
22.   Dan Smith, 'The Crisis of Atlanticism', in Baylis (ed.), *Alternative Approaches to British Defence policy*, p.234.
23.   Journalists have traced eleven utterances by Reagan on the possible imminence of Armageddon: see Richard N. Ostling, 'Armageddon and the End Times', *Time*, 5 November 1984, p.50.
24.   The phrase is from Marshall D. Shulman, 'Towards a Western philosophy of coexistence', *Foreign Affairs*, October 1973.

Comment on Chapter 3
Hugh Beach

I found Ken Booth's paper extremely stimulating and particularly enjoyed the first few pages. I think I agreed with almost every word of the last few pages, except perhaps in passing to say that the argument about hypocrisy leaves me absolutely stone cold. It seems to me that the important point is not whether or not free-riding under the American umbrella is hypocritical, but that there is absolutely no *merit* in it. And since many of the proponents put it forward as the morally and ethically desirable thing to do, this seems to me the important part of the argument. What moral merit is there in a policy which simply means that more bombs fall on somebody else – particularly if you save money in the process?

But that is *en passant,* because the comments that I chiefly wish to make are about the middle section. I cordially agree with the adoption of a 'no first use' strategy, eventual withdrawal of theatre nuclear weapons and the ultimate decoupling of NATO strategy from US nuclear strategy. Where I am stuck, and always have been, is how on earth you make a non-nuclear strategy, particularly for the Central Front in Europe, actually work. I have been thinking about this for many years now because, surprisingly or not, I suspect that very few soldiers who have direct responsibility in this area have taken the doctrine of nuclear release in any sense seriously as part of their thinking about the real world. So, what new proposals are on offer? There has been plenty of thinking on a better tactical scheme of manoeuvre. Some will remember Bogislav von Bonin back in the 1950s and Liddell Hart's book in the 1960s; one of the best for my money was written by a Colonel Burgess in the *British Army Review* of August 1970, and since he is now the Deputy SACEUR, he may not altogether thank me for reminding him of that particular contribution! However, we have had a flood of them recently – Afheldt, Brossollet, Spanocchi, Uhle Wettler, Löser – but when you come to look at them, they singularly fail to carry military conviction.[1] And I suspect that the reason that all this thinking has never really been accepted is not that the military are purblind or stupid, but that these alternative schemes do not stand up to hard-nosed analysis. When you come to look at the actual tiny menu that constitutes the characteristics of defensive deterrence – flexibility, mobility, dispersal, decentralized command, good training, defence in depth, heavy fire-power packed in small bundles – who on earth does not believe in that? The trouble is that these comments are essentially vacuous and get us no further forward.

What else do you go for? You can go for bigger conventional force levels, as in the schemes of Griffiths and Kaufman (in the famous *Economist* article of 31 July 1982),[2] and I think a bit of Booth, in so far as he believes in conscription, because the common theme of all these is that they are going to cost more money. They all entail a percentage over and above the 3 per cent per annum growth that was then being assumed, and, in the case of the egregious Mr Steven Canby, a glorious 15 per cent in addition.[3] Most people understand that the cancellation of Trident is needed, not in order to increase present provision for conventional defence but to save the remnants of what we have got. Even on present plans, half the tanks on the Central Front are not going to be modernized with Chobham armour by the turn of the century; half the armoured personnel carriers are not going to be modernized; and many of the guns in the 1st British Corps are going to be obsolescent. Everything is grossly underfunded already, and to suggest that you can go up to 3, 4, 5 or 6 per cent or whatever seems to me the veriest moonshine. Even if we did, in fact, increase the number of divisions, say, or tanks and everything else on the Central Front, it seems extremely probable that the Soviet Union would do precisely what they have always said they would do in the circumstances and up the ante themselves. Everybody is therefore left with a much more expensive defence bill and no better off – arguably worse off.

There is also the strand of what I call technological, good-life utopianism, which puts its faith in such things as small hand-held anti-tank weapons, either wielded by men on motor cycles or elevated on masts; or John Keegan's instant anti-tank ditches created by towing mole-ploughed pipes into the fields of the Federal Republic and, come the threat of war, pumping them up with high explosive and blowing V-shaped anti-tank ditches;[4] or even Bob Neild's delightful solution to the problem, which is to go out and plant more trees.[5] I cordially agree – it is probably necessary in the light of acid rain anyway – but by any reasoning it is a rather long-term solution to our difficulties! What I am working round to is that, for my money, almost the only scheme that has been proposed which shows any sign of holding water is the use of ET ('emerging technology'), or the sort of proposals produced by the European Security Study (ESECS) in 1983.[6] These point to the developments in high technology which are fortuitously coming round the corner, and which do indeed seem to make it possible to do two things: (1) doing by conventional means what has hitherto only been possible by nuclear, and that is well in sight; and (2) doing predominantly by missiles what has hitherto been only possible by manned aircraft. The advantages of the first are self-evident; the advantages of the second are twofold. First, it economizes on your most scarce resource – aircrew; and second, it decouples you from these vast immobile slabs of concrete with all the temptation to pre-emption that they bring.

However, the snags in this approach are well known. Finance is not the least of them and then there are the implications for arms control. In any case, will it work? And what happens when the Russians develop countermeasures, and when they do exactly the same themselves, which incidentally they manifestly are? And not least, of course, there is the school of thought that says that to go down this road is just as provocative, if you regard non-provocation, manifest defensiveness, as part of the aim. The Russians have told me that they regard schemes for deep attack on airfields and deep attack on follow-up forces by conventional means (and therefore guaranteed from the word go, because you do not have to wait for nuclear release) as hostile, provocative and to be avoided if at all possible. A lot more thinking is needed. Do we take this provocation argument seriously? If so, what are we going to do about it? Could we even have an arms control measure to the effect that neither side would go down the ET route? There is no clear path through this particular jungle and working it all out is going to take a great deal of time.

This brings me to the central criticism I want to make of what Ken says. He shares the same flaw as *The Church and the Bomb* (the Bishop of Salisbury's famous study)[7] and the Labour Party manifesto, in that they see what they think ought to be done as being done within the lifetime of a single parliament. The lifetime of a single parliament is very short; in Britain, as in most other democracies I can think of, it is two or three or four years. If you are going to press on regardless, it means that any thought of doing it by consultation and bringing your allies with you – of convincing the West Germans or the Americans that it is the right thing to do – goes straight out of the window. It was, oddly enough, Sydney Bailey, who was the Quaker member of the Bishop of Salisbury's commission on *The Church and the Bomb*, who highlighted this point. He said that however much goodwill a government of Great Britain had – goodwill in the special sense of wanting to travel down this route – it would actually take at the very least twenty years. Now once you have said that, you have put your finger on the key to the whole issue, because you have then totally uncoupled it from the absurdity of trying to force it through within the lifetime of a single parliament. Instead, you give time for the money to be provided (any solution is going to be extremely expensive, and, as I have said, the budget is overcommitted); you give time to investigate the arms control implications; time to persuade the Russians that this is the right thing to do; and time to persuade the West Germans and the Americans. In short, if this is your desired programme, you must be prepared to pursue it rationally and step by step, and not try to shoehorn it into what can be done by 1992.

Notes

1. Bogislav von Bonin, quoted in Hans Speier, 'German Rearmament and Atomic War', printed for the Rand Corporation by Row Peterson and Co: Evanston, Illinois, 1957, pp.75-7; Basil Liddell Hart, *Deterrent or Defence* (London: Stevens, 1960); Brigadier D. M. Pontifex and Colonel A. E. Burgess, 'A New Concept of Land Operations in Europe', *British Army Review*, No. 35 (August 1970); H. Afheldt, *Verteidigung und Frieden* (Munich: Hanser Verlag, 1976) and 'Tactical Nuclear Weapons and European Security' in SIPRI, *Tactical Nuclear Weapons: European Perspectives* (London: Taylor and Francis, 1978); G. Brossollet, 'Essai sur la non-battaille', Paris, 1975; E.Spannocchi and G. Brossollet, *Verteidigung ohne Schlact* (Munich: Hanser Verlag, 1976); F. Uhle Wettler, *Grefechtsfeld Mitteleuropa* (Munich: Bernard and Graefe, 1980); H. J. Löser, 'Raum-deckende Verteidigung', *Osterreichische Militar Zeitschrift*, No. 4, 1977.
2. P. Griffiths and E. Dinter, *Not over by Christmas* (Chichester: Antony Bird, 1983); W. W. Kaufman, 'Non-nuclear Deterrence', in John Steinbruner and Leon Sigal (eds.), *Alliance Security: NATO and the No-First-Use Question* (Washington D.C.: Brookings Institution, 1984).
3. Steven L. Canby, 'Military Reform and the Art of War', *Survival*, Vol. 25, No. 3 (May/June 1983), pp.120-7.
4. John Keegan, 'Means for Strengthened Conventional Capability', working paper for the European Security Study, Schlosshotel Kronberg, 23-28 Oct. 1982.
5. Robert Neild, quoted in *Panorama*, BBC TV, 22 Oct. 1984.
6. ESECS, *Strengthening Conventional Deterrence in Europe* (London: Macmillan, 1983).
7. *The Church and the Bomb* (London: Hodder and Stoughton, 1982).

Comment on Chapters 2 and 3
Kenneth Hunt

British defence policy is no longer the largely bipartisan affair that it was for some thirty years after the signing of the North Atlantic Treaty in 1949. Opposition parties often had their differences with the government of the day over the priority to be given to defence or over particular weapon systems or deployments, but when in office they continued with the main lines of policy – which are built around Europe – much as they found them, political rhetoric aside. Now a sharp cleavage has appeared, with the Labour Party advocating a radical shift to a non-nuclear defence.

Defence policy has not, of course, been just British in concept; allied views have influenced it strongly. Britain rests its security squarely on NATO, the mechanism by which the United States is identified with the defence of Europe and by which European defence efforts can be combined. There has been nothing to stop Britain choosing to go it alone, except good sense and the scale of the problem, but no government of either side has contemplated it. A firm link with the United States has been a main strand of British foreign policy since the war. Britain also has an evident interest in helping to preserve peace in Europe, since this is the context for its own security.

Alliance strategy

Any discusssion of British defence has to dwell heavily on Alliance affairs and particularly on NATO strategy. That strategy is one of graduated escalation, more usually known as flexible response. It is nuclear at heart. It was painfully hammered out within NATO over several years and finally adopted in December 1967. It is designed to meet any attack with whatever is required to defeat it, including the readiness to use nuclear weapons if need be. The first line of defence, and thus of deterrence, is provided by conventional – non-nuclear – forces of such a size that a major attack would be required to defeat them. These are deployed well forward, so that deterrence starts on the border. The nuclear weapons are almost entirely US-owned and controlled. American ground forces form a substantial part of the defences.

Throughout the long and intense debate over flexible response, the

United States – which initiated it – pressed hard for significantly stronger conventional forces so that if hostilities broke out, the US President would have more options open to him than just the early use of nuclear weapons, in order to meet the commitment to the defence of Europe that the United States had undertaken. Some flexibility, in other words. Europeans agreed that the conventional forces ought to be stronger, but they did not want them *too* strong. Their view was that the Soviet Union would be much more powerfully deterred by the risk of nuclear devastation of its homeland than by the costs of fighting a war on West German soil. They did not want to prepare for lengthy fighting, with all the destruction that would bring.[1] They wanted what has since been cynically described as a doctrine of conventional insufficiency: to stop short of a full conventional defence so that, from the outset, the Soviet Union would be aware that there was a risk of nuclear weapons being used. Since NATO was then judged to have superiority in battlefield (short-range) nuclear weapons, the theory was that these could be used, or held for use, against forward-attacking troops, to give military advantage or to stabilize a battle that was going badly.

The strategy was accordingly agreed on the basis that the defence would not be purely conventional. It was flexible in more ways than one, since politically it left some room for interpretation or later adjustments. Much of the intellectual force behind the European arguments was provided by Denis Healey and Lord Mountbatten, then respectively Defence Minister and Chief of the Defence Staff. They stressed that NATO commanders could not expect much larger forces – 'they had to make do with what they'd got'. The forces, however, were to be strengthened sufficiently to give a first line of conventional defence that the Soviet Union could not be confident of defeating, thereby enabling NATO at least to defer the time when nuclear weapons might have to be considered – raising the nuclear threshold, in the jargon. They were in fact strengthened over the decade that followed, when European nations generally increased their defence spending, though that of the United States went down as preoccupation with Vietnam and its aftermath increased.[2] However, Soviet forces were strengthened too, as part of a worldwide military build-up that has probably had no parallel in peacetime. It is very hard to assess the resulting military balance in Europe with precision, but some ten years after the adoption of flexible response, NATO seemed relatively no better off.[3] It was therefore still uncomfortably reliant on the early use of nuclear weapons. European war-stocks, of munitions and the like, were still low, and at best sufficient for no more than thirty days. The United States kept its own stocks at a higher level and pressed Europeans to do the same. But preparation for a long war made scant appeal to them. They wanted to deter war, not wage it on the ground where they lived. Ideas for fighting back to the Pyrenees have always looked more attractive from Boston than from Bonn. Europe remained clear that it wanted a strategy that was nuclear at heart. France left the integrated military organization because it wanted no part in extended conventional fighting.[4]

In no country in the Alliance – apart from France – did short-war thinking take a firmer hold than in Britain, under governments of either side, and notably Labour, which was in office during the critical years of the flexible response debate and for much of the decade thereafter. In Britain alone among the European countries, there is no conscription, so that the army is small, around half the size of that of France and the Federal Republic of Germany. Reserves who are properly equipped and trained are few (though they have been increased in the last five years). There are no plans for a nationwide call-up or for the mobilization of industry on a war footing. War-stocks are low. Put bluntly, planning has been for a war of weeks at most, as far as the central sector is concerned, presumably on the assumption that in the nuclear age nothing else is likely or that the resources for anything larger cannot be found. The independent nuclear force was designed to deter any nuclear war from reaching these shores.

The critics
The strategy sketched above has always had critics, obviously in the United States, where pressure for Europeans to do more for their (conventional) defence has been continually applied by Congress and succeeding administrations.[5] Washington well understands that the NATO political machinery and the European allies are prone to inertia, preferring to leave things generally as they are, and that an American kick is needed to get something done. So kicks there have been in the form of periodical initiatives for defence improvements or congressional threats, and something has been achieved, though the reliance on nuclear weapons has not materially been lessened. However, allied awareness of the dangerous nature of this has been sharpened by the growth of Soviet nuclear strength, not least in Europe.

The arrival of Soviet strategic nuclear parity not only concentrated American minds wonderfully, it made Europeans conscious that the use of strategic weapons was now much less likely, certainly on behalf of allies: a form of stalemate had appeared. At the theatre level, the development of Soviet short-, medium- and intermediate-range nuclear missiles in numbers greater than NATO's removed any likelihood there may ever have been that NATO could gain military advantage from using nuclear weapons. However, they still served the all-important purpose of deterring war or, if that failed, of deterring Soviet nuclear use. Soviet superiority in conventional forces in the key central sector remained, notably in numbers of tanks, aircraft and guns. In a speech at the International Institute for Strategic Studies in London in October 1977, the Federal German Chancellor pointed to the way in which all this undermined the NATO strategy.[6] His thinking, which was widely shared, led to the NATO decision in December 1979 to deploy intermediate-range nuclear forces (INF) in the form of Pershing II and cruise missiles. This was designed to restore flexibility to NATO escalation capacity, which had been eroded in the face of the Soviet deployment of the SS-20 missiles. Ironically, the plan to deploy missiles, in the absence of an arms control agreement to limit them, led to a public debate which naturally focused on the nuclear element in the strategy. This in turn eventually led to a major breakdown in the political consensus on defence in this country. It also led to the West German Social Democratic Party (SPD) changing its stance on INF, though probably not on the need for nuclear deterrence.[7]

Critics of the NATO strategy can now be found right across the board. There are those who have always attacked it because it does not provide a wholly or largely conventional defence, with or without nuclear weapons as a support or device for coupling Europe to the US strategic deterrent. There are some who firmly accept the need for nuclear weapons in Europe but want them removed from the forward area, because they are vulnerable or no longer have a worthwhile role. Others want NATO to adopt a policy of not using nuclear weapons first – 'no first use' (NFU).[8] Some want NATO (and Britain) to give up nuclear weapons altogether. Some accept that NATO may keep them, but they do not want Britain to have any of its own, or US ones based in Britain. Some there are who want Britain to leave NATO, break the link with the United States and organize a national, usually non-nuclear, defence. No doubt there are some who advocate no defence at all.

Change
There are, then, many who think something should be done, or should have been done a while back.[9] SACEUR (Supreme Allied Commander Europe) and others have been pressing NATO to strengthen the conventional forces, either through an incremental approach or by the use of high technology so that conventional weapons can do at least some of the things now assigned to nuclear ones.[10] Both approaches, particularly the high-technology route, would allow the nuclear threshold to be raised and permit forward

nuclear weapons to be withdrawn and dual-capable aircraft to revert to purely conventional roles.

The Alliance has in fact reached one of those periodical stages of accepting that something ought to be done, though whether this means it will find the resources for doing so is another matter. It has been brought to this position partly by determined pressure from the Reagan administration and partly by its recognition of the public concern about nuclear weapons.[11] Until recently the allies have been too preoccupied with the domestic and East-West arguments over INF; now that that issue is for the moment less troublesome, political energy has turned once more to other security problems, notably that of harnessing advanced technology. As a result, outline approval has been given for the defensive use of new conventional missiles to engage enemy forces both deep inside Eastern Europe (but moving forward to join the battle) and already in or near the front line. NATO has long planned to use aircraft for such deep strikes but, in the face of enhanced Soviet air defences, it now proposes to use missiles instead. Other programmes for incremental improvements, many already in forward budgets and covering such things as weapon systems, stores, protective and readiness measures, will go ahead as well, and Britain will be expected to play an appropriate part in them.

All this can be accommodated within the strategy of flexible response; there is no disposition at all to attempt to renegotiate this, with all the pain which that would bring. Nor is there any need: it was designed to be flexible. The changes will go some way towards meeting the criticisms of those who want nuclear weapons to play a lesser role, but they do nothing to meet the more radical complaints, in particular from those who want a non-nuclear strategy. The remainder of this paper therefore looks at some of the proposals that have been made, to see what merit or chance of adoption they may have, and then follows this by suggesting the elements around which British defence policy should be constructed.

Two radical proposals

No first use
The fear that any use of nuclear weapons in Europe would inevitably lead to a general nuclear war has prompted proposals that NATO should adopt NFU.[8] NATO has already given a pledge that it will not use any weapons except in response to attack[12] but retains the option of recourse to nuclear weapons during hostilities. By definition, NFU does not renounce the nuclear option, and most of those who advocate it recognize that nuclear weapons are still needed, both for the US nuclear guarantee to Europe and to deter Soviet use.[13] NFU is of interest to those who are against nuclear weapons only as a way-station

towards disarmament or as a means of lessening the nuclear risks they see at present.

The aim of NFU would be to prevent a war becoming nuclear, but it is far from certain that it would achieve this, since the course of a war once started is wholly unpredictable. The problem that its opponents see is that to declare NFU might be the wrong way to try to stop a war from starting in the first place, and the most important thing is to *avoid* war. NFU implies the preparedness to fight a drawn-out conventional war, something Europeans have always desperately wanted to avoid. Since they think the Soviet Union will be deterred above all by the risk of nuclear damage to its territory, there is no willingness to give up the deterrent value of possible use. To adopt NFU, furthermore, would be to create the conditions in which the Soviet Union could make war on the terms that best suited it, using its conventional and geographic advantages. NFU could be seen as divorcing the US nuclear guarantee from the fate of Europe.

The present strategy of possible first use means that if NATO is losing, it is prepared to go nuclear. NFU means that if NATO is losing it must be prepared to lose; the nuclear guarantee would be withdrawn. This is effectively what the NFU proposal advocates – not a very compelling banner for the allies to march behind. Europe is certainly not ready to subscribe to NFU; the United States is equally opposed to it, both in the administration and in Congress.

If the adoption of NFU were not to undercut the effectiveness of NATO deterrence, there would have to be 'a strengthened confidence in the adequacy of the conventional forces of the Alliance, above all the forces in place on the central front and those available for prompt reinforcement', to quote from one of the proposals.[14] One of its aims was therefore to set in train a study of how these forces might be strengthened and, as noted above, this has been happening. But it is with the idea of no *early* first use – NEFU, not NFU; of raising the threshold, not removing it. Given NATO's perceived weaknesses, even NEFU is not for tomorrow. Reaching that stage, let alone NFU, is ironically made harder by people and parties who oppose nuclear weapons, since all too often they also oppose the higher defence spending needed to rely on them less or not at all.

A non-nuclear, defensive strategy

The Labour Party has put forward a defence policy for Britain as a platform for the next general election.[15] It is non-nuclear: it would give up British nuclear weapons and require American ones to be moved from this country. It is designed for defensive deterrence and is opposed to deep-strike operations into enemy territory. It is committed to membership of NATO but would work within the

Alliance for an immediate policy of NFU followed later by a nuclear-free Europe; it wants a purely conventional defence for NATO and recommends a refusal to retaliate with chemical weapons. It accepts that there is some strength in the argument that NATO should improve its conventional defence capacity and that this might be done through new conventional weapons, but they must be purely defensive ones. Trident would be cancelled and Polaris decommissioned. Outside Europe, Britain would look to the United Nations for the protection of its national interests and not safeguard them with British forces; a political solution to the Falklands problem would be urgently sought, so that forces there could be reduced. Defence spending would be lowered over time towards the average of the major European allies, measured as a proportion of national income. The Party accepts that there should be a more independent political role for the European countries but is opposed to an EEC defence policy.

The strategy proposed by Ken Booth in Chapter 3 follows similar lines as far as its defensive nature and nuclear weapons policy are concerned. He does, however, suggest that conscription might be reintroduced in Britain and accepts the need for robust defences.

Some reactions
The NATO arguments for the retention of nuclear deterrence have been summarized above. It seems most unlikely that a non-nuclear alternative would find any support among the major countries in the Alliance. *France* would be resolutely opposed: its socialist government is as firmly attached to nuclear deterrence as its more conservative predecessors have been. Nuclear weapons may divide people in Britain but they unite them in France; they are the basis for French security, indeed foreign policy. *The Federal Republic of Germany* wants above all to deter war in Europe – not just nuclear war but any war, which would be on its soil. At root this deterrence has been provided in two ways: by the complete identification of the United States with the security of Europe; and by the link between strategic and conventional forces that American nuclear weapons in Europe demonstrate. Federal Germany is now offered in place of this a solely conventional strategy, with little or no offensive capability, which envisages fighting slowly back across the country. Quite apart from the limitation on the American commitment that this would represent, it would be seen as leaving enemy territory a virtual sanctuary. Is it supposed that deterrence will be as strong if the Soviet Union faces only the costs of fighting a war on West German soil while its own territory and that of its East European allies is to remain untouched? Such a concept seems politically unacceptable and militarily unsound, to say the least of it.

To take the military aspects further, a primarily defensive strategy hands the tactical initiative to the Warsaw Pact. If NATO forces had to give ground against heavy air and armoured assault, as they almost certainly would, then to get that ground back or to avoid retreating further, they would need strong mobile counter-attack formations supported by tactical aircraft; anti-tank weapons would not suffice. To use their mobility they would have to keep the enemy air off their backs. In part, this would be done by air defence missiles and aircraft, but this would have to be supplemented by striking at the airfields from which the enemy aircraft are operating – they could not be allowed to go back to safe havens, quietly refuel, rearm and then return to the fight. Similarly, enemy ground forces reinforcing those already in combat could not be left to come forward undisturbed; they would have to be attacked and broken up on their way forward just as NATO forces would be attacked. NATO does have a chance of defending itself if it does not have to face the whole weight of Soviet main and follow-up forces without a break. The notion that it is somehow bad to have an offensive capacity can appeal to some nervous politicians in peacetime but it is totally ridiculous once war starts. It is simply a recipe for ratcheting backwards, or even disaster, neither of which is calculated to have much appeal for West Germans.

A NATO non-nuclear policy would also seem to cast doubt on the worth of a Soviet NFU pledge. As has been said, with NFU, if NATO is losing, it must be prepared to lose. But if the Soviet Union should be losing, would it be content to lose? Or prefer to use? NATO would have no nuclear weapons and would have been at great pains to decouple explicitly from US nuclear strategy; the Soviet Union would surely be given the incentive to use nuclear weapons in Europe to reverse the tide of battle and indeed bring it to a halt. There could under such circumstances be no NATO defence left. It is very hard to see the United States being prepared to leave its troops in Europe unprotected in this way, and if they go, the whole basis of European security goes with them.

Ken Booth has remarked, in defence of the need for radical thinking, that the battlefields of strategic history are monuments to the attempts of nations to give yesterday's answers to tomorrow's questions. He might well have noted that they are also – all of them – monuments to the failure of conventional deterrence. It is after all just possible that fifteen allied nations, with changing governments, who have thought about security problems for thirty years, singly and collectively, might have managed to stumble on some of the right answers. The fact that the Soviet Union, by a different route, has finished up in the same place may make one think there is something in this.

Ken Booth has also quoted with approval (as has the Labour Party) Field Marshal Lord Carver, in this case as a military man who has spoken against nuclear deterrence. It may be worth giving here two extracts from the concluding chapter of the Field Marshal's book that he cites:[16]

Abolition of nuclear weapons would turn the clock back to the era in which the major industrial nations could think of war as an acceptable 'other means' of continuing policy . . . By abolishing or appearing to abolish nuclear weapons we should be making a Third World War more likely, and, if it started as a conventional one and lasted any length of time, there is no doubt that the nuclear weapon would reappear. We would then have the worst of both worlds. We would have lost its value as a deterrent but would suffer from its use after the war had started.

After having made the point that the deterrent to war is both nuclear and conventional, Lord Carver then answers the question of whether there should be any nuclear systems based in Europe by saying: 'For NATO's conventional forces to have no nuclear backing other than American strategic systems, while the Soviet Union had nuclear weapons clearly designed for use against Europe, would be to run an unjustifiable risk.'

The aim of the Labour Party policy is to convince the allies of the virtues of a purely conventional defence. If it failed to do so, what then? Would British forces be left in Federal Germany as an integrated part of an allied defence still based on the possible first use of nuclear weapons? This might have some attractions, since the alternative of bringing them home could be very expensive unless they were disbanded and would weaken the defences both militarily and politically. Indeed, such a step would risk an unravelling of the whole security structure that Europe has had for 35 years. But their role, if left there, would be a strange one, and British officers could hardly be left in NATO command positions, as the Labour Party would like. It is one thing for a country in the north, such as Norway, to have no nuclear weapons on its soil, but quite another to be part of a closely-woven allied defence in the central sector.

It might be remarked that when the attempt to win over other NATO members was going on, Britain's credentials as a good ally seriously interested in European security would hardly have been enhanced during the process of introducing the new Labour policy. Federal Germany would have been roundly told that its security must in future rest only on conventional deterrence; that forward defence was no longer sacrosanct; and that it should agree to barriers and fortifications being built across its territory (something opposed by all segments of West German opinion).[17] The United States would have been put on notice to remove its nuclear weapons and bases from

Britain; told that its forces in Europe must do without nuclear protection; and that Britain's relationship with the United States was long overdue for change.[18] The allies collectively would have been told that Britain would no longer abide by the NATO 1979 decision on INF; and made aware that it was the intention to reduce British defence spending over time. Taken all round, the atmosphere would not be particularly conducive to the envisaged consultation (probably no more than a euphemism for a take-it-or-leave-it decision).

Ken Booth has said that to fulfil the requirements of a non-nuclear policy it would be logical to reintroduce conscription.[19] It would, he says, stiffen the allies; send a signal to both adversaries and allies that Britain is serious about defence; and would be a small price to pay for the freedom from the nuclear burden. The trouble with this is that the likelihood of any political party paying the price of conscription in peacetime is distinctly small. Quite apart from the fact that it would be seen as remilitarizing society at a time when people are looking rather for a relaxation of East-West tensions, it would be very expensive. The figures depend on how much conscripts would be paid and whether call-up was universal or selective (which would be socially disruptive). The cost of manpower, equipment, war-stocks, training and housing could be heavy, probably £2 billion to £4 billion yearly. Even after savings from the cancellation of Trident and other things, annual defence expenditure would have to rise significantly, perhaps by as much as 15 per cent. This seems outside the realms of practical politics and is certainly not what the Labour Party policy has in mind.

An outline for British defence policy

The aims
The aims of British defence policy in relation to Europe must surely be to strengthen NATO and the US commitment to Europe. Quite apart from the fact that this provides the most effective political and military security for Europe and for Britain, it is also the cheapest. The United States bears a large part of the burden: there are some 220,000 US troops on the ground in Federal Germany, and only 55,000 British. It follows that the maintenance of a healthy relationship with the United States should remain central to British foreign policy. Similarly, the political importance of the British commitment to European security, represented by its forces assigned to NATO, must continue to be recognized. The political case for BAOR and RAF Germany in particular is powerful. The need to strengthen NATO conventional forces (discussed below) suggests that neither of these contingents should be cut, as is sometimes suggested.

Britain should also work to encourage moves towards a stronger European defence identity in the areas where this can make an improved contribution to the European political and military balance. Steps to harmonize the role of French forces with those of NATO should be welcomed, such as the talks that have been conducted between France and Federal Germany. But none of this should be allowed to engender an anti-US attitude, or to undercut NATO, which should remain the principal security mechanism. What form greater European cohesion might take is not within the scope of this paper, but given the distinctly spotty postwar record of Britain with regard to European integration, a positive and not an insular approach is required. (The Labour Party will no doubt work out its own position on Europe, which has not entirely carried conviction in the past and seems somewhat amorphous as yet.) Britain needs Europe as much as it needs us.

The strategy
The strategic aim should be to raise the nuclear threshold in Europe but not remove it. Nuclear weapons cannot be disinvented or wished away; they exist. As a Marxist might say, they are an objective fact. We therefore have to learn to manage them with safety while trying to reduce them.

The Soviet Union seems certain to keep nuclear weapons, which means that they will always be just over the border and able to be targeted on Europe, whether a European nuclear-free zone is created or not. As Lawrence Freedman has said, a nuclear-free zone is not a nuclear-safe zone. NATO must therefore be able to deter Soviet nuclear use, and only nuclear weapons can do that. We are rightly scared by the thought of nuclear war and so is everyone else. In the quotation already given, Lord Carver remarked that if nuclear weapons appear to have been abolished, war could once more be thought of as politically acceptable. It is an inescapable paradox of nuclear deterrence that the will to conduct nuclear war must be demonstrated in order to prevent war at all. So nuclear weapons have to be retained. Nothing deters like nuclear deterrence.

It is improbable that the major West European powers will spend much more on defence in the absence of a serious crisis. Some may not spend as much as they have been doing. Demographic factors will make it difficult to maintain manpower levels; Federal Germany, for example, faces sharply lower manpower intakes as a result of the falling birthrate from the 1960s on.[20] Britain, too, will have to recruit its volunteers from a shrinking manpower pool. The consequence of these two factors is that NATO is likely at best to have present manpower levels and that spending on equipment, war-stocks, consumables and training could increase only incrementally, if at all.

This should not prevent the tactical concept and defence posture being slowly changed towards NEFU. Ideally, the conventional defences should be made strong enough to permit NFU, but, for the reasons already mentioned, this should not be declared or adopted. The concept should remain based on forward defence, which does not prevent tactical flexibility. Forward defence is a political imperative for Federal Germany, since 30 per cent of its people live in a strip within 200 kilometres of the border and 25 per cent of its industry is also there. But it is also necessary so that deterrence should start on the border. The defence cannot depend on fortifications, as the Labour policy recommends, since West Germans will not accept this. This is not just a matter of environmental and social problems, which are big enough, but because such structures in peacetime would dramatize the division of the nation and the confrontation between East and West.[21]

Enemy territory simply cannot be left as a sanctuary, with the NATO countries that were being attacked left to bear the devastation of war alone. Consequently some nuclear weapons in Europe must be able to reach Soviet territory – of which more in a moment – and conventional weapons should be able to target Warsaw Pact rear areas in Eastern Europe as well. A priority for new conventional missiles should be the ability to attack enemy forward airfields – replacing the aircraft with the role now, and so releasing them for other tasks – in order to reduce the enemy air offensive against defending forces and installations. Another important task will be operations against enemy armoured forces in contact or immediately behind the line. A third but more difficult task for advanced missiles with their 'smart' warheads will be to engage enemy forces deep in Eastern Europe but moving forward (the follow-on forces attack – FOFA – to which NATO has given preliminary approval). The development of such weapons and the target acquisition capability to make them effective will, however, require much money and many years yet.[22]

Considerable resources should go to counter-attack formations, armoured and air-mobile, to counter Soviet penetration or to regain lost ground. French forces, if willing to cooperate, as now seems possible, could be valuable here as a mobile reserve specialized in air-mobile operations. Cross-border operations, as envisaged by the US Army AirLand Battle doctrine (which has not been adopted by NATO), should not be part of the concept. This is partly because they are politically divisive (the Labour policy rejects them), but essentially because they are best left until the operational time arrives, when their tactical and political advantages and disadvantages can be allowed to speak for themselves.

Most soldiers are acutely aware of the problems posed by the Soviet offensive *chemical* capability, against which NATO has, except for the United States (and France), only a defensive counter. They would much prefer an offensive capacity, which they consider would deter Soviet chemical use. But chemical weapons are an emotive issue in the Alliance, and there would be no consensus at all for the acquisition of an offensive capacity. Arms control efforts to outlaw them are pursued instead, so far unsuccessfully. If chemical weapons were to be used by the Soviet forces and NATO was committed not to retaliate in kind – the Labour policy recommends that this should be the British position – the military situation could become hazardous, bringing the use of nuclear weapons nearer. If NATO were to have no nuclear weapons and had renounced chemical retaliation – the full Labour policy – the military balance would become very sensitive, to put it gently. There is in fact no NATO or British political pressure to have offensive chemical weapons (though conceivably the United States could provide some in an emergency), but giving up the formal right to retaliate ought to be in exchange for some Soviet measure that would provide the necessary confidence. The withdrawal of all chemical weapons from Europe should be the aim.

None of the measures outlined above are new, but not too many are yet in train, principally for lack of money. However, some of them *are* tomorrow's ideas, which technology is only now making possible. As some of them are carried out, the perceived need for battlefield nuclear weapons would be eliminated. This should be a very early aim; they already seem undesirable. Similarly, aircraft fitted for the dual nuclear or conventional role should soon revert to the latter. But some nuclear weapons there must be in Europe, well back and made survivable by being mobile. They are needed to deter Soviet nuclear use, to respond to it or, in extreme circumstances in war, to be used first against military targets. By their presence alone they could compel Soviet forces to disperse, making the task of the defence that bit less difficult; and some would hold Soviet territory at risk, just as NATO territory is at risk from the SS-20 and SS-22 missiles. Above all they would be there to deter war. There need be relatively few.

Some of these weapons could be the Pershing II and cruise missiles that form part of the INF being deployed under the 1979 decision. If that decision – to deploy in the absence of arms control agreements that make them unnecessary – is to remain viable, Britain must continue to adhere to it. The requirement that US cruise missiles leave this country would very probably nullify the decision as a whole, doing great political damage within the Alliance and leaving the Soviet Union in a very advantageous position. Britain should therefore abide by the decision and continue to host the missiles. But there seems no military case for NATO's matching the SS-20 numbers; only a political one. All that are needed are sufficient missiles to be able to engage the necessary targets, a figure well below the 572 now set (which was set high for a number of reasons, including bargaining some away through arms control). Making the deployment hostage to an arms control agreement, though politically understandable, has had the effect of making roughly equal numbers a goal. There is no real military need for this.

Arms control obviously plays a part and certainly should do; it is the other side of the coin of strategy. It must be sought earnestly, not merely to get numbers down or to outlaw some systems (including chemical weapons), much less merely to conciliate public opinion so that it will support defence budgets, important though this is. It must be sought because it is an essential part of the political process in Europe, by which better East–West relations might be brought about. European and American views may not always coincide here but can usually be brought together. However, one should not be too optimistic about the results of arms control, at least in the short term. The nuclear warheads released from forward systems could certainly be used to bargain with or just given up as not necessary, which seems more sensible. There is nothing wrong with unilateral measures if the result is not unilateral disadvantage.

Out-of-area problems

Britain can clearly no longer contemplate deploying round the world the large forces and garrisons it once did. Nor is there any need to do so, now that decolonization is nearly over. But Britain's altered circumstances have not stopped British forces from performing smaller tasks effectively: for example, underpinning the security of newly-independent Belize; assisting Oman to prevent a hostile presence on the shores of the Straits of Hormuz; sharing the patrolling of these straits and helping clear Red Sea mines. It is useful to have small forces available for such tasks, which can rarely be foreseen, or for minor garrisons while political solutions to residual problems are sought. The Falklands aside for a moment, this presents no great problem. Most of the units needed in a hurry can be and are found by double-earmarking: using forces out of area in peacetime that are earmarked for Europe in war. Very little is required for overheads which are not usable for some other function as well.

The Labour Party policy is opposed to moves towards an independent British Rapid Deployment Force, which seems rather to be making a mountain out of a molehill. It would look for the protection of national interests through the United Nations. Whatever the UN is good at (for example, providing observers and interposing forces between opposing sides), it has not been noticeably good at protecting national interests. Nor is it by its nature likely to be. It can pass resolutions but cannot get them obeyed. It will rarely try to right wrongs and is almost unable to take sides, except in ideological groupings. To respect the need for the UN and to encourage its efforts is one thing; to look to it for the protection of British interests is quite another. The idea is either a figleaf or politically naive.[23] Of course Britain should not set out to have large intervention forces, but the House of Commons has a habit of calling for Britain's causes to be upheld. It can usually be done at no great expense. Britain is not yet reduced to the status of Luxembourg.

The *Falklands* was an aberration, though sadly a necessary operation. There was a failure to recognize a threat – Argentine intentions rather than capabilities, which were evident. The tiny garrison kept as a result was not sufficient to deter the invasion, which led in turn to the conflict and the present onerous commitment. If the garrison is to be substantially reduced, there must be confidence either that there is no longer a threat or that the forces are big enough to deter it. To risk another invasion would be criminal. No doubt there will be negotiations for a political solution, perhaps there should be soon. But until they succeed a garrison will have to be kept, though it can become smaller when the airfield is ready. Parliament has never shown readiness to negotiate the sovereignty away, and that seems to be the Argentine view of what negotiations are for.

Lastly, what place should there be for *Trident* in British policy? The need for a British independent nuclear deterrent has never seemed to me to be self-evident. If it did not exist, I doubt if it would now be invented. However, I have slowly and reluctantly come to the conclusion that in this changing and imperfect world a force should be kept. The present cost is small and the insurance worth having. But what if the cost turns out not to be small? If the opportunity cost of Trident meant that the conventional forces were significantly weakened? Then I think alternative forces would have to be looked at, possibly ground-launched cruise missiles in this country or some smaller submarine-launched system. No strategic system would be cheap and none would be as good as Trident, and in the climate of an agonizing reappraisal there would obviously be the alternative course of giving up the strategic nuclear deterrent altogether, though the tactical nuclear weapons, air-delivered, which Britain also has, could be retained. If the costs of a strategic nuclear force could be kept from denuding the conventional forces that Britain assigns to NATO, then I would keep it, in any practicable form. But in any case, I have come to the conclusion that Britain should remain a nuclear power in today's world. At the end of the century? That remains to be seen.

Much may depend on the progress of the US Strategic Defense Initiative (SDI) and the Soviet reaction to it, which will doubtless include the retention of substantial offensive nuclear forces which can still hold Europe under threat. At this stage it would still be my preferred option that Britain should remain a nuclear power. But I would fully expect and accept that British nuclear weapons would figure in arms control negotiations in some way or another. The outcome of those could be a determining factor.

Notes

1. There were around 50 million casualties in World War II, when weapons were far less destructive than modern conventional ones are now.
2. See *The Military Balance 1984-85* (London: International Institute for Strategic Studies, 1984), pp.156-7.
3. The yearly assessments in *The Military Balance* (see for example pp. 148-53 in the 1984-85 edition) are probably the best there are. They have the virtue of being free from advocacy and politically neutral. It is not unknown for politically inspired assessments to make a worst-case analysis or wish the threat away so as to fit in with cherished ideas. Another useful snapshot was provided by John J. Mearsheimer in 'Why the Soviets Can't Win Quickly in Central Europe', *International Security*, Summer 1982.
4. France crudely termed the concept 'trading European space for American time' and adopted a strategy relying on nuclear deterrence.
5. In the 1970s, Senator Mansfield was very active in promoting Senate Resolutions that required Europeans to do more or have some US troops go home. Others have from time to time assumed his mantle. The latest, though for friendly reasons, is Senator Nunn, whose similar resolution in June 1984 sent a similar message that the Senate was unhappy, though it failed by a vote of 55-41. The administrations have launched such initiatives as 'Alliance Defence in the Seventies' (AD 70) in May 1970 and the Long Term Defence Improvement Programme (LTDP) in 1977.
6. Helmut Schmidt, *Survival* (London: IISS, February 1978), p.4.
7. A leading member of the SPD defence community, when recently asked by the author about the form the party defence platform might take, said, 'You can be sure we're not going to do anything crazy like the British Labour Party.'
8. See 'Nuclear Weapons and the Atlantic Alliance', *Foreign Affairs*, Spring 1982. See also 'A German Response to No First Use', *Foreign Affairs*, Summer 1982.
9. See, for example, Kenneth Hunt, 'Alternative Conventional Force Postures', in Kenneth A. Myers (ed.), *NATO – The Next Thirty Years* (Boulder, Colorado: Westview Press, 1980).
10. For example, Robert Komer, 'Is Conventional Defense of Europe Feasible', *Naval War College Review*, September-October 1982, pp.80-91. Also Bernard W. Rogers, 'The Atlantic Alliance', *Foreign Affairs*, Summer 1982.
11. The Reagan administration pressure centred around a project which has been called 'emerging technology' (ET). Public concern was of course articulated by the various campaigns for nuclear disarmament such as CND in Britain.
12. Reiterated at the Bonn Summit of NATO in June 1982.
13. See the NFU article in *Foreign Affairs*, Spring 1982, cited above in Note 8, p.764.
14. See NFU article in Note 8, p.759.
15. *Defence and Security for Britain* (The Labour Party: Statement to Annual Conference 1984).
16. *A Policy for Peace* (London: Faber, 1982), pp.104-5 for the first passage; p.106 for the second.

17. *Defence and Security for Britain*, op.cit., p.39.
18. *Ibid.*, p.20.
19. Ken Booth, 'Strategy and Conscription', in John Baylis (ed.), *Alternative Approaches to British Defence Policy* (London: The Macmillan Press, 1983), pp.154-90.
20. For a succint description of the problems, see *Financial Times*, 12 November 1984.
21. The Labour Party policy document rightly makes much of the need for lowered tensions and for better East–West relations but appears to overlook the symbol of confrontation that the construction of barriers would represent. The effort should surely be to remove the physical barriers of barbed wire and minefields built by East Germany, not erect new barriers, albeit of a quite different kind. They would be a hostage to Warsaw Pact propaganda.
22. For a description of the concept sketched here, see Donald R. Cotter, 'Potential Future Roles for Conventional and Nuclear Forces in Defense of Western Europe' *Strengthening Conventional Deterrence in Europe* (London: The Macmillan Press, 1983) – Report of the European Security Study (ESECS).
23. It is sometimes difficult to see *Defence and Security for Britain* as a serious national defence policy. It has more the marks of an exercise in riding Jimmy Maxton's two horses. The one on the left seems to have been pulling a bit hard.

4   American Reactions to Shifts in European Policy: The Changing Context
Michael Clarke

It is impossible to forecast exactly how the United States will react to future British defence policy, any more than it is possible to guess what that defence policy will be – anything from a continuation of present policies, under tighter budgetary constraints, to a radical non-nuclear stance adopted by a future Labour government. There are, however, two general certainties upon which one can build an analysis: the fact that transatlantic arguments are taking place in a new context and American reactions to *any* future British defence policy must therefore take account of this; and the fact that there are contradictory trends within the US defence establishment itself which lead to opposing pressures on the European allies.

The new context of transatlantic debate
NATO is always in a state of flux: in any alliance of sixteen states this is almost a condition of its existence. Some argue that since this is undoubtedly true, its present difficulties cannot be regarded as fundamental. The debates which currently rage between the United States and the Europeans, and among the European members of NATO, have all been seen before, the argument goes; they raise insoluble problems over which we ponder periodically but about which we can do nothing useful. In the end, we can only fall back on our resigned acceptance that for the West (and in many respects for the East) there is more or less no alternative to NATO as it is presently constituted. Yet if the transatlantic arguments have all been heard before – about the proper relationship between Europe and the United States, the level of the nuclear threshold, the costs of appropriate force levels – it can hardly be doubted that they are now taking place in a new situation.

In a last, rather candid article as NATO Secretary-General, Joseph Luns summed up the change. Whereas in the past, 'NATO took its armament decisions in full unity without having to take into account public sentiments; nuclear strategy was a matter for a handful of experts', now, 'we are indeed witnessing a healthy re-politicization of the entire discussion of the East–West relationship'.[1] Harold Brown, former Secretary of Defense, wrote in the autumn of 1982 that 'a substantial breakdown has taken place in the domestic consensus on nuclear politics in Europe and the United States'.[2] Clearly, something has happened. Dr Luns's 'healthy re-politicization' and Brown's 'substantial breakdown' have several dimensions, which are all of some consequence to current Alliance debates. In the first place, there is a clear strategic element in this new politicization of NATO. It is customary to note that both superpowers now exist in a condition of mutual strategic vulnerability. It is, however, certainly true that the arms race never looked so bad to Western publics, even in the late 1950s, in the depths of the cold war, when there was a powerful perception of overall Western superiority. This factor cannot be discounted, but it is a somewhat glib and abstract strategic explanation of a more pervasive political phenomenon. More immediately, since 1977, NATO politicians have had to take clear and public decisions about modernizing nuclear forces and introducing new weapons in order to safeguard the flexible spectrum of deterrence. As a policy of the 1960s, flexible response originally had very few implications for NATO's nuclear force posture. Once the doctrine of flexible response embodied in MC 14/3 had been adopted in 1967, it was, for all nuclear purposes, operative. The existing NATO forces would from then on be deemed flexible and the nuclear weapons which backed them up were already substantially deployed. For over ten years, new generations of dual-capable aircraft were the only major additions to the nuclear arsenal. In the late 1970s, however, NATO was faced for the first time with the problem of *introducing* new nuclear weapons as part of a flexible doctrine. Thus NATO has had to spell out, to justify its deployment decisions, what is meant by flexible response, why nuclear weapons are part of it, and what threats it is designed to face.

All of these lasting questions invite dynamic answers, and, as it happens, the tough decisions which supplied such answers have not been handled well by the Alliance. The issues of the neutron warhead were mismanaged from the intra-Alliance viewpoint; they brought out into the open unwise thinking aloud about the options for nuclear release and added to the large degree of uncertainty sparked off by the debate surrounding the approval of Presidential Directive 59 by President Carter in July 1980, which was intended to improve America's ability to sustain a protracted, and limited, nuclear exchange. They also happened to coincide with some predictable divergences over the handling of East–West relations and the responses to the crises in Iran and Afghanistan. The cruise and

Pershing II (INF) deployments, partly in response to this, reflected a learning process in NATO and were claimed to have been well-handled on an intra-allied basis. Yet they were, by general consent, very badly handled in relation to the electorates of Europe, and the INF decision turned out to be the single most important issue for some years that needed to be well-managed within the *public* domain, rather than merely within the NATO elite. In the event, it has been far more bruising and has cost NATO more domestic cohesion than might ever have been imagined.

Secondly, there is a symbolic dimension to the new context of NATO debates which gives nuclear issues a unique political potency. Nuclear devices always carry a heavy symbolic value, quite apart from their practical role of making the allies equal risk-sharers, and this has acted as a form of political cement between NATO governments. To decision-makers, parliaments and publics, nuclear weapons represent a simple symbol of Alliance cohesion (and, in Britain's case, of some residual independence), since they ensure that any future war involving their use would be both widespread and disastrous. Yet this symbol of shared danger is also a symbol of absolute danger. It now seems that the heavy symbolic value of nuclear weapons is set to work against NATO governments in their domestic public relations with the same political force with which it cements allied relations between governments. Nuclear symbolism operates powerfully in both direc-tions and may indeed be now emerging more as a force of disunity than cohesion within NATO. In some respects, current criticisms are very hard on NATO governments. There are many weapons in NATO's nuclear arsenal more worthy of opposition than cruise missiles, for example, but cruise deployments represent a symbol much more powerful than a dual-capable 155mm shell. There are many conventional weapons, particularly in the 'emerging technology' categories, which threaten to be more destabilizing than some nuclear systems; but nothing quite carries the publicity of a nuclear-tipped, high-technology, non-recallable, new missile. British governments often claim that anti-nuclear opposition is fostered by people who do not understand much about nuclear weapons. It is fair to point out, however, that the impressive consensus of NATO's first 30 years was fostered by politicians who were equally ignorant.

Nuclear symbolism now tends to polarize the debate in Europe between governments and their critics. Whereas, in the 1960s, governments could mobilize the public's commonsense instincts to support the belief that massive (Soviet) explosive power could be compensated by equal explosive power; now the critics can mobilize a more recent commonsense instinct, the belief that state-of-the-art technology for deploying such overkill is probably just plain dangerous. Commonsense may not be the best guide to policy in either case, but it provides a political force that can be powerfully exploited.

In a third dimension, it is important to acknowledge that any new politicization in NATO such as Dr Luns recognizes has become a *party* politicization. As a result, anti-nuclear opposition in Europe is very unlikely to succeed in preventing any specific NATO modernization programme or collective decision. But, for the same reason, it will not disappear quickly and it can now probably mobilize more uncommitted opinion and thus exact a higher political price for any decisions comparable to that taken over the INF deployments. As a party-political issue, nuclear policy will be debated crudely and with great passion, and, for better or worse, it is not likely to go away. In Britain and the Federal Republic of Germany, the major opposition parties are committed to pro-NATO, anti-nuclear stances; in the Netherlands, the governing coalition has been forced to defer the issue of cruise missile deployment in order to survive; in Belgium, the cruise issue has been temporarily settled but will undoubtedly re-emerge at the next election; and in Denmark the powerful parliament has used the budget to suspend, in effect, its government's powers of choice over nuclear issues.[3] Unless one believes that the adoption alone of an anti-nuclear defence policy is, in itself, sufficient to bar the West German SPD or the British or Dutch Labour Parties from ever again holding office (and the political history of Europe does not give this strong support, if only because defence is not the electoral issue in Europe that it is in the United States), then it is reasonable to suppose that these parties will some day be back in government. It may be true, as critics point out, that non-nuclear policies will never get a party elected in Europe, but it is equally true (as critics often ignore) that they will not keep such parties out of office when they are favoured by other factors such as the swing of the political pendulum or persistent economic recession. And whether their present leaders like it or not, these parties will probably be carrying into power with them anti-nuclear commitments that will have been confirmed at successive party conferences.

The party politics of the European democracies can never adequately be discussed in generalized terms, but the underlying trends show some coherence. Neutralism in Europe remains essentially extra-parliamentary. Anti-nuclear opposition, on the other hand, has become parliamentary, has already figured in governing coalitions and will continue to do so. NATO, in other words, is likely to face a situation, at some time in the 1980s, in which one of its larger and perhaps one or two of its smaller European allies will be led by governments who are committed, by coalition partners or party faithful, to some anti-nuclear stance. If the United States perceives such a situation as having the same degree of symbolism as the INF deployments, then the damage to the Alliance will be at least as great. In case this seems too fanciful a scenario, let us recall that even if the anti-nuclear opposition makes no further headway in Europe, narrow governmental victories on nuclear defence issues and further INF deployments will still not provide anything like the powerful, silent consensus which existed prior to the late 1970s. This constitutes the general context within which the transatlantic debates must now be set.

The more particular trends that will condition the American response to future developments in British defence policy are contradictory. This is the second major reality with which future Anglo-American defence relations must cope. It is possible to discern in America the strands of an essentially 'conservative' orientation which would require Britain to do more of the same, and a 'reformist evolutionary' orientation which would be receptive to changes in British policy as long as they contributed to a rejuvenated NATO. Apart from pulling in opposite directions, such trends are also internally paradoxical. They are not 'conservative' and 'reformist' trends in the party-political sense, since many radical right-wing desires to break or change the old relationship between the US and the Europeans can be found in the conservative camp. Similarly, in the reformist camp there are those liberals who look to NATO reform as a way of preserving the traditional transatlantic relationship and safeguarding America's 'coalition defence' approach to its security. What distinguishes conservatism and reformism in this analysis is the attitude to NATO: the distinction between those who demand that the allies keep up with increased US defence efforts and are prepared to see them left behind if they do not; and those who see a need for reform in both European *and* US defence policies as a means of adapting NATO to the changed circumstances of the 1980s. The evolving US military doctrine and tactics of ground combat, for instance, have come to embody elements which would be quite compatible with a non-nuclear British defence policy, as well as elements which clearly would not. It is therefore the task of European defence analysts, and reformers, to try to identify and isolate such contradictory and paradoxical elements.

A conservative orientation

The globalism of the Reagan administration's foreign and defence policies has proved to be a powerfully conservative factor in its approach to NATO. There are a number of long-term demographic and economic trends in American society which suggest that its traditional Eurocentredness may be diminishing. In 1979, US trade with the Pacific Rim countries was worth $91.8 billion as compared with $92.9 billion with Western Europe. By 1983, Pacific Rim trade had risen steadily to $133.8 billion, while the value of trade with Western Europe had risen only to $104.9 billion. Between 1970 and 1980, US population growth in the West amounted to 32.9 per cent, as opposed to a 0.2 per cent growth of population in the Northeastern states over the same period.[4] These trends will presumably be reflected in policy at some stage in the future, though it is impossible to specify how. It may well be, however, that the Reagan administrations represent their most tangible expression to date and have shown signs of a much more immediate switch of attention to the Pacific Rim. Lawrence Eagleburger, in analysing European defence policies, has pointed on more than one occasion to the possibility of a reorientation of American interests towards the Pacific; and Richard Burt has officially, and pointedly, commented that now 'we have new foreign policy elites that are interested in other parts of the world'.[5]

This represents both a short- and a long-term trend away from such a previously high concentration on Europe and is part of a more assertive, globalist policy which emphasizes conservative geopolitics over the more accommodating strategies which seek to promote and manage interdependence. A decade ago, the United States prepared for a '1½ war contingency'. Now it prepares for what members of the Joint Chiefs of Staff describe as 'global strategy' and it is keen to see the Europeans cooperate in this endeavour.[6] There is every indication that the second Reagan administration will continue this trend of the first. However, this poses problems for European governments who are less geopolitically minded, draw different lessons from US interventions in Lebanon and Grenada and resent US attempts to tighten the denial of (European) high-technology exports to Warsaw Pact countries. Above all, European governments have been subjected to some significant domestic pressures with which the President has not had to contend, since the Reagan administration has 'talked up' the Soviet threat since 1980. In the NATO context, the globalist strategy demands that the INF deployments and strategic nuclear modernizations should be carried through, while the conventional component of NATO's forces is thoroughly modernized in order to restore the full spectrum of a flexible deterrent response. In this sense, the globalist strategy demands that Britain and the other European allies do more of the same. As one State Department official expressed it, modernized theatre nuclear forces show up unmodernized conventional ones – especially to Congress.[7] If the present force structure is unsatisfactory, the answer lies in a better mix of modernized forces,[8] both nuclear *and* conventional. The global strategy, therefore, has not only diminished the relative importance of Europe in American eyes; it has also emphasized the implicit requirement (soon to become very explicit) that the allies do more to support American policy, both physically and politically.

The significance of current US defence spending is not in the absolute size of the budget – America is, after all, a very rich country – but in the underlying trends. While defence spending has fluctuated up and down since 1955 and is now on a steeply rising path, it has generally taken up a declining proportion of the US gross national product. This trend began to be reversed from 1978, however, and projected defence expenditures will absorb a higher proportion of GNP, certainly until 1988, when it may be around 8 per cent, even on the basis of sustained economic recovery. If the recovery is less sustained, as seems increasingly likely, the proportion will be higher.[9]

In addition, defence budgets of over $300 billion are being accompanied by what seems to be a persistent federal deficit of upwards of $200 billion. In 1983, the Congressional Budget Office (CBO) forecast that the annual federal deficit is likely to reach $270 billion by 1988, and will still be above $200 billion even if the recovery is sustained and produces a high employment and income level.[10] The deficit appears to be remarkably persistent and, as the CBO points out, can only be reduced by remedial action. The defence budget absorbs almost 30 per cent of federal spending and becomes a prime target in any policy which must either raise taxes or cut federal outlays.

There is, however, a structural difficulty in doing much about the present defence budget in the next five years. The emphasis of the Reagan build-up has been on equipment procurement and investment, and this creates momentum for certain systems and reduces the amount of the budget that might be available for adjustment in future years when new systems are being financed. In 1983, 'prior commitments' absorbed 34 per cent of the total defence budget. In 1988, they will absorb 43 per cent, when 'pay and retirement' proportions will have fallen by 11 per cent and 'current investment and operations' will have remained virtually static.[11] In general, therefore, there will be even less scope for discretion in adjusting the budget than presently exists. To this we must add the ironic reality that if weapons programmes are as undercosted as they have been in the past, then even the total projected outlays of $1.6 trillion will prove inadequate to finance the Reagan defence package.[12] The American defence budget, the biggest in history, is underfunded for what it seeks to achieve.

Already, this has begun to produce quite specific pressures which increase American conservatism in relation to the politics of European allies. The arguments about burden-sharing have resurfaced in a more divisive form than previously. It is inaccurate to maintain that such arguments are merely cyclical reappearances of latent problems. For one thing, the present burden-sharing argument comes at the somewhat ignominious end of NATO's '3 per cent solution'. Allied contributions to the Long Term Defence Programme, which this initiated, have not been at all bad, but they have consistently fallen short of the full total. The annual reports from the Secretary of Defense to Congress on allied contributions have been generally critical in the last two years, recording an average increase in non-US NATO expenditure for 1983 of 1.9–2.1 per cent, as against a corresponding US increase of 7.6 per cent.[13] This, however, is somewhat misleading. The reports have been criticized for excluding information on host-nation support.[14] Also, the Department of Defense calculates that 56 per cent of its total spending is effectively spent on NATO. This means that US defence spending *on NATO* as a proportion of its GNP is around 3.7 per cent, about average for the other allies.[15] In political terms, however, such detailed calculations are not the point. The figure of 3 per cent takes on a massive importance when it is not met in purely financial terms. Senator Levin, whose legislation initiated the annual Secretary of Defense reports, described 'at least half of the NATO membership' as having 'failed this basic test of political and military will'.[16]

The present debate about burden-sharing is also unique in that the European allies are facing some of the congressional backlash that really belongs to Japan. As Japanese economic competition has persistently accompanied a failure to increase Japanese defence commitments, so congressional irritation has grown quickly with its allies in general, along with a perception that burdens *must* be more equitably shared in the future. Far from easing pressure on the European allies, Japan, by spending less than 1 per cent of its GNP on defence, serves to illuminate the whole issue and increase congressional conservatism in the face of budgetary crises in defence.[17] Finally, the present debate is unique because the complexion of Congress has changed since the early 1970s. Mansfieldism was never successful in Congress because of an alliance between conservatives and those in the centre. Now, however, the conservatives would not leap as instinctively to NATO's defence; in the pursuit of globalism there is a greater willingness to act unilaterally, if necessary.[18] It is no coincidence (indeed, it has an intrinsic political significance) that Senator Nunn, who helped defeat Mansfieldism in 1974, is now leading a congressional campaign to pressure the allies into greater contributions.[19]

The issue of burden-sharing, therefore, will almost certainly dominate transatlantic debates in the immediate future, and it seems clear that it will not be merely ritualistic. The administration appears set to try to do more of the same on a global scale, and Congress seems certain to demand that, as part of the process, the Europeans do more of the same on a regional scale. Although European defence ministers have gone out of their way during 1984 to stress the real contributions their countries make to NATO defence, it is certain that Congress will use the threat of troop-withdrawals to put more pressure on the European allies. In June 1984, Senator Nunn attracted unexpectedly large support for his amendment to the Defense Authorization Bill, which would have reduced the number of US troops in Europe by up to one third, beginning in phased withdrawals from 1987 (the necessity and extent of the withdrawals being determined by the European's annual performances). His amendment created considerable resentment in European circles and was defeated (55 to 41) thanks to extensive lobbying by the White House. But his staff have confirmed that it is almost certain to be reintroduced, and if it is defeated again, it will very likely be by a rather narrower margin.[20] In lieu of the Nunn Amendment, however, Senator Cohen introduced and had passed (by 94 to 3) a measure to impose a cap on US troop levels in Europe of 324,000 (the level on 31 March 1984) if the allies do not meet certain targets. This makes little practical difference, but it is the first time in NATO's history that a specified limit has been set on US forces in Europe.[21] In fact, the withdrawal of US troops from Europe is not, in itself, certain to save money. Both the Department of Defense and the General Accounting Office seem to agree on that; indeed, certain troop withdrawals could even cost more.[22] These arguments, however, do not seem to weigh heavily with a Congress faced with immediate cost pressures and a growing determination to make the allies follow their lead.

Apart from demanding such physical contributions from the allies, the present globalism of the Reagan administration also imposes political demands which militate against anything other than more of the same in British defence policy. In particular, there is a symbolism in nuclear weapons, as noted earlier, which seems to be both powerful and volatile. If nuclear weapons are the symbols of European protest about defence policies, it is perhaps inevitable that a commitment to their continued deployment should be regarded in the United States as the acid test of loyalty to NATO. The anti-nuclear protesters in Europe have become identified with a latent anti-Americanism, so that nuclear weapons have become an issue of confidence in US leadership of Europe. NATO's nuclear deployments have always been regarded as a tangible political commitment to the sharing of risks. Indeed, much of the acrimony surrounding the INF deployments was stimulated by this symbolic function.[23] As Senator Nunn, who is not given to hyperbolic statements about defence, put it in 1981, the decision to carry through the INF deployments as planned is now 'a test of the ability of the Alliance to implement any difficult decision'.[24]

It can be argued that nuclear and conventional forces in Europe are so interdependent that a substantial reduction in nuclear facilities in Western Europe would leave US forces so vulnerable that there would be an unanswerable case for their withdrawal. If they were denied the nuclear umbrella – particularly in respect of short-range and dual-capable battlefield systems – then on grounds of sheer military prudence, US troops should be withdrawn from the theatre.[25] This, however, is a tenuous argument even in military terms. Although it is entirely credible to argue that US troop-withdrawals could be the outcome of a substantial denuclearization of Western Europe, it is virtually certain that the motive for withdrawals would be political rather than military: a retaliation for the lack of Alliance commitment that a retreat from nuclear weapons would imply.

One of the apparently unshakeable premises of American political life is the belief that anti-nuclear sentiments are closely associated with neutralism. Henry Kissinger pointed to what he discerned as 'barely disguised neutralism' in Europe in 1984.[26] However mistaken this may appear from a European perspective, there is little doubt that the spectre of neutralism is never far from the surface in American discussions of the Europeans' contributions. And as with all pervasive assumptions, it is closely linked to particular symbols and images, in this case nuclear ones. Any radical change in the nuclear component of a European defence policy – for whatever reason – would therefore have to overcome a general official and congressional suspicion that it was being undertaken in response to the pressures of anti-nuclear groups. In the Federal Republic of Germany, where neutralism in Europe will be most crucial if it does develop, Jonathan Dean has pointed out that, 'Public support for neutralist positions . . . is likely to become more vocal and more perceptible rather than more widespread . . . Change in the Federal Republic's international orientation, whether for good or ill, will result far more from Washington's actions and views than from Moscow's'.[27]

In these general respects, therefore, there is a distinctly conservative orientation in US defence policy – in its globalism, its budgetary restraints, its demands for greater allied contributions and its emphasis on the importance of nuclear weapons as a symbol of commitment. It is clear, however, that present trends are contradictory. On these, and other, issues there are also some indications of a less conservative trend which may be receptive to new initiatives.

A reformist orientation

The conservative pressures in US defence policy stem mainly from short-term considerations. They are, in large measure, reactions to the problems in foreign and defence policy of the mid-1970s. Reformist pressures, on the other hand, arise from a longer-term appreciation of some of the structural problems of defence policy.

Truncated defence budgets suggest unbalanced, inefficient forces, and pose very hard choices. Whatever the pressure on US allies to do more, a defence budget crisis creates introspection. A prominent 'military reform movement' has emerged in the 1980s. In 1981 a 'military reform caucus' consisting of 20-30 senators and representatives was formed. Its membership is now around 60 congressmen and its existence has helped galvanize a like-minded group of supporters inside the military establishment. The movement draws its support not only from liberals who are traditionally suspicious of the defence establishment, but also from Republicans and conservative Democrats, and it includes a small core of defence analysts who are not noted for any liberal biases. The appearance of this movement also coincides with a new generation of military planners in the Pentagon who, independently, have influenced some policies towards a new appraisal of what constitutes military effectiveness.[28]

The military reform movement is united essentially by a concern for the size of the defence budget, but also by a conviction that military efficiency is being sacrificed for firepower equations and systems analysis, and a strong suspicion that modern weapon systems offer diminishing effectiveness.[29] As Jeffrey Record has pointed out, there is reason to be sceptical about the prospects for the reform caucus in the legislature.[30] Nevertheless, the very existence of a recognizable movement at such a high level (Congress), operating inside the Pentagon as well as outside, and drawing substantial support from conservative elements, indicates the importance of a growing struc-tural critique of the US defence posture. Steven Canby, for example, points out that NATO consistently outspends the Warsaw Pact but gets rather less for its money and suffers, not because of inadequate resources, but because of 'a doctrine emphasizing positional defense of linear lines with firepower'.[31] And, at a general level, this movement may be in tune with a growing public mood that Lawrence Kaagan has perceived: 'While anxious to have "the best defence that money can buy", Americans are now less than certain that current or anticipated outlays are in fact buying the "best".'[32]

There is therefore some willingness, which may be growing, to reconsider the structural basis of US defence spending. As Robert Komer, who has been involved in directing and assessing US military performance longer than most, has observed, 'something has got to give'. In particular, 'we are liable to end up eventually with dangerously unbalanced forces and a severe "readiness crunch" as readiness programs are sacrificed by Congress to keep funding big ticket procurement items . . .'.[33] In relation to NATO, the analyses of the reforms seem to indicate that radical changes will be necessary in the military structure if *any* form of defence is to be maintained with military adequacy. Present military pressures point towards more effort, from everyone, to repair NATO's conventional force deficiencies in sustainability and readiness. Economic trends indicate that this effort is unlikely to be maintained after the next couple of years. And reformers – and those inside government whose job it is to worry about future requirements – may be helping to make acceptable the view that only thoroughgoing changes in NATO's conventional posture can reconcile that contradiction. It may well be that radical reform in NATO forces and doctrine becomes a prerequisite just to stand still in military terms.

As part of the same recognition of structural problems, the US military is clearly involved in a major evolution of its battle tactics. The present debates surrounding the adoption by the US Army of AirLand Battle concepts embodied in the 1982 edition of the *FM 100-5* field manual, and General Rogers's follow-on forces attack (FOFA) plan for NATO and a series of other ideas, including *CounterAir 90* and the deep strike concept, are still very much in progress and it is impossible to say what the outcome will be.[34] It is clear, however, that this disparate evolution of military doctrines is based on some common assumptions. Firstly, there is an assumption that force sizes will not be substantially increased. NATO will have to do the job with more or less the size of forces that it has now. Secondly, the technologies of deep strike, precision-guidance and real-time target identification (if they work and if they are affordable) promise to give defending forces a significant advantage, if they can be integrated into battle plans efficiently. Thirdly, and possibly in the absence of such extensive 'emerging technologies', the tactical emphasis must be put back on soldiering: on flexibility, movement and local initiative. The development of smart weapons, in fact, is some way down the road behind the development of smart commanders. Finally, in the particular context of NATO, the emphasis must be not to hold a thin, defensive line, so brittle that its only real reserves are the nuclear forces, but rather to exploit Warsaw Pact vulnerabilities by launching local offensives to disrupt and confuse any attack, and to put firmly onto the Pact the onus of initiating nuclear strikes.

Such ideas are inevitably controversial within NATO, not least, for political reasons, in the Federal Republic. Nevertheless, the British Army of the Rhine and the Bundeswehr follow these debates carefully. The BAOR is experimenting with the concept of 'framework defence', which would be generally compatible with AirLand Battle. And the Bundeswehr, which must ultimately be the linchpin of any NATO-wide innovations, has gone a certain way down the road towards greater flexibility.[35] The political commitment to forward defence still remains paramount in the Federal Republic: 'any conceptual model of defence involving the surrender of territory is unacceptable',[36] but military reality in the Bundeswehr's own *Army Regulation 100/100* accepts the necessity for military flexibility in any operations on the Central Front.

The tactical evolution in US battle tactics, wherever it is going, raises important questions for the role of nuclear weapons in the European theatre. As far as the AirLand Battle concept is concerned in *FM 100-5*, the battlefield is supposed to be 'integrated' in conventional, chemical and nuclear warfare. This integration of the battlefield has a somewhat murky rationale and has been badly served in some incautious documents and Pentagon briefings.[37] The reality, however, of nuclear weapons in the AirLand Battle concept is likely to be different, for the concept will demand a much greater separation between nuclear and conventional forces. For one thing, AirLand Battle tries to put the emphasis back on soldiering. Nuclear release would be antithetical to the military logic of this. It would destroy the whole purpose of trying to fight more efficiently in a defensive battle and turn the conflict at the very least into an exercise in area retaliation. Secondly, nuclear release procedures themselves – complex as they already are[38] – would be even more questionable in a more fluid battle, as has been well noted by many within the US Army.[39] Thirdly, a future air/land battle would be won or lost behind the lines, where a sophisticated command and control structure and good mobility are essential. AirLand Battle, if it were adopted, would give NATO a very powerful stake in maintaining clarity behind the front.[40] A move across the nuclear threshold would be the single most obvious way of cancelling out the advantages that AirLand Battle would capitalize upon. An integrated battlefield it may claim to be, but this is not the way the reality of the concept seems to be moving.

This brings us to those reformist orientations directly concerned with NATO, as opposed to US defence policy alone. Arising partly out of reformist military trends, there is a clear movement against the continued stockpiling of battlefield nuclear weapons, and NATO, in addition to a programme which scrapped 1,000 warheads by 1980, announced in October 1983 that a further 1,400 would be withdrawn within the next five years.[41] Some analysts claim that although these numbers seem impressive (the battlefield stockpile will have been reduced from 7,000 to 4,600 warheads by 1989), the reduction is no more than a rationalization of the stockpile. Modernized warheads, particularly the flexible, 'dial-a-yield' 155mm shell, and the 8-inch, and *Lance*, neutron warheads, will be introduced to make the stockpile more effective.[42] This is certainly true, and hardly surprising, since the military are likely to be more interested in rationalizations than reductions. Nevertheless, it is very significant that battlefield nuclear weapons have become the centre of a larger argument about the role of all nuclear forces in NATO. Ironically, INF deployments may have been the key which unlocked the battlefield nuclear weapons issue, by warning that nuclear weapons were bad for the public's nerves. It is difficult to find anyone in Washington who does not express opposition both to the principle and the stockpiling of these weapons. Such condemnations range from Kaufmann's influential analysis that battlefield nuclear weapons are a military liability, to the assertions of Robert McNamara that NATO is both technically and politically self-deterred from ever using them.[43] In 1983, Congress blocked funds for the modernized 155mm shell – the first time it has attacked funding for a NATO system that is only ammunition. Senators were also determined that the proposed new Joint Tactical Missile for the US army and air force would not be deployed in any nuclear role. This, as one experienced Senate staff director pointed out, was an important – half-conscious – signal which Europeans were failing to read: Congress was taking an interest in the level of the nuclear threshold as part of its greater interest in NATO's conventional capabilities, and it would not support indefinitely an arrangement which allowed a low nuclear threshold to be a substitute for real European defence efforts.[44]

Another trend promoting more American flexibility within NATO might be defined as the backlash from the INF deployments. The extent and depth of the European opposition to cruise and Pershing II missiles was an unpleasant revelation to most US policy-makers, and although protest in Europe may well diminish, it is unlikely to disappear. Norman Birnbaum is quite emphatic: 'The notion purveyed in our [US] press, that the peace movement in Europe will now subside, is devoid of substance.'[45] It is impossible to say how much this view is now shared by the American policy elite, but there does seem to be a general consensus that enough blood was spilt over the INF debate to ensure that no one wants to repeat the experience. Thus, while the issue is still the focus of some continuing tension between the US and the Europeans, it *has* been constructive to the extent that it has reinforced the learning process (perhaps one should say, the cyclical, relearning process) of Alliance diplomacy. New nuclear deployments within NATO are very unlikely in the present climate, and even developments in existing systems are being handled rather more carefully. NATO policies which would help avoid rows like the one over INF are to be welcomed. There is a sense in which the US has put its response to NATO's nuclear problems on 'hold' until it has fully assessed the results of the INF deployments. This could, in fact, give the Europeans some cards to play in the event of a change in defence policy, since the US seems inclined to proceed with some caution for the time being.

A final element which could favour a reformist orientation, paradoxically, is the consistency with which both European and American publics seem to be loyal to NATO. In this respect, the public has been more consistent than the policy elite on either side of the Atlantic. Support among the American public for NATO, and the continued presence of US troops in Europe, seems to have averaged around 55 to 60 per cent, with about 25 per cent opposed, over the last fifteen years. It was at its lowest (48 per cent) in 1974-5 and at its highest (74 per cent) in 1980, in the wake of the Afghanistan invasion. Levels of support are lower for other US commitments, such as those to Japan or South Korea, and very low indeed for any new commitments that the US might take on. Opinion is immediately more fickle when nuclear weapons are brought into the equation of foreign commitments.[46] As David Calleo points out, the American public's opinion on foreign policy is far less volatile than that of the 'upper stratum', which has almost exclusive influence in the media. 'As more sensitive pollsters suggest, it is not the public that is demanding unilateral world hegemony . . . In America, at least, it is the elite and not the public that has failed.'[47]

The parallel is almost exact in Europe. While there is a varying measure of protest and disquiet about specific nuclear deployments in Europe, there is a fairly solid and consistent trend of support for NATO. Opinion-poll findings in the last three years have confirmed the general popularity of NATO but have shown a specific scepticism about some of its nuclear deployments.[48] And while leftist parties in Europe, particularly in Britain and the Federal Republic, encompass neutralist elements, these do not generally figure prominently in their policies. Hans-Jochen Vogel, the SPD leader, made it clear in 1983 that 'for us, the Alliance is not up for discussion', and he stressed his attachment to the Alliance on his visit to Washington in February 1984.[49] The latest statement on the future defence policy of the British Labour Party makes its support for NATO clear from the outset. In the Netherlands, the coalition government of Ruud Lubbers has fudged the INF deployment schedule, but has played on popular support for NATO to maintain its stand on defence policy. In

Italy and Belgium, the commitment to NATO has never been in doubt. Opposition to the INF decision has been muted, particularly in Italy, where the anti-nuclear movement has been orchestrated by (though it did not originate in) the Communist Party, which paradoxically continues to support Italy's membership of NATO. Neutralist sentiment generally remains confined to the far left, without much party representation: the European Nuclear Disarmament group in Britain, the leadership of the Campaign for Nuclear Disarmament and some pacifist groupings in the Dutch Interchurch Peace Council, the IKV. The most notable instance of neutralism in a parliamentary context currently is the Green Party in the Federal Republic.

Europe is not, therefore, suffering from creeping neutralism or significant anti-Americanism, however much its elites fluctuate. The consensus that NATO is the essential framework for the defence of West European countries is not in doubt even if some of its policies are.[50] Ironically, it is in Greece and Spain, where nuclear issues are not prominent, that the NATO consensus is under real threat. Both states appear to be engaged in a long and genuine reappraisal of whether their essential security interests are best served within NATO. In these countries neutralism *is* an issue. There is virtually no questioning of NATO on such grounds in the core countries of the Alliance.

This essential consistency in public attitudes seems to be ignored by the policy elites, who disagree with one another and who pit their differing perceptions of world power against each other in a latter-day battle of the Atlantic. Reaganism is taken as hegemony; protest as neutralism. It may well be, however, that NATO is more robust than politicians and academic observers usually think. The *policies* of NATO may be facing structural crises, and it is certainly true that publics are likely to be influenced by policy elites. It is also true that crises of NATO policy can be mishandled to the point where public support evaporates. Nevertheless, NATO's *existence* is not such a fragile blossom, and it may be that there is more scope for adjustment than competing policy-makers normally acknowledge. Arguments that NATO would unravel if one of its major members embarked on a radical departure in defence policy are neither accurate descriptions of NATO's usual behaviour, nor helpful contributions towards NATO's task of coping with adjustments among its members.[51]

Alliance management

Since there are many possible variations of defence policy and innumerable different circumstances in which NATO might find itself, it is fruitless to try to predict US reactions, say, to a Kinnockled Labour government that was committed to carrying through the sort of defence policy outlined in *Defence and Security for Britain*.[52] This paper has tried to sketch in two diverging trends, whose differences are magnified by the fact that NATO is presently in a transitional phase. Without trying to make forecasts, however, it is reasonable to assume that the scope for accommodation between a determined incoming anti-nuclear Labour government and an out-going Reagan administration would not be great.

As far as nuclear issues are concerned, a British government could probably cancel Trident without provoking much US reaction one way or another. Many in the Pentagon would accept the cancellation of the programme as long as the money saved were spent on NATO defence, as is assumed in the Labour Party document. Beyond this, it is possible that Britain could move out of the business of operating battlefield nuclear systems. This would be more sensitive than Trident cancellations, since it would have greater implications for other allies. Nevertheless, such a move is conceivable. It could represent a rationalization of effort which in some respects would be helpful: taking dual-capable systems – artillery and aircraft – out of the nuclear equation in order to dedicate them entirely to conventional defence, which is where they should always be, by most estimates. It might also coincide with a general run-down of battlefield nuclear weapons to quite low levels of mobile, flexible, delivery systems, operated chiefly by the United States.

The crucial issue, for a future Labour government, would be US nuclear bases in Britain. There would be no way of classing this as an independent force decision, or as a rationalization. On this issue, the geographical importance of operational bases in Britain – particularly for the Eastern Atlantic – lies in the infrastructure that they provide for US and NATO operations. The symbolic importance of *removing* American nuclear forces from Britain would prove to be a massive obstacle. The reactions of US policy-makers- and congressional observers to this prospect have ranged from a pensive bewilderment at what the effects might be, to a catalogue of the retaliatory acts and the political and military fall-out that would result.[53] It also seems clear, however, that while US bases in Britain are vital to NATO, the physical problems that the loss of *strictly nuclear bases* would pose are not nearly as formidable as the symbolic/political damage that such a loss would inflict upon the established consensus of the Alliance. A senior staffer on the House Armed Services Committee thought that Congress simply 'couldn't get used to it'; it would be a clear case of 'decoupling', 'a disaster'.[54]

It is also likely that the carrot of a Labour non-nuclear policy – to maintain, or even spend more on, conventional defences – would not command sufficient approval in Washington to offset the negative effects. In the light of present economic trends in British defence policy, it is highly likely that considerably more will have to be spent anyway just to maintain existing commitments.[55] It also seems clear that after the experience of the '3 per cent solution', US policy-makers regard the commitment of funds to defence with some scepticism and would rather wait-and-see what actual results are forthcoming. Certainly, the direct results of this half of the policy would seem very long-term compared to the short-term impact of an announcement of the closure of US nuclear bases.

If this represents a general picture of the limits to accommodation, what could conceivably increase the scope of agreement on such issues? What, in other words, would give the reformist tendencies more weight than the conservative ones? An obvious, if glib, answer must surely be to work for increased understanding between the United States and the European allies. At present, a heterogeneous US military machine (even less cohesive since Reagan's assumption of office, for all his increased spending) confronts a variety of military machines in Europe and governments who are essentially asymmetrical in their security and economic intersts. But if this is the inevitable condition of a transatlantic alliance, there is no reason why the attention of leaders to NATO relations needs to be as sporadic as it has been. In particular, the present government, and any future government, should make a significant effort to impress on the US policy elite that NATO *is* in a state of change. No future British government will be able to meet Washington's expectations if the US in the late 1980s really wants 'much more of the same' from the allies. A business-as-usual approach by the Europeans, born out of fear of creating ripples in NATO, is a self-defeating strategy. Even a staunchly pro-nuclear Conservative government in Britain has an interest in encouraging reformist trends within US defence policy; it simply could not keep up with any extension of the conservative trends in America identified above.

More specifically, the time is right for a much greater effort at leadership on the part of the Europeans. The Europeans have traditionally allowed the US to make NATO policy; have stood back while internal debates raged in Washington; and have then complained when they disliked the results. There is reason to believe, however, that US policy-makers would welcome a more assertive European component in NATO decision-making. For one thing, it would represent a step towards greater political unity within NATO. It would also give the United States something to react against. The problem for US NATO policy at present is that it is mainly a reflection of the internal problems of American defence policy. The NATO element of US defence policy is being driven, either by low-level military considerations, such as the US army's determination to develop new battle tactics, or by high-level political abstractions, framed by Congress or the White House, which are concerned with symbols of commitment and general concepts of the 'common defence burden'. A constructive European approach to the United States should include a European (as opposed to a NATO) threat assessment and an explicit statement of how the Europeans intend to respond to it from their perspective. This would go a long way towards focusing US defence debates where they affect NATO directly.[56] It would also strengthen public perceptions, on both sides of the Atlantic, of the seriousness of European defence efforts.[57] It would, in Stanley Sloan's words, be the basis of a 'new transatlantic bargain'.[58] The Europeans have nothing to be ashamed of in terms of their military and economic contributions to NATO, though they should, indeed, be a little bashful about their political input to the Alliance. But there is no reason to believe that the European contribution to NATO will not stand up to a renewed bargain with the US.

In the longer run, the issue of political symbolism in NATO has to be tackled by the Europeans themselves. The deep symbolism of nuclear weapons is now highly ambivalent. It works against NATO as much as for it. The single most important development that would encourage US reformist instincts would be to find a new totem pole around which NATO can unite. The nuclear totem, for so long a force of cohesion and a device to cover up incipient cracks in the Alliance, is no longer performing that role. NATO does not, therefore, have the choice of standing still. As Dr Luns himself stressed, nuclear weapons have done more than anything else to 're-politicize' the Alliance and will continue to do so for some time. The United States, however, has an intrinsically greater commitment to nuclear weapons. They represent the *only* device which can defeat the US on its homeland in the present era. There is much less ambivalence in the United States than in Europe about the role of nuclear weapons in defence policy.

It is incumbent on the Europeans, therefore, to take the lead in helping to construct a new totem pole: to devise a military arrangement which more closely links the national forces of NATO members and serves as a political symbol of collective defence. It would have to be an arrangement which creates and exploits a genuine interdependence. At whatever level the nuclear threshold is set, and however it is operated, the essential physical requirements are that US reinforcements to the NATO theatre are guaranteed, and that all of the European allies come into the fight. Nuclear weapons offer a negative type of interdependence in the certainty that everyone will suffer, but not a positive interdependence, i.e., through strengthening everyone's incentive to fight. Any new totem pole would also have to serve as a public symbol of unity to capitalize upon the general popularity of NATO, as an organization, on both sides of the Atlantic.

This is undoubtedly a tall order. It may well be, however, that holding NATO together at all for the future will be a tall order. The key to handling change within the Alliance is likely to be the speed with which it occurs. By setting a clear agenda for change within NATO, the Europeans could afford to take it relatively slowly, thereby helping the Alliance to evolve in the direction of a deeper commitment to *defence*, broadly defined, as opposed to the present rather narrow and brittle concept of defence defined chiefly in nuclear terms.

Notes

1. Joseph M.A.H. Luns, 'Taking a Parting Look at NATO', *NATO Review*, 32(2) (April 1984), pp. 1, 7.
2. Harold Brown, 'Domestic Consensus and Nuclear Deterrence', in International Institute for Strategic Studies, *Defence and Consensus: The Domestic Aspects of Western Security: Part II* (London: IISS, 1983), p. 19.
3. See Michael Clarke, 'West European Politics and Extended Deterrence', University of Maryland, *Nuclear Deterrence: New Risks, New Opportunities*, conference proceedings, forthcoming.
4. The trade figures are provided by the *Washington Post*, 22 April 1984, p. G4. The population figures are provided by *The International Yearbook and Statesman's Who's Who 1982*, p. 567. For a wider analysis, see Stanley R. Sloan, *NATO's Future: Towards a New Transatlantic Bargain* (Washington, D.C.: National Defense University Press, 1984), ch. 6.
5. *Washington Post*, 29 Feb. 1984, p. A16. Also, Lawrence Eagleburger, 'The Transatlantic Relationship – A Long-Term Perspective', *NATO Review*, 32(2) (1984), pp. 8-9. For Burt's statement, see US Congress House Committee on Foreign Affairs, Hearings before the Subcommittee on Europe and the Middle East, 'Developments in Europe, September 1983', 22 Sept. 1983, p. 41.
6. Statement by James E. Watkins, Chief of Naval Operations, JCS, *Washington Post*, 4 Aug. 1984, p. A1.
7. Personal interview, 14 Nov. 1983.
8. See for example Donald R. Cotter, 'A NATO Nuclear Overwatch Force: Modernized Nuclear and Conventional Capabilities', *Armed Forces Journal International*, July 1984, p. 61.
9. Mark Rovner, *Defense Dollars and Sense*, Washington, D.C., Common Cause (1983), pp. 9-15. A 'less sustained' recovery can be defined as any fall in annual growth rates below 3 per cent: see *The Economist*, 17 Nov. 1984, pp. 39-40.
10. Congressional Budget Office, *Defense Spending and the Economy* (Feb. 1983), p. xv.
11. Congressional Budget Office estimates, quoted in John A. Williams, 'Defense Policy: The Carter–Reagan Record', *The Washington Quarterly*, 6(4) (1983), p. 80.
12. Asa A. Clark and Thomas W. Fagan, 'Trends in Defense Budgeting: Mortgaging the Future', in Asa A. Clark *et al.* (eds.), *The Defense Reform Debate: Issues and Analysis* (Baltimore and London: Johns Hopkins University Press, 1984).
13. Department of Defense, *Report on Allied Contributions to the Common Defense: A Report to the US Congress*, March 1984, p. 49.
14. General Accounting Office, Report to the Chairman, Sub-Committee on Defense, Senate Committee on Appropriations, *Reduction in US Costs to Station Forces in the*

Federal Republic of Germany and the United Kingdom are Unlikely, GAO/NSIAD-84-130, 31 July 1984, pp. 28-9.

15. *Ibid.*, p.i. On general comparisons of defence expenditure as a percentage of GNP, see *The Economist*, 4 Aug. 1984, p. 38.

16. *Defense Week*, 5 July 1983, p. 7.

17. Stanley R. Sloan, *Defense Burden Sharing: US Relations With NATO Allies and Japan*, Congressional Research Service Report, 83-140F, 8 July 1983, p. 20.

18. Sloan, *NATO's Future*.

19. *International Herald Tribune*, 14 Nov. 1984, pp. 1, 3.

20. *Sunday Times*, 21 Oct. 1984, p. 12.

21. *New York Times*, 9 Aug. 1984, p. B10.

22. General Accounting Office, op. cit., pp. 26-7.

23. David N. Schwartz, *NATO's Nuclear Dilemmas* (Washington, D.C.: The Brookings Institution, 1983), p. 250.

24. *The Times*, 17 Aug. 1981, p. 8.

25. Personal interview, Daniel Gouré, Science Applications Inc., 31 July 1984.

26. Quoted in Richard Gwyn, 'A New Neutralism', *World Press Reiew*, 31(9) (Sept. 1984), p. 38.

27. Jonathan Dean, 'How to Lose Germany', *Foreign Policy*, No. 55 (Summer 1984), p. 60.

28. James W. Reed, 'Congress and the Politics of Defense Reform', in Clark *et al.*, *The Defense Reform Debate*, p. 232.

29. Pierre Sprey, 'The Case for Better and Cheaper Weapons', in Clark *et al.*, op. cit. Also, Franklin Spinney, *Defense Facts of Life*, Department of Defense, Office of Program Analysis and Evaluation, December 1980.

30. Jeffrey Record, 'The Military Reform Caucus', *Washington Quarterly*, 6(2) (1983), pp. 126-7.

31. Steven L. Canby, 'Military Reform and the Art of War', *Survival*, 25(3) (May/June 1983), p. 120.

32. Lawrence Kaagan, 'Public Opinion and the Defence Effort: Trends and Lessons, the United States', in International Institute for Strategic Studies, *Defence and Consensus: The Domestic Aspects of Western Security: Part I*, (London: IISS, 1983), p. 14.

33. Robert W. Komer, 'Strategy and Military Reform', in Clark *et al.*, *The Defence Reform Debate*, pp. 7, 13.

34. Robert A. Gessert, 'The AirLand Battle and NATO's New Doctrinal Debate', *Royal United Services Institute Journal*, 129(2) (1984). E. Charles Christopher, 'AirLand Battle Doctrine – into the 21st Century', *Military Technology*, Sept. 1984, pp. 59-60.

35. Canby, 'Military Reform and the Art of War', pp. 132-3.

36. Federal Ministry of Defence, *White Paper 1979: The Security of the Federal Republic of Germany and the Development of the Federal Armed Forces* (Bonn: 1979), p. 126.

37. See the present *FM 100-5, Operations*, Headquarters, Department of the Army, 20 Aug. 1982, as compared to TRADOC 525-5, *US Army Operational Concepts: The AirLand Battle and Corps 86*, Headquarters, US Army, Training and Doctrine Command, 1981. Also, personal interviews.

38. Paul Bracken, *The Command and Control of Nuclear Forces* (London: Yale University Press, 1983), pp. 165-7.

39. Col. W.G. Hanne, 'AirLand Battle, Doctrine Not Dogma', *International Defense Review*, 16(8) (1983), p. 1039.

40. Personal interviews.

41. *Statement on the Defence Estimates 1984*, Vol. 1, Cmnd. 9227-1 (London: HMSO, 1984), p. 6.

42. See, for example, William M. Arkin, 'European Nuclear Weapons Developments', *Armament and Disarmament Information Unit Report*, 4(2) (Apr. 1982), p. 12.
43. William W. Kaufmann, 'Nuclear Deterrence in Central Europe', in John D. Steinbruner and Leon V. Sigal (eds.), *Alliance Security: NATO and the No-First-Use Question* (Washington, D.C.: The Brookings Institution, 1983), pp. 38-42. Robert S. McNamara, 'The Military Role of Nuclear Weapons: Perceptions and Misperceptions', *Foreign Affairs*, 62(1) (Fall 1983), pp. 67-72.
44. Personal interview, 30 Nov. 1983.
45. Norman Birnbaum, 'Western Europe and the United States Again', unpublished paper, Federation of American Scientists, Washington, D.C., 1984, p. 12.
46. David Calleo, 'Domestic Priorities and the Demands of Alliance: An American Perspective', in International Institute for Strategic Studies, *Defence and Consensus: The Domestic Aspects of Western Security: Part III* (London: IISS, 1983), p. 3.
47. *Ibid.*, pp. 3-4, 10.
48. See United States Senate, Foreign Relations Committee Report, *NATO Today: The Alliance in Evolution*, 97-31, April 1982, pp. 77-8; Elisabeth Noelle-Newmann, 'The Missile Gap: The German Press and Public Opinion', *Public Opinion*, 6(5) (Oct/Nov 1983), pp. 45-9; and 'Opinion Roundup', *Public Opinion*, 6(6) (Dec/Jan 1984), pp. 38-9.
49. 'FRG Consensus Urged in Disarmament Issue', Foreign Broadcast Information Service, *Daily Report: WEU*, 13 May 1983, p. j3.
50. Gregory Flynn, 'Public Opinion and Atlantic Defence', *NATO Review*, 31(5) (1983), p. 10.
51. One of the clearest expressions of this point is to be found in *Statement on the Defence Estimates 1981*, Vol. 1, Cmnd. 8212-1 (London: HMSO, 1981), p. 13. Also, Francis Pym, 'The Alliance and Arms Control: Ten Misconceptions', Foreign and Commonwealth Office, 25 Nov. 1982.
52. Labour Party, Statement to Annual Conference 1984 by the National Executive Committee, *Defence and Security for Britain*, p. 8.
53. Personal interviews.
54. Personal interview, 17 Nov. 1983.
55. Malcolm Chalmers, 'British Defence Spending in the 1980s', *Armament and Disarmament Information Unit Report*, 6(3) (May/June 1984), p. 1.
56. Sloan, *NATO's Future*, ch. 9.
57. Pieter Dankert, 'Europe Together, America Apart', *Foreign Policy*, No. 53 (Winter 1983-84), p. 19.
58. Sloan, *NATO's Future*.

Comment on Chapter 4
Robbin Laird

Michael Clarke has provided a skilful overview of American defence trends and their potential impacts on the evolution of British defence policy. His central point, that 'American reactions to *any* shift in British defence policy must therefore be placed within a distinctively new context of transatlantic argument', is certainly true. One could go further and stress that any changes in British defence policy will be given meaning by Americans, primarily in relationship to the ascendancy or decline of the European component of the Western Alliance. Greater 'responsibility-sharing', as opposed to simple fiscal 'burden-sharing' by Europeans, is critical to the continued vitality of the Alliance. Britain is playing an increasingly significant role in the further development of responsibility-sharing by Europe within the Alliance.

In spite of the high quality of Clarke's analysis of US defence trends, I am not persuaded by the use of the conservative versus reformist distinction, as the means by which to explore the perceived impact of British defence policy on American interests. The reformist category simply covers too many developments on the American side, ranging from changing battlefield tactics to genuine strategic altera-tions. The effects for Britain vary tremendously, from tactical changes such as the adoption of AirLand Battle, to major strategic changes, such as the virtual elimination of battlefield nuclear weapons. In the former case, British forces would inevitably be essential to the improvement of NATO's ability to conduct forward defence; in the latter case, Britain's conventional and nuclear forces would be critical components in America's ability to resupply Europe.

Mr Clarke, unfortunately, reasserts the oft-repeated claim that America is shifting its interests to the Pacific Basin at the expense of Europe. America has been a Pacific power throughout the twentieth century, but certainly not at the expense of Western Europe. The defence of Europe remains the single most significant military commitment of the United States (even, some would argue, at the expense of home defence). It is simply that Americans seek to place more responsibility for the defence of Europe onto European shoulders. It is not a question of the American military abandonment of Europe, a course of action which, if followed, would constitute the most significant defeat in the modern history of US foreign policy.

There is one specific comment by Clarke, regarding the evolution of British defence policy, which must be treated with caution: 'As far as nuclear issues are concerned, a British government could certainly cancel Trident without provoking much US reaction one way or another'. The cancellation of Trident would be significant in American eyes, but its meaning would vary dramatically depending on the political context. If it were cancelled by a government which was serious about defence and which intended to put the money elsewhere in defence (nuclear or conventional), Americans might well not be troubled by cancellation. If it were done as a symbolic action that led to a general downturn in British defence, it would be quite another situation, and one which would seriously undercut Europe's ability to be defended.

Americans increasingly look to Europe to take a greater role in its own defence. It is useful to recover a sense of the changing strategic environment which has led Americans to this position. There is one overarching change that is shaping American thinking, namely, the emergence of the US–Soviet strategic nuclear stand-off, within which the Soviet Union has been forging a conventionally oriented option for military operations in the European theatre. (I have gone into this in my book, *The Soviet Union and Strategic Arms*, so there is no need to repeat the argument at length here.[1]

The impact of Soviet developments is to constrict American, and indeed the Alliance's, room for manoeuvre, militarily and politically. If there is to be a credible, conventionally oriented defence of Europe, then the West Europeans must (in American eyes) take the lead in providing manpower, material and (for some Americans at least) greater strategic leadership. Perhaps forward defence ought to be supplemented by some forces of territorial defence, in order to provide a much more credible conventional deterrent for the Soviets. Here, only the Europeans can provide leadership. The military staying-power of the Alliance is becoming more important in deterring the conventional forces of the Soviet Union. In the event of war, Europe must be better able to slow any Soviet advance, in order to allow American resupply. One might also add that, for anything other than a very short war, Britain and France would become critical areas for the staging of US forces. Perhaps the Anglo-French dialogue might convince the French of their critical role in this regard for European defence.

However, it is a question of a conventionally oriented, not an all-conventional, defence of Europe. Nuclear weapons remain critical to deterring Soviet nuclear use and are a hedge against the failure of conventional defence. Alliance intermediate-range nuclear forces (American, British and French) play a major part in providing such a hedge. The nuclear debate in Britain seems to lose sight of the critical interrelation between conventional forces and nuclear weapons in the defence of Europe, even if one wishes to deny it on the political/ideological or military/doctrinal level. Paradoxically, a certain nuclear capability might well be necessary for Britain if its conventional forces are to play as credible a role as possible.

In short, Britain matters to the American involvement in European defence in both the conventional and nuclear fields. Conventionally, British forces are critical to the protection of the UK as a strategic reserve for continental military activity, as well as providing forces for NATO's forward defence in the Federal Republic of Germany. Perhaps Britain's economic constraints might force choices between these conventional roles; if so, it would have a significant impact on the intra-European as well as transatlantic dialogue. Also, British (and French) nuclear forces provide a potential for 'de-Americanizing' the nuclear question in European defence. The presence of French and British nuclear forces suggests that nuclear weapons are a reliable means of defending Europe in (at least some) European eyes. British and French nuclear forces provide an important hedge against Soviet miscalculations about their ability to fight a conventional war in Europe.

Above all, Britain is a country which Americans consider to be serious about defence issues. Americans can only hope that Britain remains committed to serious defence efforts and to working with other European powers to increase the ability of Europe to contribute to its own defence.

Note

1. Robbin F. Laird and Dale R. Harspring, *The Soviet Union and Strategic Arms* (Boulder, Colo.: Westview, 1984).

5 Shifts in British Defence Policy: How Would the European Allies React?
William Wallace

All established political systems are preoccupied with their *own* maintenance first, and with their neighbours' second. So long as relations with those neighbours remain stable and unthreatening, there is a natural tendency to take those relations for granted. Attention is drawn to them only when threats appear or significant changes take place, particularly when these changes adversely affect the interests of the political system concerned. Interpretation of those changes depends not only upon their immediate and direct impact but also upon the overall image of the country undergoing them – the intentions of its government, the quality and capabilities of its political elite, the stability or instability of its society, the strength or weakness of its economy.

Governments and politicians only speculate about hypothetical developments when they consider them both possible and worrying. French politicians and writers have speculated at length about the possibility of major changes in West German foreign and defence policy, for example, because they regard such a development as profoundly threatening to the core security interests of France, and thus see even faint indications of a shift in that direction as disturbing. Britain is not seen by any of its continental neighbours as a potential threat. Its record in defence policy over the past thirty years has been that of a reliable, if at times grudging, ally whose attention has been fixed first and foremost on the transatlantic relationship. Until the late 1960s, it also concentrated on its defence responsibilities outside Europe, but it has fulfilled its commitments to European defence from 1954 onwards with a sense of obligation which has wavered from enthusiasm to reluctance and back again.

Britain is not the most important ally of any West European country. Its defence contribution is of most direct significance to Federal Germany, to Norway, to the Netherlands and to Belgium, and of considerable indirect significance to France. For all of these countries, the American commitment to Europe is of key importance.

The British contribution is assessed partly in terms of its contribution to the European balance and to the defence of the Central Front, and partly in terms of its contribution to maintaining the American commitment. Particular aspects of the British defence effort are of crucial significance to Norway and to Federal Germany, and to a lesser extent to the Netherlands. But even for these countries, the significance of any changes in British defence priorities would be assessed in terms of their impact upon the Alliance as a whole, and the consequent demands placed on its partners (and choices posed for them), as much as upon themselves, even if the changes meant the direct withdrawal of forces contributing to their national security.

Myths and symbols
Changes in defence policy give out signals about a country's foreign policy priorities and, in public expenditure terms, of national priorities as a whole. Defence commitments carry symbolic weight as well as practical significance, at home and abroad. The 1954 commitment to maintain four divisions and a tactical air force on the European continent was presented by Anthony Eden to his fellow foreign ministers at the London Conference as a gesture with strong symbolic overtones, 'for us a very formidable step to take. You all know that ours is above all an island story. We are still an island people in thought and tradition, whatever the modern facts of weapons and strategy may compel.'[1] His continental colleagues no doubt took that, alongside other evidence of Britain's reluctant and partial acceptance of the necessity of European economic and industrial cooperation, as signalling both the significance of the change and the limits within which it was set: 'thus far and no farther' was an essential part of the message.

The 1957 Review also carried messages – both intended and unintended – for Britain's European partners. Then, as now, the domestic debate on British defence policy was couched in terms of Britain's international role, the implications for Britain's relations with the United States, and the budgetary costs of Britain's international obligations. The expectations and needs of Britain's European allies were a secondary consideration. Even then, however, the problem of the relationship with Federal Germany was in the back of many policy-makers' minds, as they observed the rising costs of British forces in Federal Germany since the ending of their occupation status, the rapid recovery of the West German economy and the stately pace of German rearmament. An underlying sense of grievance about the disproportionate share of the burden of European defence which Britain's continental allies expected it to bear was already evident. Harold Macmillan, speaking as Chancellor of the Exchequer to the Foreign Press Association in May 1956, allowed himself to muse about the 'pipe dream' of a defence budget of half its present size, which (he noted) would transform Britain's economic position, solve the problem of the balance of payments, and allow a substantial tax cut. 'Of course,' he added, 'we know we can't have it, we're not going to behave in an irresponsible way . . . By and large, Britain will have to go on carrying two rifles instead of the one carried by others.'[2]

The message which the 1957 Review was intended to convey was that, in the aftermath of Suez, Britain was reasserting its position as a world power through its determination to maintain an independent deterrent and through the maintenance of its responsibilities east of Suez. The message received by its European partners was very different. The unilateral nature of the British decision, presented to its Alliance partners (apart from the United States) as a *fait accompli*, aroused a strong reaction from several continental governments. Federal Germany in particular protested against the proposed withdrawal of troops and the absence of consultation; Mr Macmillan, by now prime minister, travelled to Bonn a few weeks after the White Paper had been published to sooth ruffled feelings.[3] The attitude within Whitehall to Britain's share of the burden of European defence in the late 1950s was not unlike the attitude to Britain's contribution to the Community budget in the late 1970s, carrying with it the same instinctive scepticism about calls from others for a greater European commitment. The view from the Continent, on the other hand, was affected by Britain's parallel efforts to promote an OEEC-wide free trade area alongside the newly negotiated European Economic Community, and by Selwyn Lloyd's 'Grand Design' proposals to bring together the proliferating European parliamentary assemblies within an overarching Euro-American assembly.[4] Thus, while there must have been a degree of sympathy within France for the emphasis on national priorities, nuclear deterrence and intervention forces, the message received in Bonn, the Hague and elsewhere was that Britain was downgrading its new-found commitment to European defence in favour of priorities of little concern to its European partners.

Memory and myth play a large part in triggering the reactions of governments to each other's decisions. The predominant British image of our defence relationship with the European continent is still shaped by World War II, and was reinforced in 1984 by the ceremonies which marked the fortieth anniversaries of the Normandy landings, the liberation of Brussels, and the battle of Arnhem. That image, which extends to the whole relationship between Britain and Europe, was exemplified in the final Conservative party political broadcast before the 1984 European elections, which began with film of the Normandy landings and went on to stress the enormous contribution which Britain had made to Western Europe during and since World War II. Mrs Thatcher, if I recall rightly, indeed remarked during that programme that 'no country has made a greater contribution to Europe'. That set of memories and myths carries with it a potential rationale for a substantial cut in Britain's continental commitment. 'We have,' one can imagine a British prime minister saying, 'throughout the last thirty years shouldered a heavy burden in European defence, alongside our contributions to the air and sea defence of the North Atlantic and to the strategic deterrent forces. That burden has weighed down our economy and diverted our industrial and technological resources. Now it is time for our European partners to carry a larger share.' 'This in no way affects our established commitment to European cooperation,' he might quite possibly add; 'we are merely asking our partners to accept a more equitable division of the responsibilities of the common defence.'

Memories and myths on the Continent, however, are rather different, and focus more often on the 1950s and 1960s than on the 'glorious' period of 1944-5. The image of World War II itself is not as straightforward as some in Britain expect; informal conversations with a number of French naval officers in staff positions in 1981-2 suggested that the myth of Mers-el-Kébir[5] still had some resonance, and that it combined with the memory of Suez into a powerful but unspecific image of Britain as a hesitant European, an unreliable partner and – above all – as an 'Anglo-Saxon' power. The myth of the Nassau Agreement, of Britain's turning once again to the United States as a privileged partner, instead of accepting a European vocation in partnership with France, reinforces this image (for all that it is a myth largely without substance, since there is good evidence that de Gaulle had already decided to exclude Britain from the EEC before Macmillan went to Nassau, and very little evidence of French willingness or ability to offer any viable alternative).[6] The reinforcement of the Anglo-American relationship through the procurement of Trident, after a number of public hints and private conversations in 1979-80 about the possibilities of Anglo-French collaboration, only confirms this established image.

West German and Dutch recollections are different from the French. The Dutch armed services retain a number of traditions and ties which owe their origin to wartime exile and postwar reconstructions. These ties have been weakened for the Dutch air force by successive choices of American aircraft (and so of American training), but strengthened for the navy and marines by the steady growth of joint training and operations with the British. The West German armed services, with no acceptable history before 1956, lack such traditional ties. Politicians and officials in both countries, however, share the same recollection of Britain in the 1950s and 1960s: holding back from the ambitious proposals for a European Defence Community; giving low priority to the size or equipment of its forces in Federal Germany from 1957 on; and riding on the American coat-tails in the bitter offset negotiations of 1966-7.[7]

Sadly, the considerable credit which Denis Healey accumulated, most of all with Helmut Schmidt and within the West German government, through the Eurogroup initiative of 1968 and the European Defence Improvement Programme of 1970, was overlaid and limited by the perceived continued orientation of the British military hierarchy towards Washington, the North Atlantic and beyond and their apparent reluctance to accept the finality of their European vocation. Symbols and images, however imprecise or inaccurate, carry considerable weight here, too. At a private discussion in Bonn with a number of senior foreign and defence ministry officials, in late 1982, which compared the Anglo-German and Franco-German security relationships, the British participants were forcefully struck by the references to events of twenty or more years ago – the Franco-German military parade at Rheims in 1963, the rancorous offset arguments of the mid-1960s – to explain and illustrate current attitudes. West German defence staff still see the British as holding themselves a little apart. One remarked a little unkindly that BAOR behaves in Federal Germany rather as the British army must have behaved in India, with the intense camaraderie and introversion of a foreign posting rather than as a natural part of a common European defence on European soil. The pride with which British officials and military officers pointed to the new policy that all BAOR brigade commanders and above should be proficient in German, after thirty years in which British army officers had been spending up to a third of their career service in Federal Germany, suggests that his remark was not entirely inaccurate.[8]

These very different perceptions of Britain's contribution and commitment to European defence would raise significant problems in the presentation of any shift in British defence policy which affected continental Europe. The British government's domestic audience would understand and sympathize with a substantial reduction in BAOR in favour of the maritime role or of the independent deterrent, as redressing an imbalance which has been unfavourable for far too long. The continental audience would instinctively look for signs of Britain turning away from Europe again, as so often before. The stereotypes on both sides of the Channel are deeply entrenched, and would require great powers of diplomacy, persuasion and political leadership to be overcome. More precise interpretation of any shifts would depend upon the overall credibility of the British government and the wider framework of its external policies. Part of the difficulties which the Labour government of 1974-9 faced in persuading its continental partners of the strength of its case on the Community budget and on the adjustment of Community policies, for example, was the predominant perception in Paris and in Bonn of a government which was failing to face up to its own domestic choices: attempting to blame the Community for economic difficulties which were largely of its own making, and thus deserving (and receiving) only limited sympathy for its demands. A reduction in British defence spending which was accompanied by an economic and industrial strategy – and a redirection of public expenditure – which seemed sensible and likely to succeed would be more readily accepted by other West European governments than one which appeared to dissipate economic resources and foreshadow further decline. Such interpretations would, unavoidably, be subjective. They would differ according to the political complexion of the governments in power in other countries, draw on each government's established image of Britain and of the party in government, and be moderated and refined by the effectiveness of the British government's presentation of the reasons for any shift. In politics, what you do forms only part of the impression you make on others. The how and the why matter as much as the what; the way in which you do it, and the reasons which you give for doing it, are often as important as the action itself.

The interests of Britain's European allies

Britain's continental neighbours share three direct and immediate interests in British defence options: their potential impact on European–American relations and on the American commitment to European defence; their implications for Britain's own contribution to the conventional defence of Western Europe, in particular of the Central Front; and their implications for the further development of European collaboration in military procurement and high technology. All three make the choice of a closer emphasis on conventional defence the most attractive option, within a tighter framework of European collaboration which would in turn remain within the wider integrated structure of NATO. Few even of those who would like to see Western Europe less dependent on the United States and on its nuclear deterrent would be happy to see a crisis in transatlantic confidence provoked by unilateral action by Britain, uncoordinated with its European partners. Political opinion in Denmark and Greece might possibly applaud a unilateral British decision to withdraw from the integrated structure of NATO or to remove all American nuclear weapons and bases from British soil; but there would be few in France, at any point of the political spectrum, or in Federal Germany or Italy, who would echo such sentiments. Nor is there any discernible sympathy for a greater British emphasis on the nuclear than the conventional role. Only in France can one find public evidence of support for a continued British nuclear deterrent, and there attention is directed most often to the possibility of Anglo-French, rather than Anglo-American, nuclear collaboration.

The presentation to continental governments and publics (and the degree of coordination with them) of any radical departure from the current balance of British defence policy would thus be of crucial importance to its acceptability. A shift towards alternative defence would find a sympathetic ear within significant political tendencies in Federal Germany, Denmark, Norway and the Low Countries, the weight of that sympathy depending on the political complexion of their incumbent governments and the current balance among contending political forces within their domestic defence debates. The activities of European Nuclear Disarmament (END), with its sponsoring of research conferences and its fostering of transnational links, have intertwined with other links among the broader peace movement and among socialist and social democratic parties to create an informed Europe-wide constituency for alternative defence. It has been a characteristic of END that it assumes that Europe is now a single theatre of conflict, and that national defence efforts and security policies must be seen within that Europe-wide context. A renunciation of British nuclear weapons which was accompanied by a more active British engagement in the European debate over the future of East–West relations, the management of change and the maintenance of European stability, would not lack credibility on the left of the West European political spectrum – though it evidently *would* lack credibility for governments from the right of the spectrum. But if a renunciation of British nuclear weapons was accompanied by a degree of disengagement from European concerns, a reduction of British forces in Federal Germany, and an apparent disinclination to consult or explain, the impact would probably be almost universally adverse. The predominant image would be one of Britain slipping into self-preoccupied decline, a large country behaving with the insouciance of Denmark or Iceland, without considering the unavoidably broader range of its security interests.

The same is true for any radical shift in the Anglo-American security relationship, especially with regard to any removal of US bases from Britain. There is an evident groundswell of opinion within a number of continental countries in favour of a progressive disengagement of European strategy and security from what is perceived as the dominant influence of the United States. But there is far less support for the provocation of an immediate crisis, least of all by actions taken by one of the United States's two leading European allies without deference to the opinions and fears of its neighbours. As the papers from Phil Williams and Michael Clarke note, there is considerable nervousness within Western Europe about the current drift of American attitudes towards Europe and towards US commitment to European defence. Awareness of divergent views, of the need to represent European perspectives more powerfully in Washington and to pursue an active policy towards Eastern Europe without unsettling too rapidly the balance between the two superpowers, argues for moving in harmony, not for withdrawal or unilateral renunciation. Whatever choices are taken for British defence policy, they will self-evidently be more acceptable to our European partners if they are taken, and presented, within a European rather than a national framework.

A parallel West European concern about American technological superiority, and about the tightening of controls on technology transfers of military-related equipment and licences, has fuelled the reviving debate on collaboration in procurement. Britain has been an active protagonist in this debate. It does not want to see West European industrial collaboration centre too firmly around Paris and Bonn, and it is anxious to protect its own research and development base and overseas markets and to limit its dependence on US equipment. Michael Heseltine went so far, in his speech to the Royal United Services Institute on 3 October 1984, as to call for 'a common market in military procurement within Western Europe comparable to that which exists in the United States'.[9] This collaboration is entirely in conventional equipment, and excludes nuclear technology, though advanced aircraft like the Tornado are dual-capable and equipped for conventional and nuclear roles. A British government which wished to impose stricter controls on the exports of collaborative weapon systems to third countries, or which argued for an altered emphasis in systems under development, would find itself committed to a complicated and wearing multilateral game in the attempt to win over its partners. A government which withdrew from a number of key initiatives in European collaboration (the future European fighter aircraft, for example), in order to concentrate its resources on independent initiatives or on Anglo-American collaboration, would risk the contempt of its allies.

It is not widely appreciated at Westminster, and even less appreciated beyond, that Whitehall, the private and public dimensions of military procurement and the armed services have all become progressively entangled in a network of bilateral and multilateral cooperation from which it would now be a painful process to extricate the British participants. It may still be that, for the navy, the transatlantic network is more important than the European; for the army (and the air force?) and for the civilian officials, the European network is now at least as important, and a good deal more time-consuming. One may imagine the reaction in Whitehall, as well as in other capitals, to an incoming government which threatened to disrupt this intricate network, let alone to one which threatened to disrupt both its transatlantic and its European connections.

There remains the particular French interest in the future of the British nuclear deterrent. Others may be able to cite evidence from Federal Germany, the Netherlands, Belgium or Italy in favour of the maintenance of a British nuclear deterrent as a second 'decision-centre' within the Alliance; I have found none within the mainstream of political opinion in those countries. On the contrary, all the indications are that any decision to maintain Trident at the expense of Britain's existing continental or maritime commitments would meet with vigorous disapproval. If allowed the luxury, there are those within the defence establishments of several European countries who would prefer to see Britain maintain a nuclear capability, both as an insurance against a further drift of American opinion away from the European commitment and as a counterbalance within Europe to the French deterrent force. But few, if any, would accept the maintenance of that option as Britain's first defence priority. Many more would view with some sympathy the pursuit of a less expensive, even residual, nuclear capability which did not involve commensurate cuts in other programmes.

The question is, would collaboration with France offer such an option, and would it carry any wider benefits in terms of reorienting Britain's defence? Certainly, France would be the European country most unhappy about a British renunciation of nuclear weapons, not simply because the French elite would take this as evidence of Britain's continuing political and economic decline, but also because the French government is itself faced with a similar dilemma. M. Hernu, on taking office as President Mitterrand's defence minister in 1981, declared his intention of reversing the previous administration's slide back towards conventional forces and equipment and of concentrating resources far more on strengthening the nuclear deterrent. Three years later, after some substantial lobbying from within the French armed services and from West German ministers and officials through the Franco-German defence dialogue, French conventional forces have been reduced only marginally; the Force d'Action Rapide (FAR) has been announced as a significant additional contribution to the defence of the Central Front; and the budgetary squeeze between different military roles and between competing requirements for new equipment is becoming increasingly acute.[10]

In tactical terms, a British proposal to opt for Anglo-French nuclear collaboration, as an alternative to Trident, would be a master stroke. It would demonstrate, symbolically and practically, the extent of Britain's European commitment, and it would force the French government to transform its rhetorical suggestions into concrete proposals.[11] There would follow some hard and extremely intricate negotiations, most probably prolonged, in which the price that the French government might charge Britain for the delivery of M-4 missiles (for example) would be a crucial factor, and the necessity of American acquiescence to transfers of technology would be a major complication. There might also be implications for British access to American intelligence and satellite systems, and for Franco-German and Franco-British collaboration in satellite launching and technology. The outcome of such negotiations would be uncertain in the extreme.

This would therefore be in some ways as radical a departure in British defence and foreign policy as any other on offer. Management of the American response would be crucial; the risks of provoking American opposition, thereby raising the spectre of 'unravelling the Alliance', would be very considerable. And it would carry far less weight with other European governments than it would in Paris. A British government which reasserted its European and international standing by the pursuit of Anglo-French nuclear cooperation and the reduction of its conventional forces in Federal Germany would find itself facing much the same contradictory political and military pressures as M. Hernu faced in 1982-3.

In many ways the most attractive way forward for a British government attempting to reorient its defence policy towards closer European cooperation, without any too radical a departure, would be to try to extend the bilateral Franco-German relationship into a trilateral one, a West European *directoire* which could talk on equal terms with the United States and provide firm leadership, without becoming entangled with the squabbles, special interests or moralizing of their smaller partners. This 'European triangle' has briefly emerged, from the secrecy of the Bonn Group and the preparatory discussions of national armaments directors, into the public gaze on a number of occasions in the last five years. There was a tripartite meeting of defence ministers from Britain, France and Federal Germany in Paris in September 1983, to discuss an agenda that was officially focused on armaments collaboration but which in practice extended to a range of other subjects. At its close, it was announced that a further meeting would take place in London in May 1984. Vigorous Italian protests persuaded the participants that this would be unwise, and that such discussions were better formally subsumed under the broader seven-nation framework of the West European Union (WEU). For Italy, as an important partner for Britain in arms procurement and a fellow participant in the multinational forces in the Sinai and Lebanon, changes in British defence policy will be assessed in terms of the indications they give of Britain's acceptance or rejection of a multilateral role both within Europe and beyond. Italy and France, as Mediterranean states, share a much more active interest in a continuing British role in out-of-area operations than their northern colleagues. They feel themselves more vulnerable to disorder spilling over from North Africa or the Middle East, and are consequently more concerned to ensure a collaborative European response.

The shock of the new
From the continental perspective, it is the continuity of British defence policy which is striking. The Labour government which took office in 1964 did not cancel Polaris, despite its criticisms of the Nassau Agreement when in opposition. The withdrawal from east of Suez was reluctant and gradual, and left a residual naval presence behind. The Labour government of 1974-9 did not significantly alter the direction of British defence policy; as with the period between 1964 and 1970, the disaffection of Labour backbenchers and activists was successfully contained by the old alliance between the two front benches. The expectations of continental observers are therefore of continuity rather than change, of adjustment rather than transformation. The shock of any radical shift in British defence policy would thus be considerable, and its significance for Britain's future relations with its major partners would be that much more difficult for those partners to assess. Britain has been the loyal ally of the United States for forty years; it still carries two rifles instead of one and still maintains a residual out-of-area role as well as a nuclear deterrent and a commitment to Europe. What, foreign ministries, defence staffs, politicians and press will ask, does any substantial shift in British defence policy mean for British policy as a whole?

If any major changes are to be made, presentation will be crucial. European governments will judge the implications of any major British defence review by what it signals to them about the direction, rationale and rationality of British policy, even more than by how it affects their immediate interests. They will look for the underlying attitudes to European cooperation, as well as to the transatlantic connection, that it conveys. They will look to the alternative uses to which resources saved are to be put, judging, according to their own ideological preferences and economic approaches, whether tax cuts are a more acceptable beneficiary of the shift in resources than public investment, or welfare payments than investment subsidies. They will listen critically to the explanations put forward by British ministers and officials, and to the links which such visitors make between defence policy, security policy and Britain's policy orientation as a whole. Above all, they will look to Washington, to the American reaction and to how the British government handles that reaction, for reassurance that any adjustment will not be too violently disruptive of the Alliance and of European stability. Beyond that, we are into the realm of idle speculation.

Notes

1. Quoted in Edward Fursdon, *The European Defence Community: A History* (London: Macmillan, 1980), p. 321.
2. Quoted by William Wallace, 'World Status without Tears', in Vernon Bogdanor and Robert Skidelsky (eds.), *The Age of Affluence* (London: Macmillan, 1970), p. 203.
3. *Ibid.*, pp. 210-12.
4. Miriam Camps, *Britain and the European Community, 1955-1963* (Oxford: OUP for the RIIA, 1964), pp. 119-22.
5. Former French naval base in the Gulf of Oran, Algeria. In July 1940, a British naval force arrived off Oran with orders to prevent French warships at anchor from falling into German or Italian hands. The French refused to take up any of the alternatives offered to them: to continue to resist; to entrust themselves to the Americans; or to be scuttled in port. The British therefore bombarded the French squadron, putting three ships out of action and killing 1,300 French seamen.
6. Andrew Pierre, *Nuclear Politics: The British Experience with an Independent Strategic Force, 1939-1970* (Oxford: OUP, 1972), pp. 236-40. But note that senior members of the British Cabinet had been dropping hints about nuclear collaboration with France during the summer and autumn of 1962. Peter Thorneycroft, then Minister of Defence, 'spoke of Europe as a potential world power which must be equipped with commensurate military capability' in a speech to the WEU Assembly in Paris on 4 December. 'In closed sessions he reportedly discussed how the weapons for a European nuclear force might be procured.' (*Ibid.*, p. 224.) The French sense of betrayal after the Nassau Agreement on 21 December was thus not entirely without cause; at the very least, signals across the Channel had been confusing.
7. It is not generally recalled in Britain that we again threatened a major withdrawal from BAOR in 1966. Characteristically, the threat was made by the Chancellor of the Exchequer, James Callaghan. Tactlessly, it was issued publicly by him at an airport press conference in Bonn, on 21 July, after delivering his government's demand for a full offset of the foreign exchange cost of the BAOR. See Gregory F. Treverton, *The 'Dollar Drain' and American Forces in Germany* (Athens, Ohio: Ohio University Press, 1978), pp. 141-2. Treverton adds that 'Bonn regarded the British threat as a nuisance . . . they cared most about US troops'.
8. These paragraphs draw on research conducted between 1981 and 1983 on Britain's links with France, Germany, the Netherlands and Italy. See William Wallace, *Britain's Bilateral Links within Western Europe*, Chatham House Paper 23 (London: Routledge & Kegan Paul for the RIIA, 1984), especially pp. 65-7; and 'Defence: the defence of sovereignty, or the defence of Germany', in Roger Morgan (ed.), *Leaders, Partners and Rivals*, forthcoming.
9. Notes taken of his speech.

10. See David S. Yost, *France and Conventional Defence in Central Europe,* European American Institute for Security Research, Paper no. 7, Spring 1984, who is particularly valuable on the changing rationale for the FAR.
11. See, for example, the candid article by Paul Delahousse in *Le Monde,* 14 October 1980, 'Pourquoi Londres a choisi le Trident', which analyses the changes in French defence policy which would be needed to convince the British government that cooperation with France was a realistic alternative.

Part II   Economic Constraints

6 Long-term Trends in Public Expenditure
M. S. Levitt and M. A. S. Joyce★

This paper is intended to outline some long-term trends that will affect public expenditure in the UK and to indicate their implications for defence spending. The background to the discussion must be the Treasury's Green Paper,[1] which states the strategy for the long term as being one of deciding what can be afforded before setting plans for particular programmes. It places the emphasis very clearly on the financing implications of spending and it raises the question of why total spending should rise at all. It acknowledges that in some cases programmes will need to be increased, but it also points to the need to establish relative priorities so that such increases are offset by reductions elsewhere. And it stresses the need to consider the scope both for switching from the public to the private sector and for improved efficiency within the public sector as a means of permitting improved provision. Achievement of Green Paper objectives would represent a break with the past, since public spending has normally risen absolutely and as a share of Gross Domestic Product (GDP). It would also require a tighter approach to the control and management of expenditure.

The Green Paper eschews any attempt to make projections for individual programmes, although it outlines several sources of pressure for higher spending, for example demographic change and the rising cost of sophisticated defence and health equipment. It does consider the implications of either holding total spending flat in cost terms or of allowing it to grow at 1 per cent annually after 1988/9. It seems useful here to quantify some of the expenditure implications of certain pressures and to consider the growth of total spending on a variety of illustrative assumptions, in order to be a little more specific about the context for defence spending.

First of all, we will briefly outline developments in expenditure management over the past twenty years or so; then sketch some broad

★ We wish to record our appreciation for the comments of Andrew Britton, Kit Jones, Chris Trinder and David Worswick on an earlier draft. We are responsible for the final content of the paper and any errors.

trends over the same period in the behaviour of the main expenditure aggregates; present some illustrative projections; consider some of the implications for defence; and draw brief conclusions. The Annex at the end of the book outlines the methodology used for our projections.

Developments in expenditure management and control

Developments in the systems of public expenditure management and control have been very well described and analysed by Sir Leo Pliatzky,[2] and only a summary is required here. Following the Plowden Report of 1961, public expenditure in the 1960s was planned in relation to the volume of resources expected to be available over the next five years under the Public Expenditure Survey (PES) system. Plans were expressed in constant prices. As a result of the frequent balance-of-payments crises of the 1960s, the system gradually placed greater emphasis on short-term control than on medium-term planning. However, it was not well suited to that purpose: it was difficult to translate PES prices into cash for Estimates purposes (the basis of parliamentary control); changes in prices made it very difficult to check back after the event to see whether plans had been fulfilled; the medium-term economic forecasts upon which plans were based proved too optimistic about GDP growth; and there was weak incentive to control costs, since there was automatic entitlement to cash compensation for greater than expected inflation, provided that the 'volume' plans were on target.

A particular feature of cost increases was the 'productivity differential' or 'relative price effect' (RPE), as it became known. This was the tendency for the unit cost of government services to rise faster than the general rate of inflation. This was partly because, in the case of labour-intensive services, earnings tended to move in line with pay in the private sector, where there were offsetting productivity increases; whereas in the government sector, in the absence of unambiguous measures, productivity was assumed to remain constant. In addition, there was the apparent tendency for contractors' prices for sophisticated defence and medical equipment to rise faster than the general rate of inflation. The expenditure plans recognized the existence of the RPE, for which provision was made; knowledge of this by outside equipment suppliers cannot have helped to limit cost increases. In any event, the RPE is not an unambiguous figure; it is very difficult to distinguish between a cost increase for a given product, and a cost increase for one that offers better performance (i.e. output) as technology changes. Furthermore, conventional measures do not take into account equipment suppliers' productivity increases. It seems likely, therefore, that to some extent the RPE was in fact a disguised volume increase.

The PES constant price approach tended to ignore *financing* at the departmental level, since departments were guaranteed cash provision for their volume plans. The financing onus existed of course, but only for the Treasury, which had to arrange for the necessary taxation or borrowing. Departments had a weak incentive to control costs.

In the context of the 1976 approach to the IMF, cash limits were introduced. They applied a year ahead, but medium-term planning was still done in volume terms. In 1979, cash planning was introduced, with no automatic entitlement to compensation for higher than anticipated prices; the emphasis was firmly on cash control. In these circumstances, uncertainty about the effects of future price changes has been decentralized among spending departments, except in the case of the 3 per cent NATO target in volume terms.

The basis of the Green Paper is neither volume (constant own prices) nor cash but 'cost terms', i.e., cash adjusted for general inflation as measured by the index of GDP prices generally. This means that the Green Paper objective of holding total spending flat in cost terms involves no compensation for the RPE. If a positive RPE is anticipated, volumes of resources must be cut, or efficiency increased, or public servants' pay must rise less quickly than pay elsewhere. As for improved efficiency, the Financial Management Initiative, launched in 1981,[3] is intended to secure lasting improvements. Improved procedures and information systems are being developed so that in future the machinery for setting objectives, assigning responsibilities, controlling costs, monitoring achievements and securing value for money will be lastingly better than hitherto. So far, the pace of progress seems somewhat varied among departments.[4] We briefly return to some of the relevant issues later on.

Past expenditure trends

First, we consider how public expenditure should be measured and outline some broad trends in the UK and other countries; then we look at the growth of defence spending in particular, in relation to GDP and other public expenditure; finally, as a basis for the discussion of our projections, some recent developments in public spending are briefly discussed.

Measurement and broad trends

Interest in trends in the amount of public spending might arise for two reasons. One concerns the extent of political/administrative control over the use of real resources (as opposed to the market mechanism); the other involves the financing implications of public expenditure (irrespective of its composition), the main concern of the Green Paper. A consideration of the use of real resources requires public spending to be measured in volume terms (i.e. at constant own prices) excluding cash transfers (e.g. social security benefits which recipients are free to spend as they choose). But to meet the concern about financing, public spending as a whole is of interest, measured either in cash terms for comparison with money GDP, or in cost terms for comparison with constant price GDP.[5]

Table 6.1   General government expenditure, 1962–82, UK[a]

Percentage of GDP

	Current expenditure			Investment (GDFC)[c]	Total
	Total	Final consumption	Other[b]		
1962					
Current prices	30	17	13	4	34
1980 prices	35	22	13	4(22)	39
1972					
Current prices	33	18	15	4	37
1980 prices	35	21	14	5(24)	40
1982					
Current prices	43	22	21	2	45
1980 prices	42	21	21	2(11)	44

Source: Central Statistical Office, *National Income and Expenditure Blue Book* (London: HMSO, 1983).

[a] Central government plus local authorities.
[b] Current grants to persons (e.g. pensions), subsidies, debt interest and net overseas grants.
[c] Figures in parentheses represent percentage of total GDFC – i.e., of total gross fixed investment – at 1980 prices.

Table 6.2   Government final consumption shares in GDP, 1978, compared with 12 OECD countries

Final consumption	12 OECD	UK
Civil	15.7	15.3
Defence	2.9	4.5
Total	18.6	19.8

Source: Malcolm Levitt, 'The Growth of Government Expenditure', *NIESR Review*, No. 108 (May 1984).

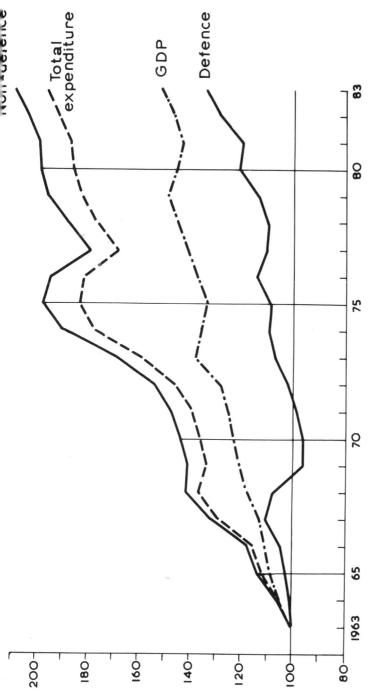

Figure 6.1 Index numbers of GDP at constant prices and public expenditure in cost terms. (Source: NIESR)

Figure 6.1 illustrates the growth of total public spending in cost terms in relation to GDP since 1963. Table 6.1 shows the share of current expenditure and investment since 1962 (general government gross domestic fixed capital formation); it reveals that final consumption has maintained a constant share in GDP in volume terms, but a rising share in current prices because of the RPE. The investment share has fallen. Other expenditure, mainly social security, debt interest and foreign grants, including EC contributions, has increased its share in volume and current price terms. By comparison with other countries, the share of current expenditure in GDP and the growth of government consumption in relation to GDP in the UK are broadly consistent with experience in comparable countries; on the other hand, cash transfers are of relatively less importance in the UK. Table 6.2 shows that defence spending is of greater importance relative to GDP in the UK than on average in other countries for which data is available.

UK defence spending and total public expenditure
Figure 6.2 shows total public spending as a proportion of GDP and defence as a share of total public expenditure. The defence share in the total fell sharply between 1963 and 1969; then remained fairly flat until 1975, since when it has tended to rise, although at a low and varying rate.

It has been suggested by Ron Smith and colleagues[6] that changes in the composition of government expenditure over this period as a whole are better explained by 'objective' factors such as demographic influences (e.g. on education and health) and the behaviour of American and Soviet military spending (as influences on defence) than by the political party in office. Others have noted[7] that total spending over this period as a whole was likewise uninfluenced by differences in ruling party (as Figure 6.1 illustrates). A broad conclusion might be that severe competition for resources between defence and other programmes was side-stepped by allowing the total to grow.*

Recent developments
Finally, Table 6.3 shows the pattern of programme expenditure in 1978/9 and 1983/4 and intentions for 1986/7. It excludes such items as debt interest and special asset sales.

---

* A way of describing this is to note that the elasticity of defence spending with respect to non-defence spending in the UK over the period 1963-83 is 0.27; i.e., a 1 per cent increase in other spending is associated with a 0.27 per cent increase in defence spending; if defence and non-defence competed, the elasticity would have been negative. (Data in cost terms: $R^2 = 0.52$, t = 4.5; NIESR estimates.)

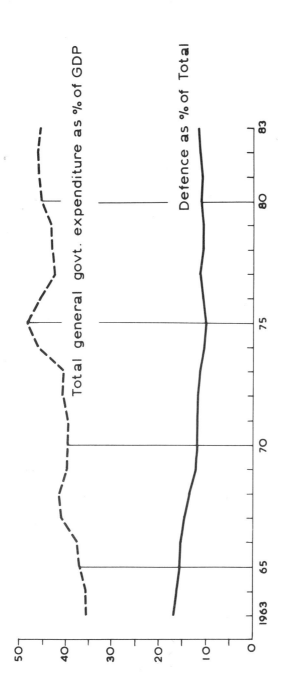

Figure 6.2   Total public expenditure as a proportion of GDP, and defence as a share of total public expenditure. (Source: NIESR)

Table 6.3   Public expenditure programmes (£bn, 1983/4 cost terms)

	1978/9 (actual)	1983/4 (estimated out-turn)	1986/7 (plan)	1993/4 (projections)		
				A	B	C
Group I						
Education and Science,UK	16.1	16.3	14.7	16.1	16.1	17.4
Health & Personal Social Services, UK	15.7	18.3	18.6	22.1	22.1	22.4
Social Security	28.0	35.3	36.5	38.1	38.1	43.4
Group II						
Defence	12.8	15.7	16.4	16.4	19.2	21.1
Group III						
Agriculture, Fisheries, Food	1.4	2.1	1.7	1.7	2.1	3.4
Law and Order	3.5	4.7	4.7	4.7	5.8	7.0
Employment	1.8	2.9	2.9	2.9	3.5	5.0
Group IV						
Energy	0.9	1.2	–0.7	–0.7	0	0
Trade and Industry	4.1	2.0	1.1	1.1	1.1	1.1
Transport	4.6	4.6	4.1	4.1	3.9	4.2
Housing	6.1	2.8	2.4	2.4	2.4	2.4
Other[a]	17.1	15.9	15.1	15.1	15.6	16.1
Total Programme Expenditure	112.2	121.7	117.6	123.8	129.8	143.5

Source: Cmnd. 9143 (London: HMSO, 1984) and NIESR projections (see Annex at the end of the book).

[a] Other programmes include expenditure on Overseas Aid and other Overseas Services, Arts and Libraries, Other Environmental Services, Other Public Services, Common Services, and all expenditure on Scotland, Wales and Northern Ireland which cannot be allocated either to Education and Science or Health and Personal Social Services.

A number of distinctions between programmes are appropriate, as a basis for considering projections of future spending in the next section. In Group I, there are programmes in which firm policy commitments and/or statutory requirements, combined with clear demographic and other influences, have in each case raised spending. They are the programmes in which the scope for flexibility available to government is the most tightly constrained, unless there are major changes in policy which can often require important legislation: eduation, health and social security. In defence, Group II, the UK commitment to meet the NATO aim of 3 per cent real growth to 1985/6 has produced expansion. In Group III, we have agriculture, employment, and law and order. Here the flexibility available to government is greater, there being no mechanistic determinants of expenditure (such as children of statutory school age), but various more or less clear pressures have played an important part in increasing spending; the Common Agricultural Policy (CAP) and world food prices for agriculture; the rising number of unemployed young people (notably the Manpower Services Commission) for employment; and rising crime for law and order. Expenditure rose in all cases. Finally, in Group IV, there are the programmes which have either shrunk or which are intended to shrink by 1986/7, and in which government has considerable flexibility (at least by comparison with the first group): energy, trade and industry, housing, and transport. (This is not to say that pressures are absent, such as the possible implications of the 1981 DoE Housing Conditions Survey, and various pressures to preserve coal and public transport subsidies.) These distinctions between the groups play an essential part in the next section on future projections.

Future prospects

The Green Paper noted several sources of pressure to spend more on particular programmes; it also considered the tax implications of holding the total flat in cost terms and of allowing it to grow at 1 per cent annually from 1988/9 to 1993/4. It is not our intention to say what is desirable for the future pattern of public spending, nor what we think is likely to happen. It is simply to make more explicit the cost implications of certain alternative assumptions concerning particular programmes. We have adopted a number of assumptions for the different groups of programmes noted in the previous section. The methodology is discussed in the Annex, but the broad approach is summarized here.

Group I: Education, Health, Social Security

For this group of programmes the demographic projections are crucial. For education, the projections to the end of this decade are broadly favourable from an expenditure viewpoint, although the proportion of the age group outside the compulsory years participating in education is also an important factor; in the 1990s, the size of the school-age population rises again. The number of the elderly, who make particularly heavy demands on the health services and whose numbers are an important factor in social security expenditure, is projected to rise over the next ten years before declining.

In the case of education, we have made a detailed analysis of unit costs in each sector, from under fives to higher education, and we have related these costs to the demographic projections. Our projections make no allowance for such pressures as greater provision for (expensive) science and technology courses or major improvements to the school building stock. In variants A and B, we assume existing participation rates for under fives, and in higher education we take the middle of the DES's projected range of student participation rates (which are a matter of some debate); in variant C, we allow higher participation.

For health and the personal social services, we undertook as comprehensive an analysis as possible of the usage of the main types of hospital and other services by different age groups, in order to estimate the unit costs of those services for each one: the elderly are particularly expensive (although our estimates are a little lower than those published by the DHSS in Cmnd. 9143). We have taken the official demographic projections and incorporated into our cost projections some modest assumptions about efficiency savings and the relative price of equipment. We have made no allowance for the cost of meeting a number of pressures for improvements, including reductions in waiting times; levelling up the less well-endowed regions to the standard of the best (i.e., without reducing provision for the latter); more rapid expansion of community care for the elderly and mentally handicapped; or an expansion of such facilities as intensive care, renal dialysis, coronary by-pass surgery, etc., to US levels. (According to estimates by the Brookings Institution, this could raise NHS costs by a fifth; the case for expansion to US levels is of course open to dispute.)[8] The health service in particular is one in which limitless opportunities for expansion exist. There are powerful criticisms of existing levels of provision and, in the face of competing demands on national resources, difficult decisions are unavoidable.

Rising unemployment has been a strong influence on the growth of social security expenditure in recent years. For the projections, we show the effect of a constant level of unemployment; a change of 500,000 in the number of unemployed would change expenditure by approximately £1 billion. The demographic projections, for example of the elderly, the build-up of entitlement to benefits under the Earnings Related Pension Scheme (ERPS), the rising trend in one-parent families and other social changes, all impose greater demands which we have attempted to allow for. An important assumption is whether benefits are uprated in line with prices or earnings. There are powerful pressures to uprate benefits in line with earnings, at least over a run of years if not in every year. Many retirement pensioners depend on means-tested benefits to supplement their pensions and income from other sources. As ERPS builds up, those with inadequate contribution records and older pensioners who retired under pre-ERPS arrangements and who have inadequate income from other sources may present a case for additional expenditure.[9] Variants A and B assume prices uprating only; we illustrate the cost of earnings uprating in variant C, but not the cost of extending ERPS benefits to non-contributors.

Group II: Defence

Spending on defence cannot be explained or projected in terms of quantifiable pressures in the same way as the social programmes outlined above. In practice, the growth of defence spending has been influenced by a number of military, diplomatic and industrial pressures. The purely military considerations have included assessments of the nature of possible military threats to the security of UK interests on the one hand, and the appropriate size and mix of UK forces needed to provide insurance, in the context of our alliances, on the other. Military considerations will point to extra UK spending when threats are perceived to have increased, as a result either of greater tension or of improved weapons in the hands of enemies. The armed forces will tend to have a preference for better weapons in any case, although they will trade off the existing, cheaper, familiar and tested against the more expensive, more sophisticated, untried and most recent. There can be no simple answer to the trade-off, and it will partly depend on the nature of the conflict in which the weapons might be needed. Foreign policy will tend to emphasize the symbolic importance, for NATO allies as well as potential enemies, of Britain's being seen to spend a significant and growing amount on defence. This symbolism, by emphasizing defence costs *per se*, involves the risk of diverting attention from consideration of the effectiveness, efficiency or maybe even the military need for spending. However, symbols matter in international relations, and in this respect the UK has an almost unique record, during a period of economic difficulties, to show its allies: the UK spends a higher proportion of GDP on defence than Greece or the USA and a higher amount per capita than all its NATO allies apart from the USA. UK defence spending has grown three times as fast as non-defence public expenditure since 1978/9. Industrial pressures in favour of UK as opposed to foreign procurement, and for those contracts that maintain UK production lines and skilled groups, can run counter to the achievement of value for money in defence spending. They also tend to cushion the industries concerned from the market forces to which other industries are subjected. This is not to say that industrial considerations are unimportant, but that they can have more to do with industrial or employment objectives than purely military objectives and that this distinction should be recognized.

We have not attempted to analyse the precise impact of the military, diplomatic and industrial pressures on defence spending in this paper; instead we have adopted a rather broad approach. We have taken a range of broad assumptions, with no attempt to make a precise allowance for any costs attributable to an equipment RPE generally or escalating Trident costs in particular. This is on the grounds that the defence block budget, which allows the MoD more discretion as to the precise composition of spending than virtually any other department, is the focus of attention. We simply assume: A – flat in cost terms after the British commitment to the NATO 3 per cent 'real' target runs out; B – growth at 2 per cent annually on average to 1993/4; and C – growth at 3 per cent.

Group III: Agriculture, Employment, Law and Order
These programmes have expanded since 1978/9 in line with such pressures as the differential between CAP and world food prices, youth unemployment and crime. The current Public Expenditure White Paper (PEWP) plans for reductions by 1986/7. We assume: A – flat after 1986/7; C – expenditure grows in accordance with past (1978/9–1983/4) trends; and B – a mid-point between past trends and future plans.

Group IV: Trade and Industry, Energy, Housing, Transport, Other
Trade and industry and housing have been cut considerably since 1978/9 and further reductions are planned; we show spending flat at its 1986/7 level. Energy has risen since 1978/9 but is meant to become negative by 1986/7, reflecting a planned turn-round in nationalized industry finances. We show the (negative) 1986/7 target in A, but zero for B and C. Transport has been level since 1978/9; other programmes have been cut. Cuts are planned for both categories. We assume: A – flat at 1986/7 levels; B and C – mid-points between a projection of past trends and future plans (but see the discussion of pay below for C)

Pay
It is important to take particular account of public service pay. The pay of the armed forces, police, doctors and nurses is linked to the growth of private sector earnings by review bodies or, in the case of the police, by a formula. It does not necessarily follow that public spending will fully reflect this link, since part of the cost of pay increases might be expected to be offset by reduced numbers or

efficiency gains. For simplicity, we assume that in the case of the defence and the law and order programmes, the link to private earnings is accommodated within overall total spending on these programmes. This assumption reflects our aggregative approach to their expenditure trends. In the case of health, where we have adopted a disaggregative approach to spending, the earnings link to private earnings (assumed to grow by 1½ per cent a year in real terms) is specifically added on to spending otherwise projected according to demographic trends. The above assumptions – i.e., for defence, law and order, and health – are common to all variants. For all other public servants, whose pay is not formally linked to private earnings, we assume in variants A and B that pay is constant at 1983/4 GDP prices until 1989/90, falling further behind private pay, after which it rises in line with private earnings. In variant C, it rises in line with private earnings over the entire period.

The projections

The effects of all these illustrative assumptions are incorporated in Table 6.3. For example, if total expenditure were flat throughout the period 1983/4 to 1993/4, it would be £121.7 billion; if it grew at 1 per cent annually from 1988/9, it would be £128 billion; and if it grew in line with GDP (assuming 1½ per cent per annum throughout), it would be £141 billion. If under variants A and B the assumption of no real pay increases for most public servants (i.e., except armed forces, police, doctors and nurses) were retained beyond 1988/9, the total would be approximately £2 billion lower.

For a period as far ahead as 1993/4, the detailed figuring in Table 6.3 is clearly artificial. Nonetheless, some broad impressions emerge. It is clear that on the illustrative assumptions chosen, total expenditure rises rather than remains flat. All programmes therefore face the problem of containing expenditure in the face of pressures of the kind referred to earlier, including those deriving from the expectations that past growth would continue. On the tightest variant, A, there is no scope for real improvements in programmes without improved efficiency or the removal of some functions from public expenditure. A does leave basic provision in the three social programmes (Group I) intact, but leaves no scope for extra defence spending beyond 1986/7 unless other programmes (Groups III and IV) are cut. Strict adherence to an objective of flat expenditure would require cuts and improved efficiency anyway. B breaches the illustrative upper Green Paper variant (based on 1 per cent expenditure growth in the final five years), but not if real pay does not rise; it permits growth beyond 1986/7 for defence, law and order, and employment as well as Group I. Variant C, implying a higher GDP share, is well above the Green

Paper upper variant. It incorporates 3 per cent defence growth and earnings uprating for social security, costing £4.7 billion and £5.2 billion respectively by comparison with variant A. *Either* – but not both – could be contained within the Green Paper upper range if everything else were held as in variant A.

In practice, if total expenditure did grow in line with the Green Paper upper variant (which the document finds less desirable from a tax viewpoint), it is unlikely that the whole of the additional resources available would be devoted to a single programme anyway. Furthermore, looking back over the past two decades as a whole, we have already seen that defence and non-defence spending have tended to grow, or be cut, broadly in line with one another, which possibly reflects some underlying social and political concensus. It is conceivable that for the long-term future to the end of the century, the defence/non-defence balance within the total may be subject to wider fluctuations.

Implications for defence
The most realistic assumption for the future must be that defence spending will grow at less than 3 per cent annually on average, in cost terms, once the NATO target runs out. (Realistic, that is, unless the Green Paper aim of controlling total spending is dropped.) All programmes will need to reduce costs and improve efficiency. In the case of the National Health Service, there has often been an explicit target in the PEWP for efficiency savings, the achievement of which was crucial to attaining the objectives of the service, given the available finance. There have been a number of investigations into the relative costliness of different education authorities with respect to functions such as teaching, catering and transport. The Audit Commission has set in train several studies of differences in unit costs across the whole range of local authority activities including police authorities. A number of central government departments are taking an interest in identifying best private-sector practice in broadly comparable activities.

Efficiency
In the case of defence spending, too, it is essential to examine the scope for improving efficiency. Academic economists normally treat defence as the classic public good, which must be publicly financed and supplied if it is to exist at all, and whose output, defined in such general terms as the 'preservation of the state from external attack', is unquantifiable. Even as far as operational units of the armed forces themselves are concerned, the latter point is arguable. But as well as 325,000 service personnel, many of whom work in support functions,

the MoD employs 237,000 civilians. It is responsible for dockyards; ordnance factories; repair facilities of many kinds;[10] settling invoices; paying pay and pensions; for catering, laundering, medical, educational and transport services; for maintaining stores and supplying material – in short, for a whole host of activities where some quantifiable output, provided at some quantifiable cost and not necessarily by the state, exists. It is also responsible for massive expenditure on equipment and R&D, and public knowledge of the NATO commitment to expanding the volume of expenditure cannot have helped to restrain costs.

In practice, however, very little information is available on the volumes of specific activities undertaken, or their costs in man-hours and in financial terms, except in extremely aggregative form. In these circumstances it is often impossible to compare the unit costs or physical productivity of management groups within the defence organization who are undertaking broadly similar tasks. And it is very difficult to judge improvements in performance over time, or to make comparisons with best practice outside, whether in the private sector in the UK or elsewhere. It is probably fair to say that the MoD is not unique among NATO defence ministries in these respects, nor among civilian departments with respect to their functions. However, defence is our main interest here. The Comptroller and Auditor-General has recently commented, with respect to the royal dockyards, on the 'dearth of relevant and reliable performance measures and indicators'.[11] No doubt a similar remark could be made of several other support services. It may well be the case that where measures of output, input, productivity and costs exist (or could be calculated in principle), some defence activities might show lower absolute productivity and higher unit costs than those in other services or in private-sector organizations engaged in similar tasks (e.g. engine servicing). The disparity might be explained in terms of higher manning levels being needed to produce faster service in military emergencies. That is, military *effectiveness* commands higher priority than *efficiency*.[12] That might or might not be a sufficient explanation,[13] but over time there should be no reason for productivity growth to be lower in-house than in best practice elsewhere.

It should be possible to devise a set of indicators of output (volume of work done), man-hours involved and unit costs which will permit, wherever possible, comparisons between the MoD and best practice outside. This set should cover as much of MoD business as possible. Rather detailed work measurement would be required, and a system to check the accuracy of the returns would need to be established. For some broad functions no convenient outside comparison might be possible (e.g. tank repair), but precise specific comparisons might be possible for certain major tasks (e.g. welding). In practice, many areas of work measurement and costing present no overwhelming obstacles – beyond that of persuading those concerned that it is worthwhile. Some areas where this approach might be applied include: equipment production; equipment maintenance; transport operations; payment of pay and pensions; payment of bills; medical services; training; catering; laundries; maintenance of files; housing services; personnel recruitment and movements; data processing; and secretarial services, etc. If such a system could be devised, it would enable standards and targets for productivity, complementing and budgeting to be set, monitored and improved.

Procurement

As for purchases of equipment from outside contractors and R&D expenditure, the main incentive to control costs, as in every other area of government spending, must be a cash constraint, although the MoD's purse has immense potential as a bargaining weapon. Here we face a dilemma between the objective of securing the best possible deal from suppliers and the pressure to maintain domestic or, increasingly, NATO production capability. But those involved in bidding for contracts have a vital interest of their own: remaining in business. Their incentive to improve their efficiency can only be weakened when they believe that their survival is as assured by the public purse as British Leyland's was in the early and mid-1970s; the threat of withdrawal of that support, and the associated management overhaul, had a considerable impact.

It is also appropriate to ask whether the strategic need to maintain domestic industrial capability should be interpreted to refer to Europe rather than the UK. Of course there are purchases from Europe, but generally as part of a collaborative deal rather than on outright value-for-money grounds. The Secretary of State for Defence recently drew attention to this matter when he noted the difficulties of attempting to arrange collaborative deals that maximize efficiency – which might mean, for *individual* projects, a divergence between financial contributions and work-sharing. The solution to this problem requires us 'to seek to square the circle by "juste retour" trade-offs across defence business as a whole, coupled with competition and efficient management at the project level'[14] (i.e., instead of seeking national 'fair shares' in the work on individual projects in isolation from one another, entire projects might be produced by different countries with a fair overall share in the work as a whole: project A goes to France, B to Federal Germany, C to Britain and so on). In any event, the spur of foreign competiton – and not just from NATO sources – and what technologies are covered by this strategic need should be rigorously explored.

In practice, a more aggressive approach to procurement and competition faces a number of constraints. The placing of contracts abroad is often unpopular if it appears that UK jobs are immediately at risk. In the case of new development, there is an inevitable range of uncertainty about future costs, which might be so large anyway as to rule out encouraging more than one firm to go ahead. However, in the end it is essential to distinguish a clear military requirement for domestic production and a more precise industrial policy goal (including employment aspects). Where a clear military objective exists, it remains important to consider how large it needs to be and whether it should be met irrespective of cost. In cases where only one domestic source makes economic sense, it remains necessary to consider the spur of foreign competition. (It is disappointing that a recent major US enquiry into 'second sourcing' did not even discuss the option of possible European sources.)[15] It is difficult to escape the impression that where new large projects are concerned basic questions are asked, but for the mass of ongoing activities and replacement this is less likely.

RPE

Finally, it might be noted that this paper includes no estimates of a defence RPE. It is possible to calculate one by comparing defence spending at current and constant prices. The trouble is that the price indicators used include contractors' input prices (which assume no productivity growth), and much of the equipment bought is subject to improved technology and enhanced effectiveness. It follows that the conventional constant price series understate true volume increases and ignore improvements in effectiveness. A recent US study has concluded that when proper account is taken of output prices – in the sense of the price of certain performance specifications – defence prices moved broadly in line with GDP prices from 1972 to 1982.[16] In short, rising unit input costs, which create an impression of the need for extra spending to achieve a given military objective, by ignoring improved productivity and effectiveness, exaggerate future expenditure needs assuming a given threat of attack.

Effectiveness and efficiency

As UK success in the Falklands so clearly demonstrated, military effectiveness in the British armed forces is extremely high. The foregoing paragraphs are simply intended to demonstrate that improved effectiveness, within tight budgetary constraints, requires increased economic efficiency. In practice, a balance needs to be struck between operational requirements and cost considerations. Some would argue that efficiency is not a neutral concept in political/

operational terms[17] and that there are dangers in placing too much emphasis on it, for example in military training,[18] not least because it makes excessive demands on the time of top military personnel and officials.[19] However, there are many possibilities for improved efficiency before these problems have to be faced.

Conclusions

There are many pressures for more public spending, whether to improve the living standards of those who are dependent on social security; to extend the entitlement to various benefits; to increase the quantity and quality of a whole range of services; to improve the capital infrastructure; to subsidize unprofitable enterprises; or to raise the real earnings of state employees. There is also a temptation, in the face of some social or industrial problem, to spend money as evidence of doing something about it almost irrespective of its effectiveness. Together the pressures are virtually limitless. Given available national resources, these claims compete with one another and, via taxation, with private individuals' claims to their own incomes. Different choices on these claims are not neutral in their effects on different income and social groups, on the quantity of public services, on the pattern of economic activity and employment or, at any rate in the short run, on its level. Consequently, any government has to establish priorities between the competing claims on its revenue, and between its need for revenue and citizens' private uses of their incomes.

Difficult choices always exist, and it is important to try to get some grasp of how those choices are likely to develop over the longer term. The illustrative projections presented above suggest that those difficulties are not going to go away. (It might also be noted that our most costly variant, C, is far from being the most expensive case one might devise.) It follows that considerable emphasis will need to be placed on increased efficiency from the available resources. In the particular case of defence spending, there seem to be several routes for improving efficiency which remain to be fully explored.

Notes
1. 'The Next Ten Years: Public Expenditure and Taxation into the 1990s', Cmnd. 9189 (London: HMSO, March 1984).
2. L. Pliatzky, *Getting and Spending* (Oxford: Basil Blackwell, 1982).
3. 'Efficiency and Effectiveness in the Civil Service', Cmnd. 8616 (London: HMSO, Sep. 1982).
4. 'Financial Management in Government Departments', Cmnd. 9058 (London: HMSO, Sep. 1983), and 'Progress in Financial Management in Government Departments', Cmnd. 9297 (London: HMSO, July 1984).
5. See also V. Imber and P. Todd, 'Public Expenditure: Definitions and Trends', *Economic Trends*, November 1983; M.S. Levitt, 'The Growth of Public Expenditure', NIESR, May 1984.

6. J.P. Dunne, P. Pashardes and R.P. Smith, 'Needs, Costs and Bureaucracy: the Allocation of Public Consumption in the UK', *Economic Journal*, March 1984.
7. F. Gould, 'The development of public expenditures in western industrialised countries', *Public Finance*, No. 1 (1983); Levitt, op. cit.
8. H.A. Aaron and W.B. Schwartz, 'The Painful Prescription: Rationing Medical Care' (Washington, D.C.: Brookings Institution, 1984).
9. M. Fogarty (ed.), *Retirement Policy, The Next Fifty Years* (London: Heinemann, 1982), discusses this point.
10. Figures from the 1984 Statement on Defence Estimates, Cmnd. 9227 (London: HMSO, 1984).
11. National Audit Office: Ministry of Defence; Dockyard Efficiency (London: HMSO, February 1984).
12. The contrast between economic efficiency and military effectiveness is brought out in 'Economy of Stores Support', Public Accounts Committee, Session 1983/4, House of Commons Paper 411.
13. The NAO Dockyard Report seems to hint at ancient Spanish customs with respect to overtime payments.
14. Speech to Rolls-Royce, 4 September 1984.
15. Analysis of the Grace Commission's Major Proposals for Cost Control; Joint Study by the Congressional Budget Office and General Accounting Office, February 1984.
16. *Survey of Current Business*, November 1982.
17. S. Rosen, 'Systems Analysis and Rational Defence', *The Public Interest*, No. 76 (Summer 1984).
18. T.J. Crackel, 'On the making of Lieutenants and Colonels', *Public Interest*, op. cit.
19. G.N. Luttwak, 'Why we need more waste fraud and mismanagement in the Pentagon', *Commentary*, February 1982.

Comment on Chapter 6
Leo Pliatzky

The press recently reported that the Defence Secretary has called for a substantial cut-back in the projections emerging, especially for the later years, from the annual exercise on ten-year defence costings. The reports are plausible because something of this sort has been highly predictable. The paper by Levitt and Joyce sets the scene.

Before I join in the crystal-gazing into the future, let me say something about the past, and about the thesis (to which Levitt and Joyce refer) that total public expenditure is uninfluenced by differences in ruling party, and that changes in its composition are better explained by 'objective' factors than by the political complexion of the party in office. I believe these propositions to be at best only partly true and that they bear an imperfect relationship to what has been happening over the past ten years.

I deal at some length with the factors governing public expenditure as a whole, and in particular with relative priorities within it, in a book to be published by Basil Blackwell in the summer of 1985,[1] and I do not want to plagiarize myself too much here and now. In brief, while I agree that the force of circumstance is very potent in frustrating fulfilment of the ideas with which governments come to office, the ideas themselves also have great potency in determining priorities. The force of circumstance is illustrated by the way in which the last two Labour governments embarked on great spending sprees but were obliged to cut back in mid-term, and Edward Heath's and Margaret Thatcher's Conservative governments set out to cut total expenditure but presided over an increase. But this is not to say that the differences in beliefs and manifestos between the two parties made no difference to the outcome. The last Labour government, for instance, increased the housing programme; since 1979 it has been more than halved. Labour increased the aid programme; since 1979 it has been cut. Social security has increased under both governments, but more so under Labour, though the increase in unemployment was much less. And so on.

Let us turn to defence. The first Wilson government adopted the 'East of Suez' policy. This, and the fact that governments were not yet committed to annual statutory upratings of social security benefits, were among the factors that enabled Roy Jenkins, when Chancellor of the Exchequer, to bring about an absolute downward kink in the long-term upward trend in total public expenditure in real terms. Under the Heath government which followed, the course of events was not unlike that which we have seen under Margaret Thatcher, so far as the defence budget is concerned. At that time the objective of the Ministry of Defence was to maintain the size and structure of the forces more or less unchanged; with rising unit costs, this meant a steady increase in defence expenditure. The Ministry of Defence also urged that any additional expense incurred for reasons extraneous to their essential role – e.g., in Northern Ireland or through purchasing British equipment even if it was more expensive – should be treated as additions to the basic defence budget. Thanks to the powerful position in Cabinet of the Defence Secretary, Lord Carrington, the Ministry initially had a good deal of success in these matters, but increasing resistance was put up by Anthony Barber, as Chancellor of the Exchequer, out of concern over the size of public expenditure as a whole. An exercise was therefore commissioned to look at the problem.

This paved the way, under the second Wilson administration, for a full-blown defence review, with a remit to reduce the proportion of GDP going to defence. From this there emerged the strategy of concentrating on NATO and eliminating other commitments, so far as possible, and a corresponding round of cuts. This did not prevent further cuts in 1976 as a result of the sterling crisis and the negotiations with the IMF. However, in the later stages of that government's time in office, after James Callaghan had succeeded Harold Wilson, the defence budget came back somewhat into favour, for two reasons: first, because of the employment which it generated at a time when unemployment had started to rise; and second, because of the role of the forces in keeping essential services going during various industrial disputes. During this phase, the undertaking in NATO of a 3 per cent annual increase in defence expenditure in real terms – though less than a cast-iron commitment – was first incurred.

Under the present Conservative government, the defence budget has until now, and in spite of the Chancellor of the Exchequer's concern about its effects on total expenditure, enjoyed preferential treatment. It was in effect exempted from the initial squeeze on cash limits. The 3 per cent annual increase has been in volume rather than cost terms. The cost of the Falklands war and its aftermath has been treated as an extra. In cost terms the increase in 1983/4 over 1978/9 was 22.3 per cent.[2] However, as under the last Conservative government, the Treasury has finally turned. The 3 per cent increase runs out in 1985/6. The implication of the figures in the last (1984)

Public Expenditure White Paper is that from now on defence expenditure will be approximately flat in cost terms – and not even flat if the underlying assumptions on inflation prove optimistic. Heavy reliance is placed on improved efficiency to effect this severe transition. More recent statements by the Ministry of Defence confirm that they do not expect any increase in real resources in the years after 1985/6.

These developments have to be seen in relation to the setback to the government's objectives on expenditure and taxation in its first five years, and its strategy for the five- and ten-year periods ahead. If we count in debt interest (which the White Paper figures exclude but which nevertheless is an outgoing that has to be financed), total public expenditure in the government's first five years rose by not far short of 2 per cent a year in cost terms. This is not a high rate of increase, but one which, at a time when revenue was adversely affected by the recession, and given the government's unwillingness to run a high borrowing requirement, has entailed increased personal taxation and national insurance contributions. The government has learned the forseeable lesson that total expenditure cannot be cut if increases are taking place in programmes that account for 70 per cent of central government expenditure: defence and health because of specific promises; and social security because of a combination of statutory and political constraints, demography and the slump.

So we come to the Green Paper strategy of stabilizing total public expenditure for the next five and perhaps the next ten years. The Green Paper recognizes that, since some programmes will still go up, others (unspecified) will have to be cut. But the government has clearly learned that, if the strategy is to have a chance, some or even all of the main programmes will have to be held reasonably stable. Defence has already been mentioned. As regards social security, Mr Norman Fowler has made a very significant statement to the effect that it is a working assumption of the current social security reviews that there will be no increase in the total amounts available for these programmes. For the time being at least, some modest continuing increase in resources is planned for the National Health Service; but in practice part of this is eroded each time that extra funds are withheld for the financing of pay increases in excess of the limited provision made for them, so that the difference has to be made up at the expense of growth in the service.

The case for the stabilization strategy, to make the whole of the gains from economic growth available for tax reliefs, is strong. The problem of high taxation on low earners is particularly acute; the 'poverty trap' is a striking manifestation of this, but only part of the problem. On the other hand, the difficulty of implementing the strategy has been demonstrated in the first (1984) public expenditure exercise to follow the Green Paper. This involved, among other things, cuts in student grants and overseas services (including at least to some extent the aid programme), which have been unpopular with the government's own supporters.

In the case of any programme involving overseas expenditure, the budgetary problem is aggravated by the current weakness of sterling. In one sense this reflects the strength of the US dollar, but the fall in the price of oil, and its effects on our oil earnings, has exposed our continuing weaknesses in international trade generally. The recurrence of concern about sterling and the balance of payments, which at one time dominated our economic policies but which ceased to do so while we were flush with oil earnings, may not be a purely passing phenomenon.

I have made no attempt here to assess the adequacy of a flat defence budget or the case for further growth in defence expenditure. I should say, however, that the increase in this expenditure in recent years, bringing it to a figure well above 5 per cent of GDP, after it had been comfortably below that mark in the 1970s, has made the problem of reconciling defence requirements with fiscal policy more acute than ever. If there is a strong case for continued growth, then the tension between defence requirements and fiscal strategy will get worse rather than better. Nor do I attempt to assess the possibility that the situation may be eased by better economic growth than is projected in the Green Paper, or by a different administration which does not give such overriding priority to squeezing out inflation and takes a more relaxed view of the level of government borrowing. I should, however, judge it unlikely that either development, if it occurred, would make it significantly easier to accommodate a continuing growth in the defence budget such as we have seen in recent years. We should not exclude the possibility that growing concern about unemployment among the government's own supporters may finally cause the Treasury team to yield to pressure for some expenditure measures designed directly to promote employment – though the government's declared strategy and objectives leave it little room for manoeuvre. However, there will be many strong candidates apart from the defence budget for any such funds.

The Ministry of Defence has so far professed a relatively relaxed attitude towards the cutting off of growth in the defence budget, and has disclaimed the need for any major defence review. This does not, of course, preclude a critical look at particular elements in the defence budget. On the other hand, any adjustment required might well be effected by applying the well-tried principle of equality of misery to the various services, rather than by discriminatory cuts in individual fields of expenditure. Meanwhile the crunch is still a little way off. In any event, though its financing may be something of a headache, one would expect Trident to survive.

Notes
1.   The book is to be called *Paying and Choosing: The Intelligent Person's Guide to the Mixed Economy* (Oxford: Basil Blackwell, 1985).
2.   Hansard, Written Answers, 13 March 1984, Cols. 77-8.

7   Defence Costs
*R.P. Smith**

Introduction

The conventional account of the dynamics of British defence policy emphasizes how the growing cost of effective forces and the poor performance of the British economy have left the cash available to the defence budget inadequate to meet the commitments that successive governments have endorsed.[1] Cash, costs and commitments have been the three forces shaping postwar defence policy. Restricted resources and the escalating cost of capability have constituted the twin blades cutting into British military effectiveness, readiness and, ultimately, major strategic roles. The task of defence budgeting has largely involved manipulating the scissors in order to minimize the disruption. Defence economists of all political persuasions have found the outcome of this manipulation profoundly depressing and are wont to utter Cassandra-like croaks on such occasions.

In principle, the mismatch between roles and resources could be solved in one of three ways: the cash available could be increased by devoting a larger share of output to defence, though at the risk of adverse economic effects that would in the long run reduce the resources for defence even further; the commitments incurred could be reduced, though the choice of cuts is controversial; or, finally, defence costs could be reduced, allowing the UK to obtain greater capability for the same amount of cash. With regard to the cash available, Britain has faced special problems because of the exceptionally dismal performance of its economy in comparison with other industrialized countries. With regard to commitments, Britain has also faced special problems associated with the adjustment to a more humble, post-imperial (and, increasingly, post-industrial) role in the world. However, with regard to costs, the problem is a general one; inflation in the military sector is seen internationally as a pervasive problem.

The two other forces shaping British defence policy, the cash available and the commitments incurred, will be discussed elsewhere in this volume; here the emphasis will be on costs. This focus seems

*This paper draws on work done under the CNRS/ESRC-financed project on the British and French defence efforts.

appropriate, partly because costs are such an important influence shaping the defence budget, and partly because there often appears to be some confusion about what is involved. The term 'defence inflation' is best regarded as a convenient shorthand to epitomize the implications of a range of difficult strategic, tactical, social and economic choices. Used in this way it is a useful and unobjectionable metaphor. However, there is a danger that the metaphor will gain a life of its own and eventually be seen as an independent causal factor, rather than as a consequence of particular choices. There is no evidence that defence suffers from a particular problem of inflation, but defence costs do act as a useful focus for discussing a range of economic, social and military problems that will shape policy.

Symptoms

When people refer to inflation, there is the idea that some commodity or output increases in price or costs more. Let us consider what output might be being referred to in the case of defence inflation. The cash provided through the defence budget is used to buy various inputs: to hire civil servants and members of the armed forces from the labour market and to buy stores and equipment from private firms. These inputs, together with the existing inventory of human capital and hardware, contribute to the provision of forces, which can be measured in terms of the number of particular types of tank, aircraft or soldier, etc. (the items found listed in the *Military Balance*). These forces provide military capability, expressed in such terms as potential lethality or the probability of winning particular types of conflict. Except in actual combat, capability is not normally observed and must be surmised. Military capability contributes to security, which is measured in terms of attainment of ultimate policy goals, a subjective judgement. Thus, when we are talking about costs, we could be talking about the cost of the inputs, of particular types of forces, of effective military capability, or of security.

This description of the process as a linked input/output system distinguishes categories that are often confused, and emphasizes the variability of the intervening processes. Whether or not more cash will buy more forces depends on the level of input prices, the efficiency of military industry and the maintenance and depreciation of existing stock, none of which can be regarded as fixed. Whether forces provide military capability depends on morale, training, tactics, logistics, and the theatre of engagement. Vietnam is a case in which the size of US forces contributed little to capability. Whether military capability contributes to security depends on national objectives, strategy, and the nature of the threat. Britain's nuclear capability contributed little to Falklands security.

Such linked systems are not peculiar to military output. An annual computer budget is used to acquire staff, hardware and software, which, together with the existing inventory, constitutes the system. This can be described in terms of the number of the CPU's memory devices, systems analysts, etc. The system has potential capability which can be measured in terms of memory capacity, retrieval times and number of calculations per minute. This computing capability contributes to the ultimate ends of keeping customer records, conducting research, or whatever. The intervening variables are also important in the computer example, and many businesses have acquired very powerful systems only to find them quite inappropriate to their commercial needs; just as many nations have acquired expensive armed forces which have proved quite inappropriate to their security needs. Most people would say that defence costs have risen while computing costs have fallen. At a shorthand level this seems obviously true, but it is difficult to know what that means. In the sense that spending on the national computing budget has grown much more rapidly than spending on the defence budget, computing costs have grown faster. In terms of performance characteristics, computing costs have fallen. Megabyte per dollar spent on memory devices has risen rapidly, but so no doubt has megadeath per dollar spent on nuclear devices.

It may appear perverse, but one can put forward a strong argument that the cost of defence equipment has fallen. Imagine that defence planners have, say, £5 billion to spend on equipment and can buy either from the current Defence Sales Catalogue at current prices or from the 1964 Catalogue at 1964 prices. From which Catalogue will they choose to equip their forces? Choosing from the 1984 Catalogue suggests that they get more for their money now, that defence equipment prices have actually fallen over the last twenty years. In order to judge the movement in the price of capability, imagine the planners being offered a Catalogue with not only 1964 products and prices but also 1964 threats. There are clearly some factors (Falklands and Ulster perhaps) which might lead them to regard the 1964 package as better value despite the obsolete equipment, because the threat at that time was less.

The simplest measure of the cost of defence is the amount we pay for it, the defence budget, though as is well known the budgetary cost may not represent the true economic or opportunity cost. Conscription may reduce the budgetary cost but leave the true cost unchanged or increased. The indirect benefits of arms exports or technological spin-off may make the true cost of defence smaller. The displacement of investment and the pre-emption of scarce R&D skills, with consequent effects on growth, may make the true cost larger.

Anomalies of definition further complicate the costing. However, ignoring these issues, between 1973 and 1983 the budget increased at 16.5 per cent per annum, while money GDP at factor cost only grew by 14.7 per cent p.a.[2] Most of this was of course 'inflation', and at 1980 prices the budget increased by 1.1 per cent per annum. This correction for inflation uses the price index for defence calculated from the *National Accounts*. According to this, during 1973–83 defence prices rose at an average annual rate of 15.18 per cent as compared with only 13.54 per cent for all output prices. From 1980 to 1983, the annual average growth rates in prices were 9.5 per cent for defence and 7.5 per cent for all output. This is the notorious relative price effect. Defence prices, as measured in the *National Accounts*, tend to rise about 2 per cent p.a. faster than the general rate of inflation.

Two points should be made about these figures. Firstly, the relative price effect for defence is almost exactly the same as that for central government total final consumption as a whole. Over the 1973–83 period, central government prices went up by 15.6 per cent, slightly more than defence, and from 1980 to 1983 by 9.5 per cent, exactly the same as defence. Thus, on the basis of these numbers, defence does not suffer any more inflation than the rest of government. It should be noted that an alternative estimate of the relative price effect for defence can be obtained from the constant price figures in the 'Statement of the Defence Estimates' (Table 2.1 Cmnd. 9227-II). This is calculated by a different method from the *National Accounts* series and is on a fiscal rather than calendar year basis. From year to year there are quite large differences between the two price series, although they do seem to average out over a longer run of years. Defence prices have been politically more significant than other public sector prices in recent years. With the switch to cash planning, 'funny money' (the volume target in 'Survey Prices') was abolished elsewhere in Whitehall. However, it lived on in the MoD because the commitment to NATO of 3 per cent growth had been made in 'real' terms. The MoD was thus able to argue for compensation for differential inflation long after other departments.

Secondly, these indexes are input price measures; they say how much the prices of the type of goods and services bought by defence increased. No allowance is made for productivity growth or quality change because of the difficulty of measuring output. They are quite a different type of measure from the GDP price index with which they are compared, since that is predominantly a measure of output costs. In fact movements in the relative price effect are dominated by relative wage movements in the public and private sectors, and by the general rate of growth of productivity, together with a smaller effect

from import price movements because of differential import pro-
pensities. These are factors which are peripheral to the major issues
normally associated with defence inflation. The published price index
is very useful for certain specific questions, but it cannot be used to
answer general questions concerning the cost of defence.[3]

With volunteer armed forces (and civil service), personnel costs are
largely determined by general labour-market conditions. In the short
run, quite large differential movements are possible, but if wages are
kept substantially below those available elsewhere, in the longer run
recruitment difficulties and loss of trained personnel will lead to some
adjustment. Determining the levels available elsewhere is not a
straightforward exercise. The Review Body on Armed Forces Pay
aims 'to ensure that the Services can attract and retain the people they
need by providing a fair reward for the work they do. We believe that
implementation of our recommendations based on this approach has
been a major reason why recruitment and retention in the armed
forces has been largely satisfactory in recent years, although we
recognize the part that the general economic climate has also played.'
Public Money[4] comments: 'That seems a rather throw-away manner of
dealing with the effect of over 3,000,000 unemployed on the relevant
labour-market.' After reviewing the report, *Public Money* concludes:
'It is difficult to see how, in the present economic climate, any
combination of labour-market criteria, comparability and judgement
could lead to awards of between 8 and 10 per cent. But that is what the
review body recommended.' Conscription as a method of cutting
personnel costs is discussed in the next section.

When people talk about defence inflation, what they normally have
in mind is the rising unit cost of equipment. The White Paper gives a
figure for major items of defence equipment of between 6 and 10 per
cent faster than the rate of inflation.[5] These price increases refer to
different generations of the same family, which differ in quality and
performance. It you upgrade from a Mini to a Rolls, you should not
blame the extra motoring costs on inflation. With cars, there are a
variety of methods of constructing quality-corrected prices, in order
to judge what the true inflation is. Quality is measured by composite
indices based on function. In principle, these could be applied to
weapons, using indices of effective lethality for instance, but it is not
clear how useful such measures of true inflation would be. Like death
and taxes, increasing unit cost from performance enhancements in a
particular family of weapons seems likely to be always with us. It
represents the outcome of a series of linked processes which feed back
on each other.[6] To use an evolutionary simile, it resembles Cope's rule
of phyletic size increase: that body size tends to increase fairly steadily
within evolutionary lineages, until the family dies out. Weapons tend

to show a similar trend. I am sure contemporary defence economists would have been making dire predictions from extrapolations of the length of sarissas, the thickness of fortress walls, and the weight of knightly armour. The predictions are inappropriate because the family gets displaced.

Cost escalation, like that of Chevaline from £250m to £1000m, is sometimes regarded as evidence of a special problem in defence inflation, but the essence of the problem here is forecasting, not inflation as such. Forecasting failures of this sort may reflect wrong economic predictions; the well-known hazards of projecting costs for uncertain technological developments, which is equally difficult in civilian markets; bureaucratic tactics (getting the camel's nose into the tent with a low initial estimate); or merely more widespread inefficiency. But these are all problems in their own right that are not specific to military projects, and not symptoms of inflation generally.

The argument in this section is that defence inflation is not an inexorable alien force, but merely the economic manifestation of a tendency by defence planners to choose expensive solutions to a large variety of distinct military and technical problems. One way of illuminating the attractiveness of high-cost solutions is to consider the objections to the various cost-reducing proposals. The next section contains a necessarily brief review of suggested remedies and the obstacles they face.

Remedies

Cheap-and-cheerful weapons

There seem to be at least three separate arguments for changes in the type of weapon deployed. One is that the trade-off between numbers produced and performance, both in terms of production cost and combat effectiveness, has shifted so as to make a new quantity/quality mix optimal. This is comparable to a commercial company deciding to replace the mainframe-oriented Data Processing Department with distributed micros. A second argument is that the conventional families (tank, combat aircraft, warship) have reached the end of their evolutionary road. In this case, the best way to counter the increased effectiveness of enemy weapons is not the direct approach of trying to match or beat them on comparable performance characteristics, but the indirect approach of using different types of systems which exploit the potential of new technologies. It is also argued that the high cost of incidentals, platform, protection, etc., in the existing systems means that little firepower is obtained for the money invested, and that everything from the infantry section to the naval frigate is under-gunned. A third argument is that the high performance weapons are so complicated, temperamental, and unreliable that they would not operate in practice.

The economic considerations of these issues are relevant for providing estimates of the trade-offs (costing how many tanks we could have instead of Trident, or how many anti-tank missiles instead of Challenger), but the central issues are military. Any judgement as to whether expensive-and-miserable weapons will perform better than standardized, mass-produced alternatives depends on assessing the likely location and conditions of conflict, countermeasures to be faced, readiness, and the like: traditional military imponderables. Adoption of different types of weapon systems would also involve, if they were to be used effectively, changes in tactics, deployment and force organization, which would be disruptive and threatening to the existing framework.

Standardization/collaboration
The objectives involved in this case are clear: to reduce unnecessary duplication of programmes and conserve defence resources through greater standardization and interoperability of weapons. This can be achieved by division of labour in development; harmonizing operational requirements; exchanging technical information; exploring opportunities for cooperation, through dual-production capacity; licencing; or reciprocal purchasing. These have long been NATO goals, but the difficulties are so great that they make it hard for them to become more than pious principles. Collaborative programmes suffer a substantial cost penalty and time delay, and are hard to cancel if they fail to meet expectations. Nations are reluctant to surrender industrial capability, and the politics of allocating production are acrimonious. It has been argued that by collaborating Britain has merely created competitors to whom it has transferred technology. There is a fear of putting too many eggs in one basket; diversity of available weapon systems can be regarded as a tactical strength. National procurement schedules or requirements rarely overlap. Kenneth Warren MP presents the case against collaboration very strongly with regard to the European Fighter Aircraft.[7]

Exporting
There seems no doubt that over the last decade some industrialized countries, including the Soviet Union, have derived substantial balance-of-payments benefits from arms exports. Exports also appear to offer the opportunity to spread overheads, to extend production runs, to provide economies of scale, and to aid the acquisition of high-technology expertise. In economic terms, the arguments for an export promotion strategy are not straightforward. Over recent years

the market has become very much more competitive, with Newly Industrialized Countries (NICs) becoming significant exporters for the first time.[8] The arms with the greatest export potential, which are often relatively low technology, may not be the same as those required by domestic armed forces. The political and technological uncertainties, and the uneven nature of production and demand, make this a high-risk area economically. The deals can be very complicated,[9] and when account is taken of counter-trade (barter), offset deals, the foreign exchange cost of credit terms, the risk of disruption of the transaction by political factors, the insurance against the risk of non-payment and the marketing costs, the overall economic position can easily be adverse. The debt overhang faced by Third World countries also seems likely to inhibit the growth in the market. Effectively the exports, though profitable to the companies concerned, are being heavily subsidized by supplier governments in order to maintain a domestic arms industry.

Competition
It is widely argued that in commercial terms the arms industry is inefficient because within a country there is often only a single producer and a single customer, which creates a cosy symbiotic relationship insulated from the fresh breeze of competition.[10] The poor performance by many arms firms which attempt to diversify into civil markets lends support to this view. As it is usually put, this argument fails to distinguish two sorts of inefficiency. One is organizational (slack management, lazy workers), which competition might dispel, if, as in so many other sectors, the UK firm does not simply go out of business or stop producing in Britain. The other is structural. The high-cost, low-productivity methods employed may be the most efficient way of producing the small numbers required, custom-designed to changing ministry specifications. Domestic competition with multiple design teams, the need for liaison with more contractors, and shorter production runs for each, could increase structural inefficiency. Competition can cut costs, but if it is to do so it means accepting imports, making the best of weapons not designed exactly to meet British idiosyncracies, and the loss of part of the present defence industry.

The US has a long tradition of trying to promote competition in the arms industry: for instance, the US navy's second-sourcing of the Phoenix AIM-54C after the 'serious deficiencies' in those supplied by the Hughes Aircraft Co. This is more viable in the US, since the production runs are longer and there is less threat from foreign competition. But, in the Phoenix case, the government will have to fund tooling-up of a second production line; so there are costs even there.

Bureaucratic reorganization

Attacking military bureaucracy has mass-market appeal; the bureaucracy is unpopular with the right, and the military with the left. In addition, there is no shortage of spectacular examples of military 'waste, fraud and mismanagement'. The Department of Defense's $90 screwdriver is currently a favourite example in the US. However, the distinction between organizational and structural inefficiency applies as much to the MoD as it does to the contractors. It would be nice to remove organizational inefficiency,[11] but much is structural; a large bureaucracy is an inevitable cost of trying to meet goals that are widely thought desirable. Much of the stunning complexity of defence procurement arises from conflicts between these goals. The requirements of auditing, political acceptability, control of quality and cost, mediating between the conflicting interests of different groups, and flexibility, all require a large bureaucracy. Abolishing the MoD Procurement Executive and letting the services negotiate directly with contractors might produce better weapons more cheaply, but only at the expense of scandals which would violate the conventional, though perhaps inappropriate, expectations about what constitutes good management.[12]

When Geoffrey Pattie, then Minister of State for Defence Procurement, said, 'You have to have every sprocket laid out on the table with its price and specification agreed before you can go for fixed price contracts,'[13] it may have surprised corporate buying departments or private purchasers, who make fixed price contracts all the time without such problems. However, a defence contract could involve a manufacturer providing a system to meet specified operational requirements for a particular price; and in development the manufacturer could discover that by using different electronic components that have now become available, the system can be made better and at a quarter of the price. This is not uncommon with electronic developments over military planning timescales. The manufacturer meets, or more likely beats, operational specifications, and the military get the system at the planned budget. But this is a political disaster because of the profit levels the manufacturer has realized. Detailed costing and specification avoids that sort of scandal. The example is also unrealistic in assuming that a fixed set of operational requirements could be agreed in advance.

Civilian resources

Conventional and, even more, nuclear, defence uses a very narrow spectrum of resources provided by specialist suppliers. It seems obvious to many that by using relatively cheap and easily available civilian resources, capability could be inexpensively increased.[14] This applies to civilian manpower, transport and communications facilities, and products. It often appears to an outsider that by the end of the long development times required to produce customized, ruggedized, application-specific, military electronic systems, comparable cheap mass-produced civilian alternatives are available. The military argue that these civilian systems would not operate effectively in combat conditions, though this has to be balanced against the evidence that many military systems do not operate effectively anyway. But this argument brings us back to military judgements about what contributes to capability in likely conflicts.

The general economy acts as a reservoir of strategic resources: supply of essential materials, high-technology skills, adequate food and fuel supplies. The importance of these is usually only appreciated in conflict; in peacetime the military provide for their current needs in their own way. Although this inevitably results in a lack of preparedness in conflict, it is probably better not to base industrial decisions on anticipated military requirements. Predicting strategic requirements is hazardous, and self-sufficiency on security grounds tends to be the last refuge of inefficient industries who cannot provide any other argument for protection.

Improved productivity
In engineering terms it is not immediately obvious how military product development differs from commercial new product development against the competition. The commercial solutions involve a combination of the use of new types of equipment together with changes in organizational structure. This has enabled industries as different as cars and computers to halve the time required for the development cycle and sharply reduce production costs. The new equipment tends to use CAD/CAM (computer aided design/manufacture) and raises the possibility of more automated and flexible manufacturing systems which would be suitable for the low-volume batch production typical of the defence industries. This contrasts with the traditional productivity-boosting mechanization which was confined to high-volume standardized products. Breaking down organizational barriers has been central to this process of cutting costs and development times. The methods used include appointing project champions outside the traditional hierarchy; establishing relatively independent interdepartmental product teams; and switching from serial to parallel development of product and production process.

There is no doubt that were the need to arise, in for example the traditional type of protracted war, these options could be put into operation rapidly, to ensure fast development and mass production of the needed weapons relatively cheaply. But this misses the point. The long development times, the small numbers produced, the lack of investment in mass production and process development are not problems to be solved; they are the solutions to the requirements of the system. In general, they are efficient adjustments to the pattern of British defence procurement, ways of spreading the load while maintaining a minimal production capacity.

Conscription

Although Britain spends a lower proportion of its budget on personnel than most of its allies, a return to a system of national service might appear to be a way to cut wage costs. In addition, demographic trends might suggest that recruitment could become more difficult, though this is likely to be offset by high unemployment levels. When various countries are compared, a very clear pattern emerges of higher real incomes being associated with higher expenditure per member of the armed forces, since it becomes efficient to switch to a more capital-intensive defence posture and to economize on the relatively expensive factor, labour. Countries with conscription, however, tend to adopt a more labour-intensive posture. Statistical analysis suggests that moving from a volunteer army to one that is half conscript reduces the average budgetary cost per member of the armed forces by about 40 per cent.[15]

The arguments for and against conscription are primarily military and social, about the size and composition of the armed forces, rather than economic.[16] The budgetary, though possibly not the economic, cost of military manpower could be reduced by conscription, but the current UK judgement seems to be that this would be more than offset by the military and social costs of the change. An argument, more common in the US, is that volunteer forces tend to be drawn from 'disadvantaged' (the euphemism varies) groups in society who lack technical training and skills. This raises a whole set of questions about the prevailing image of service in the armed forces, the general educational level in civil society which provides the reservoir of skills, the technical complexity of the weapon systems employed, and the difficulty of manpower planning. In a British context, conscription seems unlikely to solve such skill shortages.

Diagnosis

The arguments above should not be interpreted as suggesting that cost-cutting measures are necessarily misplaced; clearly they are highly desirable and to be applauded. Nor should the arguments be interpreted as suggesting that the defence industries, services, or MoD are particularly efficient; or that the force posture chosen is militarily effective. The argument is merely that the high-cost solutions adopted are chosen for what appear to the defence decision-makers, acting collectively, to be compelling reasons. The remedies proposed all fail to meet explicit or implicit objectives; they can reduce budgetary cost only at the expense of surrendering other goals. There are a range of explanations for the preference for high-cost solutions in the military sphere, but three important influences are uncertainty, multiple goals, and system linkages.

Military planning inevitably faces great uncertainties about potential conflicts, technological possibilities, weapon performance, production cost, and political priorities. Qualitatively, these uncertainties are no different from those that face a computer manufacturer planning corporate strategy and product development: is the technology feasible; will the machine work; can it be produced to target cost; will the market want it; how will the competition respond? The difference is that commercial battle happens, and the winners and losers are decided by the market. In military planning, the battle rarely happens and the evaluation remains hypothetical. The only experience available rapidly becomes dated, of dubious value and potentially irrelevant. This means that differences of opinion cannot be decisively settled, and the result is an expensive caution that requires preparation for almost any eventuality. This risk-aversion is reinforced by the knowledge that the consequences of wrong decisions in the military sphere can be disastrous.

The ultimate objectives of an organization (UK security in the case of defence planners; profits in the case of a firm) are usually too vague and distant to be much use in operational decision-making. What happens, therefore, is that the means to the ultimate objective (selling more, cutting costs; smart turn-out, faster aircraft) become the goals of sub-units of the organization. This is, in general, an effective division of labour, as long as the intermediate goals do in fact contribute to the ultimate end. It can happen that when circumstances change, the intermediate goals lose their relevance but are retained nonetheless; the spirited defence of the military usefulness of the cavalry is the standard example.[17] Irrelevant intermediate goals persist because of uncertainty about the appropriate means to meet the ultimate objective. The cost and difficulty of designing systems to meet multiple military goals are bad enough, as experience with Tornado and the Army Boot indicate. There is also a set of other intermediate goals such as maintaining a domestic defence industry, ensuring politically acceptable contractor profitability, being able to choose customized hardware, and wishing to protect particular jobs or traditions. Economists are fond of trying to persuade decision-makers to specify precise goals: exactly what they are trying to do, where and to whom. Reality, with its committee bargains, pressing interest groups and uncertain eventualities, is not like that. Instead, the proliferation of objectives and compromises over hard choices produce high-cost solutions.

In general, complicated interacting systems limit the scope for cost-reducing innovation. Innovations are easiest in discrete components which do not interact with numerous other elements. When a component must fit into a highly coordinated system, compatibility requirements restrict how it can be used. New and better ways of doing things cannot be adopted because they do not fit in with the rest of the system, or can only be adopted in a technically inefficient way. Major innovations thus tend to be introduced first in discrete elements with minimum interactions and single goals. Hence integrated circuits in arcade war-games are more advanced than those used in real war-games. Since military organizations are highly integrated and weapon systems tend to have very demanding compatibility requirements, the problem is extreme, but it also arises in civilian technology. Two areas in which it was expected that semiconductors would have very rapid applicability, namely telecommunications (the transistor was invented at Bell Laboratories) and automobiles, were in fact slow to adopt them.[18] Robustness and reliability were important considerations, but the constraints imposed by fitting them into complicated systems were crucial in restricting their use.

The system constraints can be technical, financial or social. Interfacing digital and analogue signals, for example, has been an important technical system constraint.[19] The social constraints arise from bureaucratic/emotional obstacles to fitting the new element into existing organizational structures and traditions. There are many military examples of this. Financial constraints arise from large existing investments that would need to be written off in any change.[20] It is easy to get locked in, since the uncertain benefits of change never look big enough to offset the sunk costs. In commercial life, competition forces adjustment; in the military arena, the peacetime evidence is less compelling and the system linkages inhibit the cost-reducing innovations.

Conclusion

The escalating cost of capability has been a major factor shaping British military posture, and the manner in which this problem is confronted will condition future defence policy. The cause of the problem is not inflation, as the term is normally understood; in fact there does not seem to be any meaningful sense in which the prices of forces, capability or security can be said to have risen. The evidence usually cited in this respect needs to be interpreted with some care.

The cost growth arises because defence planners have chosen to adopt expensive solutions to the military problems they face. In monetary terms, the thoroughly monitored procurement of small numbers of high-performance, highly-customized traditional weapons, produced domestically and operated by volunteer forces, is a high-cost approach. There is no shortage of proposed remedies, but the brief review of a selection of them suggests that costs could be reduced only at the expense of surrendering other explicit or implicit goals of policy.

There are a variety of reasons why the preference for high-cost solutions is more prevalent in the defence sector than in civilian life generally. The relative lack of evaluation in combat, for which we are all profoundly grateful, does mean that disputes about effectiveness can persist unresolved for a long time. Uncertainty about what really contributes to security and the maintenance of national interests means that subsidiary goals proliferate which can only be met by high-cost compromises. The need for everything to fit into a tightly interconnected military system restricts the adoption of many cost-reducing innovations.

Past experience indicates that when budgetary pressures bite, economies do get made, albeit in a destructive and self-defeating way that is designed to minimize disruption of existing arrangements. The façade is expensively maintained while the roof is allowed to continue leaking. If we wish to continue to live in a stately home and are willing to ignore the puddles and the complaints from the bank manager about the expense, that is our choice. But it is very unfair to blame inflation for our predicament.

The point of this paper is to attempt to clarify the issues involved in defence costs rather than propose solutions. However, to pursue the metaphor in the preceding paragraph, my advice to the impoverished aristocrat would be to surrender his grandiose aspirations, move to a suburban semi-detached and spend his declining years in relative comfort. In the case of the UK, this would involve cutting the share of output devoted to defence to the average of our European allies, relying much more on them for imports of arms, and reducing our commitments accordingly.[21] Of course, such a remedy would not meet many of the goals of current policy.

Notes

  1. David Greenwood and Lawrence Freedman give very clear statements of this position in John Baylis (ed.), *Alternative Approaches to British Defence Policy* (London: Macmillan, 1983). It is also advanced in Dan Smith and Ron Smith, *The Economics of Militarism* (London: Pluto, 1983).
  2. These data come from the UK *National Accounts 1984 Edition*, previously called *National Income and Expenditure* (London: HMSO, 1984), Tables 9.2 and 9.3.

3. An example of the specific questions it can be used for is given in Dunne, Pashardes and Smith, 'Needs, Costs and Bureaucracy: the Allocation of Public Consumption in the UK', *Economic Journal*, March 1984.

4. *Public Money*, September 1984, p. 58. The quotation from the review board is cited there. See also *Public Money*, December 1984, p. 13.

5. Cmnd. 8529-I (London: HMSO, 1982), para. 403, p. 27.

6. D.L. Kirkpatrick & P.G. Pugh, 'Towards The Starship Enterprise – are the current trends in defence unit costs inexorable', *Aerospace*, Journal of the Royal Aeronautical Society, 1983. This article also makes it clear that the problem is not primarily one of technological change (which tends to be cost-reducing) nor of inflation (since quality differs). Not adopting new technology would not solve the problem. Although I cannot produce the figures, I feel sure that the cost of keeping a troop of cavalry at Knightsbridge barracks would show real growth when compared with that for more modern weapon systems.

7. *Financial Times*, 15 Jan. 1984, p. 13.

8. The presence of a Brazilian contender in the competition for the new RAF basic trainer illustrates this trend. It is ironic that it is said to be the failure of a Ferranti missile-fire-control system in 1972 that galvanized the Brazilians into developing their own production (*Business Week*, 22 Oct. 1984, p. 37). Both this *Business Week* article and the 1984 *SIPRI Yearbook* (London: Taylor and Francis) provide evidence of the increasing competition in the international arms market.

9. The Belgian purchase of military vehicles from Bombardier described in the *Financial Times*, 13 July 1984, seems to be a classic case of complexity.

10. As an *Evening Standard* article of 26 Sept. 1984, prompted by AEW Nimrod delays, puts it, 'In practice, much of our British hardware is inferior, arrives late and proves much more expensive than the competition.' The government's efforts to introduce competition are described in Cmnd. 9227-I (London: HMSO, 1984), pp. 16-17.

11. This is the purported objective of MINIS and the like as described in Cmnd. 9227-I (London: HMSO, 1984), pp. 12-16.

12. E. Luttwak in 'Why we need more "waste, fraud and mismanagement" in the Pentagon', *Survival*, Vol. 24, No. 3 (May/June 1982), reprinted from *Commentary*, argues that this concern with micromanagement at the expense of strategy reduces military effectiveness and increases costs. There are similar disputes about service bureaucracies. Maj.-Gen. J. Frost in *2 Para Falklands* (London: Sphere, 1983) puts great emphasis on the need for established HQ organization, whereas it has been common to regard such structures as fat to be trimmed. Nor does the popular tail–teeth metaphor, used to justify such moves, seem so obvious in terms of animals like squirrels, for whom the tail plays an essential function.

13. Quoted in an interview in *Technology*, 9 Jan. 1984, p. 19.

14. For instance, Air Marshal Sir Frederick Sowrey, 'An Unconventional Approach to Defence Resources', and John L. Clarke, 'NATO Neutrals and National Defence', both in *Survival*, Vol. 24, No. 6 (Nov./Dec. 1982).

15. The econometric estimates are reported in R.P. Smith & A. Humm, 'Capital-Labour Substitution in Defence Provision', Birkbeck College, mimeo. *European Security*, May 1984, p. 6, gives figures for the striking differences in the monthly wage paid to conscripts in NATO countries.

16. C. Mellors and J. McKean, 'The Politics of Conscription in Western Europe', *West European Politics*, Vol. 7, No. 3 (July 1984), p. 25; and K. Booth, 'Strategy and Conscription', in J. Baylis (ed.), *Alternative Approaches to British Defence Policy* (London: Macmillan, 1983).

17. Edward L. Katzenbach, Jun., 'The Horse Cavalry in the Twentieth Century: A Study in Policy Response', *Public Policy*, 1958, reprinted in Endicott and Stafford (eds.), *American Defence Policy* (Baltimore: Johns Hopkins University Press, 1977), p. 360.

18. Ernest Braun and Stuart Macdonald, *Revolution in Miniature*, 2nd ed. (Cambridge: Cambridge University Press, 1982).

19. As another example, John Kinnear of GEC Avionics, explaining the delays in AEW Nimrod, has said: 'The hundreds of black boxes which make up the radar's electronics work well individually, but not together.' *Evening Standard*, 26 Sept. 1984.

20. For instance, the US retains the NTSC colour TV system, the first developed, despite its poor quality, because of the large cost involved in converting to the better systems now available.

21. The implications of such a move are discussed in detail in J.P. Dunne and R.P. Smith, 'The Economic Consequences of Reduced UK Military Expenditure', *Cambridge Journal of Economics*, Sept. 1984.

Comment on Chapter 7
*D.L.I. Kirkpatrick**

Smith's paper on 'Defence Costs' is a perceptive survey of many of the important issues in defence economics. It is particularly useful that his paper distinguishes between three different types of defence inflation: the year-to-year budgetary inflation measured by the defence price deflator; the growth in unit cost between successive generations of weapons; and the escalation in the estimated procurement cost of a new project during its development. It also clearly identifies the factors which differentiate the change of the defence price deflator in a given year from that of the GDP deflator. It is important that this difference – the relative price effect, which averages about 1½ per cent per year – should be explicitly recognized, not only because 1½ per cent of the defence budget is a lot of money, but because failure to take proper account of it over a decade would produce an inadvertent but significant real cut in the defence procurement programme. Thus Smith's conclusion, that 'there is no evidence that defence suffers from a particular problem of inflation', requires some qualification: defence inflation does have some characteristic features, but these have been identified and understood.

It is also useful that he has identified the multiple goals which influence defence planners. Their aims are to provide enough military capability to ensure national security, but keep down the cost of doing so; to maintain a domestic defence industry that will provide independence of policy and security of supply, but expose it to the blasts of international competition; to ensure that the industry's profits are high enough to encourage investment for productivity, but not high enough to provoke political storms; and to provide UK forces with the equipment they want when they want it, but simultaneously to seek collaboration with, or exports to, countries with different military requirements and budgetary problems. These aims are pursued amidst extreme uncertainty and long timescales, where the consequences of any misjudgement could be disastrous. An appreciation of the influence of these multiple goals and of other

---

*The views expressed in this paper are those of the author and do not necessarily represent those of the Ministry of Defence.

aspects of government policy, such as the aim of reducing the Public Sector Borrowing Requirement, is essential to a good understanding of UK defence policy.

Smith reviews several of the remedies proposed to reduce the cost of raising and equipping defence forces, and only a few points need to be added to his analysis. Collaboration can yield substantial savings by sharing the development cost and obtaining economies of scale in production, but additional costs can arise from encompassing divergent requirements, duplication of trials and tooling, integration of different national methods and procedures, and extra travel, transport and administration. However, the size of these savings and penalties does vary widely between different projects and depends on the chauvinism of the politicians, military officers and manufacturers involved. Exports reduce the cost of defence equipment for the MoD only if the foreign customer accepts a share of the cost of development and of the (comparatively expensive) first units delivered: in a highly competitive market such customers are rare. Competition in the supply of defence equipment for UK forces has both economic advantages and disadvantages, as in the civilian economy. One disadvantage arises from the government's duty (unlike a private consumer) to ensure that the fairness of its choice is above suspicion; so the selection process requires large teams of evaluators with specialist advisers to assess the alternative proposals. Productivity in the defence industry continues to increase, but current developments are no more than the latest steps in a series of improvements in methods and techniques which have not in the past yielded any dramatic reductions in defence costs. Smith's review indicates that there are no magic solutions, and his conclusion that 'the remedies proposed all fail to meet explicit or implicit objectives' cannot be faulted.

But Smith did not sufficiently emphasize the serious problems for UK defence policy which arise from the sustained growth in the unit cost of major weapon systems between one generation and the next.[1] This growth is caused mainly by the need for rival nations to improve progressively the quality of their weapons, in a rational response to changes in technology and to developments in the perceived threat.[2] Each nation must avoid allowing its own forces to fall into a position of qualitative inferiority relative to its rival's, thus offering that rival the opportunity to obtain advantages by the use or the threat of force. Each nation therefore undertakes improvements of its own forces whenever it knows or believes that its rival is making improvements. The two nations or alliances thus establish a vicious circle in which more effective weapons procured by one nation increase the threat to a rival nation, thereby stimulating it to advance its technology to produce, or to procure, more effective weapons for its own forces to counter the threat.[3]

More effective weapons from a particular family tend to have higher development and higher unit production costs. The former mean that governments find it more difficult to take a decision to proceed, and that new projects are launched less frequently. For both these reasons, the scope and cost of the development programme tend to increase. Similarly, higher unit production costs mean that fewer weapons can be procured, so there is less scope for investment and for learning in production, which leads in turn to a further increase in unit production cost. This combination of positive feedback loops causes the unit costs of procurement to rise by a greater extent than that which would result directly from the increased effectiveness of the weapon system.[4]

Although it is widely recognized that the unit costs of major weapon systems are increasing from one generation to the next, the scale of the increases, their prevalence and persistence, and their implications for UK defence policy are not always appreciated. The unit production cost of RAF combat aircraft, for example, has been rising since World War II at about 8 per cent per year in real terms, equivalent to a fivefold increase between one generation and the next.[4] The costs of warships, tanks and missiles have risen at similar rates, and comparable trends have been observed in other allied nations.[5] In the past, such increases in unit production cost (well above the real growth of GNP or of the defence budget) have been accommodated by reducing the number of weapon systems procured, and the corresponding increases in development cost have been accommodated by funding development programmes less frequently.[6] This strategy has been widely adopted and has generally been successful. The RAF, for example, has maintained its overall capability while the composition of its fleet has changed, so that it now deploys smaller numbers of aircraft with individually greater combat effectiveness: the 165 Tornado F2 interceptors now entering service can face the contemporary threat with as much confidence as 1,400 Hunters and Javelins faced the threat of their time.

However, if unit costs continue to rise, this strategy leads ultimately to a point of absurdity where the forces deployed are so few in number that they are vulnerable to unserviceability, accident, sabotage and pre-emptive attack; where one weapon is expected to accomplish several roles (in several places at once?); and where geriatric equipment is expensively maintained in service despite its dubious effectiveness against newer enemy systems. For a particular type of weapon system, this point depends on the scale of the budget available, so it is reached first by small nations, later by medium powers like the UK, and lastly by the superpowers, who set the pace in the technological arms race. In 1966, the UK decided that its force of aircraft carriers was approaching the point of absurdity and consequently undertook a fundamental reappraisal of the role of the Royal Navy, the structure of the fleet, and its cooperation with land-based air power. Today it appears that the UK will soon face similar reappraisals, since several other major weapon systems are moving towards the point of absurdity and may reach it in the next generation.

The rise in unit costs and the trend towards a smaller number of more expensive projects may also pose serious problems for the MoD (Procurement Executive) and for the defence industry. When the procurement budget consisted of many small projects, it was comparatively simple to ensure, by judicious programme adjustments, that the annual (real) defence expenditure varied only slightly from one year to the next, and so remained compatible with the government's revenue and its non-military expenditure, neither of which can easily be altered sharply. In the future, with fewer but larger procurement programmes, it may prove very difficult to maintain consistently either the smooth trend of total defence expenditure or the traditional division of that budget between Services. At the same time, the workload on the various sectors of the defence industry may fluctuate more violently than in the past, and demand unprecedented flexibility in manning levels or work transfer between factories and organizations.

Thus, whereas the scale of the defence budget produces at present only an uncomfortable diversion of the nation's resources, the rise in unit costs appears likely before long to present critical problems in several areas of weapon procurement which will demand reappraisals of the structure of UK forces, of the funding of procurement, and of the organization of the defence industry. But it would be irresponsible to decide to evade these problems by equipping UK forces with second-rate weapons, taking little account of the potential of technology or the nature of the threat. Such a policy would be extravagantly wasteful, because forces equipped with outclassed but still costly weapons could make no significant contribution towards the nation's objectives in a future conflict and would suffer severely as a result. A cheap-and-cheerful weapon system should be procured only if it is good value for money and is better fitted to its task than a donkey at Aintree.

The validity of Smith's comparison of the MoD to a crumbling stately home might be disputed, but it is more important in conclusion to contest his denial of any meaningful rise 'in the prices of forces, capability or security'. Although it is true that technology has reduced the cost of a given capability, the defence budget needed to achieve the same degree of national security has risen because of developments in the threat. In that sense, the price of security has risen and may continue to rise in future.

Notes

1. The prediction that in 2054 the entire US defence budget will purchase just one tactical combat aircraft is given in N.R. Augustine, 'Augustine's Laws', American Institute of Aeronautics and Astronautics, New York, 1982.
2. The rational procurement policy which leads to the unit costs of weapon systems increasing between one generation and the next is described in D.L.I. Kirkpatrick, 'A rationale for the rising unit cost of defence equipment', unpublished.
3. A good example of such a cycle of technical leapfrogging may be found in the development of battleship shells and armour prior to World War I: it is described in W. Manchester, *The Arms of Krupp* (Boston: Little, Brown, 1968).
4. The five vicious circles thus found are described more fully in D.L.I. Kirkpatrick and P.G. Pugh, 'Towards the Starship Enterprise – are the current trends in defence unit cost inexorable?', *Aerospace*, May 1983. This paper also presents the growth in recent years of the unit cost of RAF combat aircraft.
5. See for example S.J. Deitchman, *New Technology and Military Power: general purpose military forces for the 1980s and beyond* (Boulder, Colorado: Westview Press, 1979); P.G. Pugh, 'Of ships and money: the rising cost of naval power', *Warship*, 32 (October 1984); and J. Martre, 'La Bataille contre l'escalade des couts', *Air & Cosmos*, 887.
6. Data on the reduction in the number of major weapon systems deployed by the UK is quoted in Sir John Charnley, 'Aeronautical research: some current influences and trends', *Aeronautical Journal*, October 1982.

8　Defence Procurement and Industrial Policy
Keith Hartley

The problem

Modern weapons are not only expensive to develop and produce, but their real unit costs have been rising with each generation of new equipment (see Table 8.1). As a result, nations are developing fewer new types of expensive weapons, purchasing smaller numbers of each type, and consequently failing to exploit scale and learning economies in production. There is also an incentive to continue operating an expensive weapon for longer periods before seeking a replacement.[1] Fewer new types creates pressures from both the military and the domestic industry's scientists to ensure that each new project incorporates the latest technology, and this leads in turn to elaborate and lengthy development programmes and ultimately to even higher development costs. Increasingly, the domestic defence industries of small and medium-sized nations, typical of Europe, are required to undertake technological 'leaps' as they seek to maintain their capability to develop advanced weapons. Technological leaps can be costly, since a nation's defence industry does not have the benefits of continuous previous experience in the form of information and knowledge which accrues from undertaking a succession of relatively small technical advances. Moreover, the trends towards fewer new types and shorter production runs has implications for the size, structure and skill composition of the domestic weapons industries which can be supported by a nation's armed forces. Fewer new types and greater time intervals between the start of each new project creates difficulties and extra costs in maintaining domestic design and development expertise.

These problems are not unique to the UK. NATO is often criticized for being an inefficient organization in the procurement and supply of military equipment. There are believed to be too many similar types of weapon and consequently major inefficiencies in each nation's defence industries, as demonstrated by the wasteful duplication of costly R&D in member states and the relatively short production runs, particularly in Europe. The desire for independence

Table 8.1   Weapons costs, 1984

(a)   *Estimated programme costs (R&D and production)*

Weapon system	£m
Sting Ray torpedo	1,570
EH-101 helicopter	1,200
Sea Eagle air-to-surface anti-ship missile	595
Mechanized Combat Vehicle (MCV-80) variants	373
Air-Launched Anti-Radiation Missile (ALARM)	300

(b)   *Unit production costs*

Weapon system	£m
Nuclear-powered fleet submarine	235.0
Type 22 Frigate	160.0
Tornado F2	19.0
VC-10 tanker	11.9
Chinook helicopter	4.7
Fleet minesweeper	4.5
Challenger tank	2.3

(c)   *Trends in unit production costs of successive generations of equipment*

Weapon system	Period between replacements (yrs)	Real cost increase
Combat aircraft	15	×3.75
Guided weapons	13	×3.50
Armoured vehicles	20	×3.50
Frigates	12	×3.00
Helicopter	11	×2.50
HE shell	11	×2.00
Trainer aircraft	14	×1.50
Median	13	×3.00

Source: Statement on the Defence Estimates, 1981, 1983, 1984 (London: HMSO).
Note: Figures are approximations, all converted to 1983/4 prices.

and security of supply has meant that NATO is characterized by a variety of separate defence industrial complexes, each capable of developing and manufacturing either a complete, or a limited, range of modern weapons. At one extreme, the USA, Britain and France have the capacity to design, develop and manufacture advanced combat aircraft, missiles, aircraft-carriers, nuclear-powered submarines, nuclear weapons and main battle tanks. Italy and the Federal

Republic of Germany are intermediate cases with more limited capabilities in combat aircraft, warships and tanks. At the other extreme, nations such as Belgium and the Netherlands have some aircraft manufacturing capacity (e.g., the F16 co-production) and the Dutch also have a warship industry. Table 8.2 shows the number of NATO states with the industrial capacity to develop and manufacture combat aircraft, warships and tanks, together with an indication of the total number of different types currently being developed and/or produced within NATO. The table also shows the typical *total* output for each nation's armed forces, as well as the *annual* output in NATO and the Warsaw Pact. It can be seen that there is duplication of weapons development capabilities and substantial differences in the scale of output between the USA and the major European arms producers. Such evidence often leads to proposals for standardization.

Standardization as a solution
From a NATO perspective, the 'ideal' solution to weapons procurement emphasizes the military and economic benefits of standardization. The aim is to improve efficiency in the use of NATO defence resources by 'increasing cooperation and eliminating unnecessary duplication among Alliance nations in research, development, production, procurement and support of defence systems and equipment'.[2] One expression of this aim proposes to eliminate 'needless' duplication through 'healthy and controlled competition', which would result in rationalization, specialization, fairness and equity in all procurements, together with trade liberalization, offsets and the removal of all restraints.[3] Rarely are such aims critically evaluated. If standardization and collaboration are so attractive, why has the record been so unimpressive? Not much recognition is given, either, to the implications of standardization for industrial structure, the behaviour of firms, market performance, and public policy. NATO standardization requires a NATO industrial policy. Consider some of the questions which have to be answered in formulating such a policy:

1. What is 'unnecessary, needless and wasteful' duplication in R&D? How can successful R&D projects be identified in advance? Will the elimination of competition (wasteful duplication?) in R&D lead to problems of monopoly – e.g., higher prices, inefficiency, lack of dynamism and restricted choice? And who will choose the winners and on what criteria?
2. What is 'healthy and controlled' competition? If rivalry is controlled, can there be competition in the form of continuous rivalry between firms? Significantly, the concept of 'healthy

Table 8.2   Duplication in NATO

Weapon system	Number of NATO nations developing and manufacturing	Total number of different types currently being developed and/or produced in NATO	Typical total national output per type				Annual output (1981)	
			France	UK	FRG	USA	NATO	USSR
Combat aircraft	5	14	200–400	200–400	175–325	1,000–2,600	900	1,350
Destroyers/frigates	8	16	2–13	8–25	4–6	30–46	20	9
Main battle tanks	4	4	2,000	700–800	1,800–3,600	7,251	760	2,000

Sources: *Soviet Military Power*, US Government Printing Office, Washington D.C., March 1983; *Flight International*, London, 26 May, 1984; H. Lyon, *Modern Warships* (London: Salamander Books, 1980); R. Bonds (ed.), *Modern Tanks* (London: Salamander Books, 1980).
Notes: (i) Figures are approximations, indicating orders of magnitude and are based on 1980-4. (ii) National output per type refers to output for the nation's armed forces, i.e., domestic sales only; but French tank output includes exports. (iii) Annual output for NATO excludes France.

and controlled' competition is not defined nor in general use in standard economics textbooks.

3. What controls on competition are to be exercised so that it results in 'fairness and equity' for all members of NATO?

NATO standardization will have to be based on an industrial policy which creates an efficient industrial structure capable of responding to the uncertainties of defence procurement that inevitably accompany *future* demands for equipment. Often, the model for NATO industrial policy is based on the Warsaw Pact solution, which seems to avoid duplication and leads to the economies of long production runs (see Table 8.2). But the fact that the Warsaw Pact's output is standardized and produced in large quantities does not necessarily mean that its industrial structure is more efficient (i.e., operating at a lower cost). The lack of competitive rivalry within the Warsaw Pact can lead to inefficiency in both development and production. It can also be misleading to assume that all weapons industries operate on an identical and most efficient cost curve and that the Warsaw Pact is producing towards the bottom of such a curve while NATO is some considerable distance from the lowest point. Cost curves can have different positions and different shapes. Evidence is lacking on the relative efficiency of arms industries in the Warsaw Pact and NATO.

An alternative method of achieving standardization requires the creation of a competitive NATO free trade area for weapons, with no restrictions on the entry of new firms into national markets. This would allow each nation to specialize in the development and/or production of those weapons in which it has a comparative advantage and to reap the benefits of international trade and exchange. Estimates suggest that the introduction of competition and the creation of a free trade area for NATO weapons markets might lead to substantial cost savings, possibly in the region of 20 to 30 per cent.[4] But if there are major cost savings from competition and free trade in weapons markets, why have governments opposed such policies? An obvious explanation is that most NATO states dislike the expected outcome of a competitive market and prefer to retain their independence. They recognize that competition and free trade will require a reallocation of defence resources within and between NATO members. European states expect to be amongst the losers, particularly in high-technology weapons: hence their opposition to such reallocation and the loss of independence. There are also likely to be worries and disputes about the *distribution* of gains and losses. The potential losers in a NATO free trade area fear that they will not be compensated and that they will be worse off after the policy change. In the circumstances, nations are willing to pay any extra costs for domestically developed and manufactured weapons. An independent defence industry enables a country to avoid undue dependence on foreigners, guarantees security of supply and provides the bonus of jobs, technology and balance-of-payments benefits from domestic procurement.

Not surprisingly, a domestic defence industry will form a major interest group that seeks to influence government policy in its favour. Such a group will oppose procurement policies which will adversely affect its income, particularly efforts to open up the domestic market to rival foreign firms with the possibility of buying weapons from abroad. In other words, even if some form of NATO standardization is regarded as desirable (the appropriate form has to be specified), its advocates have to recognize that the achievement of the ideal cannot ignore the presence of domestic defence industries in the member states. Is it possible to formulate a policy which will move the different defence industries in NATO towards an agreed standardization objective? What are the likely problems *en route* to this objective? What are the implications for the UK defence industry? A starting-point must be the stylized facts about the size and efficiency of Britain's arms industries.

The UK defence industry

The UK defence industry provides some 700,000 jobs. Weapons production is particularly important in aerospace, electronics and shipbuilding, with firms such as British Aerospace, British Shipbuilders, Ferranti, GEC and Rolls-Royce being major recipients of MoD contracts. Defence is also a major spender on R&D as well as a source of substantial export sales (Table 8.3).

UK defence markets are often non-competitive, especially for advanced technology equipment, for which there might be only one or relatively few domestic suppliers. In 1982-3, some 20 per cent by value of equipment contracts were awarded on the basis of competitive tendering.[5] The market is dominated by the government, which is a monopsonist (single buyer) able to determine technical progress, the size of the domestic arms industries, their competitiveness, prices and profitability. A government commitment to maintaining a domestic arms industry means that its national suppliers are protected from the rivalry of other domestic and foreign firms. Such protection, together with cost-based contracts and government regulation of defence profits, provides a market environment which is likely to be inefficient. Critics point to waste, fraud and mismanagement as reflected in low productivity, the 'gold-plating' of weapons, cost escalation, delays in delivery, cancellations and unreliable equipment. Indeed, UK evidence shows an average saving of over 30 per cent following the introduction of competition for defence contracts.[6] But

Table 8.3   The UK defence industry, 1984

(a) *Direct and indirect industrial employment (people thousands)*

(i)	MoD expenditure on equipment	405
(ii)	MoD expenditure on other material and stores	160
(iii)	Exports of defence equipment	145
	Total industrial employment	710

(b) *Defence expenditure (£m)*

(i)	Total UK defence expenditure	17,033
(ii)	Industrial analysis of UK defence expenditure	6,954
	including: Aerospace	2,092
	Electronics	1,292
	Petroleum products	916
	Ordnance, small arms, explosives	522
	Shipbuilding and repairing	516
(iii)	MoD expenditure on R&D	2,097
	including: Military aircraft	508
	Ships and underwater warfare	390
	Other electronics	340
	Guided weapons	314
	Total extramural R&D	1,543

(c) *Exports*
Overseas sales of UK defence equipment (£m, 1984-5)   2,600

(d) *Major UK defence contractors*

(i) Receiving over £100m p.a. for MoD equipment:	(ii) Receiving £50–100m p.a. for MoD equipment:
British Aerospace (Aircraft Group)	British Leyland
British Aerospace (Dynamics Group)	General Motors
British Shipbuilders	Hunting Associated Industries
Ferranti	Racal Electronics
GEC	Thorn EMI
Plessey	
Rolls-Royce	
Royal Ordnance Factories	
Westland	

Source: Cmnd. 9227 (London: HMSO, 1984).

once again, proposals for improving efficiency through introducing and extending competition in UK weapons markets will encounter opposition from established producer groups, who are likely to suffer from greater rivalry. Even the 1984 commitment to competition as the means of achieving the 'best value for money, the most efficient use of industrial resources and the stimulation of innovation and new ideas' is subject to limitations. 'We need a strong indigenous defence/ industrial base; . . . and the limited number of British suppliers of certain advanced defence equipment is also a constraint on competition within the UK.'[7]

Such assertions are typical of the many myths of UK defence policy. Little effort is made to define a 'strong indigenous defence/ industrial base'; why such a base is required; its minimum size and industrial composition (i.e., which industries?); and the costs of supporting such a base. Nor, in the case of 'advanced equipment', is it explained why competition cannot be provided by allowing foreign firms to bid for UK defence contracts. Presumably, defence policy is the outcome of a complex process involving a variety of agents in the political market-place. Voters, political parties, bureaucracies, UK and foreign defence contractors, together with NATO, the USA, European interests and other pressure groups, will all seek to influence British defence policy. Figure 8.1 shows the various agents in the political market and some of the linkages or channels through which they seek to influence policy. The existence of such a complex set of interrelationships means that policy proposals which appear attractive to one group (e.g. voters) are likely to be modified as they proceed through the political process. Proposals for more competition, more standardization and more collaboration, each of which appears to offer substantial cost savings, are often rejected by governments which seem to ignore obvious opportunities for making people better off. They prefer to buy weapons from expensive domestic firms and to protect British industry, jobs and technology. Changes which appear so attractive to economists often fail to recognize the influence of actors in the political market-place and their impact on policy formulation.

Is a defence industrial policy needed?

Are weapons different from, say, bananas, cars, computers, motor cycles and videos, many of which the UK willingly buys from abroad? The standard argument is that a domestic weapons industry provides independence, guaranteed supplies and equipment designed for national requirements, so that the UK is not dependent on the willingness of foreigners to provide military equipment for national defence and security. In other words, it is believed that, left to market forces, the UK defence industry would be too small: hence the need for government support to maintain an industry at the size which is socially desirable. This argument raises a number of questions:

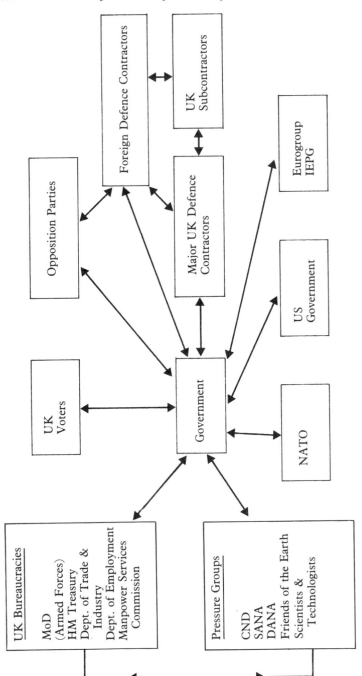

Figure 8.1   Linkages in UK defence policy

1. What are the aims of UK defence policy and what is the relevance of industrial policy to these aims? Indeed, should industrial policy be the proper concern of the Ministry of Defence or the Department of Trade and Industry? Here problems arise, since the MoD Procurement Executive is seeking to reconcile the conflicting interests of buyers (armed forces) and UK suppliers. Presumably, the armed forces need access to markets which will supply defence equipment efficiently (assuming they have limited budgets and specific defence commitments). If so, the armed forces might be left to determine whether they are willing to pay extra for British equipment.

2. What are the costs and benefits of different sizes of domestic defence industry – e.g., 10 per cent smaller? What is the optimum size and structure of the weapons industry (problems arise because there are a number of industries)? How much are UK citizens willing to pay for the independence associated with a national defence industry?

3. How can voters express their preferences for different weapons procurement policies? Given the limitations of the voting system as a means of registering collective preferences, there are considerable opportunities for politicians in power to exercise discretion in determining the size of the defence industry which is socially desirable. They can then rationalize their decisions by referring to defence as an industry which is vital to national security and which also provides major benefits in the form of jobs, technology and the balance of payments. In some instances, defence contracts might be allocated to important or marginal constituencies!

The meaning of industrial policy in relation to defence procurement needs clarification. It embraces size, structure (number of firms) and entry conditions in the R&D, production and repair phases of a weapon's life cycle. Nor is the UK defence industry a single, homogeneous entity: it includes a variety of industries such as aerospace, electronics, engineering, ordnance, shipbuilding and vehicles, with a mix of publicly and privately owned firms. For UK governments, there are four broad options for defence industrial policy: first, a buy-British policy; second, a competitive policy of shopping around and buying weapons as cheaply as possible from either within the UK or abroad; third, collaborative projects can be undertaken, sharing both R&D and production work (e.g. Tornado); and fourth, a weapon developed abroad can be produced domestically under licence or on a co-production or work-sharing basis (e.g.,

European co-production of the F16). Clearly, a government can adopt different mixes of these policies, and its preferred combination will depend upon an assessment of their relative costs and benefits. What is the extent of the gains and losses, and who gains and who loses from the alternative policies? In other words, sensible public choices require an information framework which identifies and quantifies the effects of alternative procurement policies. The government's emphasis on value for money suggests five performance indicators which might be used to assess the policy options:[8]

1. *The effects on defence expenditure.* What are the implications for present and future unit costs of equipment (i.e., R&D, production and spares prices)? For example, estimates are required on the net current value of buying British compared with, say, importing weapons over a specified period (five, ten or fifteen years). In some instances, the procurement choice will depend on the ratio of development to production costs. For example, where R&D costs are many times the unit production costs of a weapon, the UK often buys foreign equipment or seeks a collaborative programme.

2. *Advanced technology and spin-off.* Are there technological benefits to the UK from buying British? And are any such benefits restricted to the defence industries, or do they spill over into the civilian economy (spin-off)?

3. *Employment effects.* What will be the implications for the total number of present and future jobs in the UK, their skills and their regional location?

4. *Balance-of-payments effects.* In the form of exports and import savings.

5. *Weapons characteristics and the contribution to UK security.* For example, performance of the equipment; time-scales from initial order to first delivery and completion of contract; cost escalation; delays; quality escalation or failure; and implications for UK defence output (security). Throughout such appraisals, consideration needs to be given to the extra costs of incremental improvements in performance.

To illustrate the approach, consider the choice between buying British weapons and importing defence equipment. To make the choice, basic issues must be clearly specified and critically evaluated with supporting quantitative evidence. Also, it has to be recognized that decisions are made with uncertainty and that mistakes are always likely to occur.

The case for buying British

The following arguments, which are often used to justify buying British, need to be assessed:

1. *Britain gains high technology* which is reputed to be vital to maintaining a national defence industry. Questions arise as to which military technologies are so vital; whether the technology is vital regardless of costs; whether there are alternative methods of acquiring the technology (e.g., cheap prototypes; licensing and licensed production); and whether today's technology is relevant for the next generation of weapons (i.e., how costly is a gap in technology?). It is also often claimed that military R&D results in valuable spin-off for the civilian economy. If it does, how valuable is such spin-off? Could the desired results have been achieved more efficiently through direct support of civil R&D? Indeed, is there too little spin-off, so that Britain is failing to make full use of the results of defence R&D? If so, why is defence R&D not being used by civil firms? In this context, it might be useful to compare spin-off from government R&D with that from private R&D establishments.[9] However, there is the problem of the hypothetical: what would have happened in the absence of defence R&D? And there is a more fundamental worry: spin-off is a bonus, but it is more properly the concern of the Department of Trade and Industry than the Ministry of Defence.

2. *There are balance-of-payments benefits.* The economic logic of this argument needs to be clearly set out and evaluated in the light of the following points:

   a. With floating exchange rates, why worry about the balance of payments? However, the policy objectives of UK governments can change. If the balance of payments becomes an objective of government policy, then it has to be shown that the balance-of-payments contribution of a domestic defence order will coincide with a *future* balance-of-payments problem.

   b. Are the balance-of-payments considerations the proper concern of the Ministry of Defence or the Treasury?

   c. What is the evidence on the balance-of-payments contribution of domestic defence orders and the relationship between the domestic market and exports (including civil home and export sales of defence equipment such as transport aircraft)?

   d. Would the resources currently employed in UK defence industries make a greater contribution to the balance of payments if they were used elsewhere in the economy? This argument can be tested by examining the evidence on the balance-of-payments performance of other UK industries.

3. *There are employment benefits.* It is often claimed that cancellation of domestic defence orders will result in job losses, Exchequer costs and the emigration of highly skilled labour. This raises a set of questions, some of which can be tested:

   a. What are the quantities involved? How many jobs are likely to be lost, in which skills and in which regions?[10] It has to be remembered that most changes in policy and in the economy involve gains and losses in jobs. The question then is whether the potential gainers from the change can more than compensate for the potential losers.

   b. What happens to the labour which is released from the defence sector? Is it re-employed in other sectors? If so, which other sectors, and how quickly does the reallocation occur?

   c. What is the employment (and unemployment) experience of other industries which have suffered major reductions in sales? Examples include cigarettes, coal, cotton textiles, motor cycles and steel, together with the response of civil firms to the current recession. Are there any major differences in the responses of defence and civil firms to a reduction in demand (and/or an increase in the exchange rate)? What are these differences and why do they exist?[11]

   d. What assumptions are being made about the workings of the labour market? Which labour market (local, regional, national, different skills), and how long will it take to remove any unemployment?

   e. What are the Exchequer costs of cancelling or not buying British equipment (e.g., lost tax revenue, social security payments to the unemployed)? It has been suggested that because of the Exchequer costs, a price differential should be applied to overseas purchases. For example, some estimates suggest 10 to 15% of the contract price in the first year, depending on how quickly the labour market removes unemployment.

4. *The UK avoids becoming dependent on a foreign monopoly.* This argument, too, needs to be clearly set out and critically evaluated:

   a. What does it mean, especially when there are alternative nations willing to supply equipment? What are the risks of relying upon imports?

   b. What are the costs of *independence?* For example, the UK might have to purchase its high-technology weapons from a small-scale British monopolist!

c. What are the costs of the alternative methods of achieving *some* independence – e.g., licensed or co-production; international collaboration; buying off the shelf and stock-piling?

d. What is the experience of other countries – e.g., Israel, South Africa, Netherlands, Belgium?

e. What is the *minimum size* of UK defence industry required for independence (compared with the existing size)? Which areas, if any, should the UK retain? How can these activities be retained? And what are the costs of the alternative methods of retaining a reserve of capacity?

For many of these arguments, the important question is whether the resources currently employed in UK defence industries would make a greater contribution to technology, jobs, the balance of payments and, ultimately, human satisfaction, if they were used elsewhere in the economy. Central to any choice will be the implications for the defence budget: what are the costs of buying British? Two examples are illustrative: first, the estimated programme costs of the Sting Ray Torpedo were £920m compared with a US buy of some £200m (1979 prices); second, the original decision to purchase TSR-2 rather than American F111 aircraft was equivalent to protecting the UK industry with a tariff rate of between 90 and 135 per cent! Admittedly, other considerations such as operational requirements and the quality of weapons enter into any choice. Nonetheless, such examples indicate that buying British might be costly and that substantial cost savings might be available through importing.

The case for importing

The arguments for importing defence equipment can be summarized as follows:

1. *Imported weapons are cheaper.* Are they, and how much cheaper? Is it the case that foreign equipment is cheap, but you have to pay for the spares? In other words, life-cycle costs must not be ignored. And, if foreign equipment is cheaper, which types of equipment should be imported and why are they cheaper? For example, American equipment might be cheaper because of the ratio of R&D to production costs and because the scale of US industry allows it to exploit scale and learning economies.[12] Or is it the case that foreign equipment is cheaper

because foreign governments subsidize their defence industries? If so, should the UK accept 'free gifts' from foreigners and specialize in other things? It must also be remembered that unanticipated changes in the exchange rate can adversely affect the cost advantages of foreign equipment.

2. *Resources will be released for other more valuable uses.* This claim raises the following questions:

   a. Will a reduction in UK defence spending increase the economy's rate of growth and/or lead to increased expenditure on, say, state health and education? What will be the effects on growth and the balance of payments, etc., of increased expenditure on the NHS (i.e., how do the costs of defence spending compare with the costs of NHS expenditure)?

   b. Will a reduction in UK military R&D spending reduce total R&D spending, and will this reduce the economy's growth rate? Or will civil R&D (private and public) increase?

   c. How do UK firms respond to the loss of defence contracts to foreign firms? Do they release labour, or do they withdraw work from subcontractors? How many jobs are lost, and which type of labour is involved (e.g., scientists, skilled or unskilled workers)? Do UK firms minimize the effects by obtaining offsets and/or diversifying into other markets (military and civil)? Or are UK firms likely to respond by reducing their prices to compete with imports?

3. *Imported weapons can be available before domestic equipment.* Is this correct? If so, how much sooner is the foreign equipment available, and how does it compare in terms of performance and reliability? For example, as a result of the UK decision to purchase Nimrod AEW aircraft rather than participate in NATO's AWACs programme, there have been considerable delays in delivering the equipment to the RAF.

Nations cannot avoid choices in weapons procurement. If they are reluctant to import and wish to retain a domestic defence industry while seeking economies in weapons costs, they are often attracted by the prospects of international collaboration. A group of nations might agree to share both R&D and production work, or sharing might be confined to production work only, as in co-production arrangements.

International collaboration: is it worthwhile?
Collaborative ventures involving two or more nations in developing and producing a weapons project are often presented as a model for standardization and for creating a European defence industry capable

of competing with the USA. Current examples involving the UK, France, the Federal Republic of Germany and Italy include the Jaguar and Tornado strike aircraft, the Alpha Jet Trainer, helicopters and missiles. In the ideal case, European collaboration is supposed to lead to cost savings from the sharing of R&D expenditures, together with the scale and learning economies from the pooling of orders (e.g., the Tornado output of 809 units consists of 385 for the UK, 324 for Germany and 100 for Italy). For aircraft, a doubling of cumulative output is likely to lead to a 10 per cent reduction in unit production costs. However, political bargaining between the partner governments, bureaucracies and contractors creates considerable potential for inefficiency in collaborative ventures. In aerospace projects, this inefficiency can arise from:

1. The equality of work-sharing. Each partner nation demands its fair share of each sector of advanced technology and production. Work is allocated on equity and bargaining criteria rather than efficiency criteria. This means that procurement is *not* based on the principles of specialization and comparative advantage.
2. The duplication of development and production work, with each partner often demanding its own flight-testing centre and final assembly line.
3. The administrative and organizational costs resulting from excessive government bureaucracy and from duplicate organizations for procurement and supply. In other words, there are substantial transaction costs in establishing, running and monitoring collaborative arrangements.
4. Each nation demanding modifications for its order and thereby raising R&D costs and reducing the production economies from a long run of one type.

The result of political bargaining is that joint projects might take longer to develop and involve higher costs than a national programme. Critics have asserted that the delays on joint ventures can be measured by the cube root of the number of partners, while the collaboration premium on R&D approximates to the square root of the number of nations. If one applies these rules of thumb to the proposed five-nation European fighter aircraft, development time might be 70 per cent longer and R&D expenditures could be some 2.24 times the outlays on a national project! Experience with existing joint aircraft projects indicates that they involve *higher* R&D costs when compared with a national programme, possibly an extra 30 per cent. Joint production is also likely to be inefficient. If one assumes a 5 per cent collaboration premium on production work and a doubling of output compared with a national programme, a joint venture might save 5 per cent on unit production costs. This means that even with some collaborative inefficiencies, joint ventures can result in cost savings compared with a national project. However, the estimates of savings derive from comparing collaborative and national ventures. Ideally, a comparison is required between a joint venture and the cheapest supplier in the world market.

An alternative option to joint development and production is some form of licensed or co-production, or a work-sharing arrangement. These usually involve cost penalties, in the form of no learning economies and relatively short production runs, when compared with buying directly off the shelf. For example, the F16 co-production programme resulted in an extra 34 per cent cost penalty for the Europeans, compared with a direct purchase from the USA.[13] In return, the European nations believed they obtained benefits in the form of jobs, technology transfer, industrial modernization, military standardization and future export possibilities. Presumably their willingness to pay an extra 34 per cent reflected the value they placed upon these benefits. A similar example occurred with the UK purchase of Phantom aircraft, which involved a cost penalty of an extra 23-43 per cent, compared with a direct buy from the USA.

Conclusion
There are no cost-free policies, and difficult choices cannot be avoided. With a limited defence budget, any extra costs of buying British means less equipment for the armed forces with possible delays in delivery. In the case of aircraft, a broad, illustrative ranking of some of the cost implications of alternative procurement policies is shown in Table 8.4, using 100 as the base point for comparisons.[14] Faced with such information, voters might question the desirability of current UK procurement policy.

Table 8.4   The costs of aerospace policy options

Policy	Unit cost index
1. Buy USA	100
2. Buy UK (i) Average	130–150 (assume 140)
(ii) TSR-2	190–235
3. Joint projects	<125
4. (i) Co-production: F16	134
(ii) Work-sharing: UK Phantoms	123–143

If society wishes to introduce more cost efficiency into weapons procurement, then competition is a possible solution. A competitive procurement policy for the UK would have the following characteristics:

1. A willingness to shop around for weapons and not to restrict purchases to UK firms.
2. Abolition of entry barriers into the UK market, allowing foreign firms to compete for British defence business.
3. Competition which would not be restricted to a single specification. Rivalry is required for alternative specifications, which would indicate the extra costs of achieving different operational requirements.
4. Competition that applied at the design, prototype and production stages of procurement.
5. Competitively determined fixed-price contracts with penalty clauses for poor quality and late delivery.
6. These competitive principles would be applied to collaborative projects, the aim being to allocate R&D and production work on the basis of efficiency criteria and comparative advantage. Compensation should be offered to the potential losers from such a policy (e.g., manpower policies in the form of mobility, training and income deficiency payments).

Clearly, the introduction of real competition into UK weapons markets will be opposed by those firms currently benefiting from protection. Change is likely to be costly, but taxpayers will be eternally grateful!

Notes

1. D.L. Kirkpatrick and P.G. Pugh, 'Towards the Starship Enterprise', *Aerospace*, Journal of the Royal Aeronautical Society, May 1983, pp. 18-23.
2. P. Mitchell, 'Increasing the combined operational effectiveness of NATO's forces: the role of the Military Agency for Standardization', *NATO Review*, March 1984, p. 17.
3. A.H. Cornell, 'Collaboration in weapons and equipment', *NATO Review*, October 1980, p. 19.
4. K. Hartley, *NATO Arms Co-operation: A Study in Economics and Politics* (London: Allen & Unwin, 1983).
5. Cmnd. 9227-I, *Statement on the Defence Estimates 1984* (London: HMSO, 1984), p. 17.
6. *Ibid.*, p. 17.
7. *Ibid.*, p. 17.
8. Ministry of Defence, *Value for Money in Defence Equipment Procurement*, Defence Open Government Document 83/01 (London: October 1983).
9. I. Maddock, *Civil Exploitation of Defence Technology* (London: NEDC, 1983).
10. J.P. Dunne and R. Smith, 'The economic consequences of reduced UK military expenditure', *Cambridge Journal of Economics*, Vol. 8 (Sept. 1984), pp. 297-310.

11. K. Hartley and E. Lynk, 'Labour demand and allocation in the UK engineering industry: disaggregation, structural change and defence reviews', *Scottish Journal of Political Economy*, Vol. 30 (February 1983), pp. 42-53.
12. K. Hartley, *NATO Arms Co-operation* (London: Allen & Unwin, 1983).
13. M. Rich *et al.*, *Multinational Co-production of Military Aerospace Systems* (Rand, R-2861: Santa Monica, California, October 1981).
14. It must be stressed that the ranking is based on the *acquisition* costs for military aircraft only. Ideally, life-cycle costs are required and the examples need to include other weapons (e.g., missiles, warships, tanks). Also, the buy-US option usually requires at least some UK modifications, suggesting an index of 105.

Comment on Chapter 8
Farooq Hussain

There are a number of defence procurement problems for both the United Kingdom and the Alliance that have been presented in Keith Hartley's paper. The first of these concerns the effective application of research and development (R&D) resources to the design of technologically advanced weapon systems. Inefficiencies in the procurement process occur at a national level through the inability to manage adequately economies of scale, and for multinational collaboration through conflicting objectives and requirements. Hartley also raises important issues regarding the scope of departmental responsibilities for the formulation and execution of military procurement and industrial policy. For the purposes of this comment, there are two areas that may deserve some further expansion. The first concerns better collective use of the Alliance's R&D resources, and the second concerns improvements in NATO's procurement programmes.

In 1979, when Robert Komer launched his initiative for better armaments collaboration within the Alliance, William Perry, then the Director for Defense Research and Engineering at the Pentagon, posed a number of still unresolved questions.[1] If NATO's scientific expertise generally leads that of the Soviet Union and in many cases is significantly better funded, why does it take the Alliance so much longer to field weapon systems? The result has been that it is frequently possible for the Alliance to be discussing the implications of advanced military technology for arms control, while systems actually deployed are old and qualitatively inferior to comparable Soviet ones. This problem is particularly prevalent in conventional weapon systems: the Alliance not only takes much longer to deploy a given system, but once in service it remains there for long periods without significant upgrades in its performance (if these are possible).

If the Alliance's R&D base is stronger than that of the Soviet Union, then is the weakness in its application to military procurement due to unnecessary duplication, as is frequently suggested, or to other causes? Keith Hartley's paper suggests that there is an incentive for both the R&D and industrial establishments to produce technologically advanced weapons in order to compensate for the long periods between weapon system replacements. When a new system is being considered, the R&D and industrial establishments view it as an opportunity to maintain a capability at the cutting edge of their special skills. Hartley suggests as an alternative that the European military-industrial complex might adopt an incremental approach of small technological jumps from one generation of system to the next. This is very similar to the Soviet Union's method of deploying systems and gradually improving their capabilities as experience with the system grows.

This proposal does not seem very satisfactory for the following reasons. The principle strength of the Alliance's R&D base is that it is highly innovative. A cursory examination of a ten-year period in most sectors of science and technology with direct military applications shows that the advances come not from incremental improvements alone, but from dramatic changes brought about by new discoveries. But are the benefits worth the price? Another factor that needs to be considered is that the incremental approach will not be acceptable in the commercial sector. Although it is commonplace to assume that military R&D is the most advanced, this is rarely true today except in a very few areas where there are limited, if any, commercial applications to be considered. In computing, the commercial development dictates the kind of systems that can be considered for future military application. Many of these applications have led to very dramatic improvements in the cost-effectiveness of military forces. The potential hazard of the incremental approach is that weapon systems may become even less cost-effective than they are already, because their development could become very isolated from the pace of scientific and technological advance.

The problem for the United Kingdom and the Alliance would not seem to rest so much on the fact that advanced technology is expensive as that its application to the development of weapon systems is embroiled in the conflicting objectives and priorities of national policy and Alliance politics. For example, NATO manages a collective infrastructure budget and attempts to harmonize national procurement requirements with the collective interests of member nations. The infrastructure budget is spent heavily on the development of the NATO Integrated Communications System (which is several years behind schedule and uses for the most part commercial telecommunications technology), and cannot afford a replacement satellite. Another area is the NATO pipeline system for the distribution across Europe of petroleum, oil and lubricants. This system is made available to the commercial sector and is run profitably. The requirements for certain types of improvements to the NATO Air Defence Ground Environment also come from the infrastructure, and the programme for NATO Airborne Early Warning is managed by yet another NATO agency. There already exists within the Alliance a vast structure of committees and subcommittees capable of discussing any type of procurement coordination imaginable. The sad fact is that with a few exceptions the bulk of the NATO coordinated spending for the improvement of Europe's defence is spent badly.

Initiatives for collaboration between member nations in the procurement of weapon systems are made nationally and coordinated by the Alliance. The only executive authority held by the Alliance is over the management of the infrastructure-funded programmes. It follows that the chances of offering nationally sensitive procurement decisions to NATO for management are slim. In cases such as the NATO Frigate, the problems associated with an alliance-managed collaborative development are apparent and do not lead to improved cost-effectiveness, though this may not be the only criterion by which these programmes are judged. However, there is a contradiction in endorsing collaborative programmes on the basis that they help maintain industrial capability, while at the same time worrying about rising defence budgets. Hartley raises the additional problem of the differing priorities and interests between the various national ministries and industries. Thus, in negotiations for collaboration, the flexibility of the participants is constrained by the pressures of national interests. These pressures are always most severe in major weapons programmes; they need not be so in smaller ones.

Perhaps the most important issue arising from Keith Hartley's paper is whether present plans for future collaboration in defence procurement have sufficiently clear objectives and sobriety (as a result of past experience) to be successful. For military R&D, it is unlikely that much more coordination is either possible or useful. Ideas for a European DARPA,[2] for example, often fail to take into account the number of costly projects initiated by that agency which had to be abandoned as they failed, or were less successful than alternative approaches. A multinational agency entrusted with the pursuit of high-risk, high pay-off projects and given significant funding does not seem entirely suited to the mood of present times. There is not as much duplication in military research and development as is sometimes supposed. The difficulties that arise occur when two organizations from different countries are unable to share data to resolve problems of common interests. The present circumstances suggest that the prospects of improving the exchange of information between American and European scientists, beyond existing arrangements, will be poor. However, there can be no doubt that a detailed examination of the R&D process within the Alliance would be worthwhile, especially so if full account were taken of the independent R&D activities of the commercial sectors that are relevant to military applications. At a national level, a better sharing of interests and objectives in military R&D between the governmental R&D establishments and industry could indeed be of enormous value. Nor at present is there any office in NATO HQ capable of providing information on how the R&D activities of the member nations and those collectively undertaken by NATO agencies are set up, how they are progressing, or how much they are costing.

There can be little doubt that improved procurement collaboration will stimulate some sectors of industry in Europe, and that breaking the protectionism of the larger defence manufacturers to help smaller industries would be beneficial both to defence procurement and to the industrial health of individual nations. What is less obvious is how collaboration in defence procurement can contribute to reducing the rising costs associated with the development of new generations of weapon systems. If one major objective of collaborative procurement of weapon systems is to show the United States that Europe is doing more for its own defence, that effort should not be measured by the numbers of new systems likely to be developed and deployed, because the chances of significantly affecting the present pattern of procurement, with or without further collaboration, look bleak.

Notes
1. Robert Komer was Undersecretary for policy in the US Department of Defense at the time.
2. DARPA: Defense Advanced Research Projects Agency, part of the Department of Defense, Washington D.C.

9   Conclusion
John Roper

Much of the discussion on the first five papers turned on the implications of the end of consensus on defence policy. This is not a phenomenon unique to Britain; the discussions on the possible deployment of Enhanced Radiation Warheads (the Neutron bomb) and of cruise and Pershing II missiles, and the deterioration in East–West relations following the Soviet invasion of Afghanistan, have led to a prolonged public debate on defence in most West European countries.

The discussion of new systems, and in some cases of their war-fighting capabilities, and the end of détente have caused many who had previously taken the invulnerability of nuclear deterrence for granted seriously to consider the risk that nuclear weapons might be used. This in itself has reduced confidence in deterrence, since the build-up of nuclear weapons is itself seen as threat, one which in the view of some is as serious as the threat they are intended to deter. What is now at issue is the fundamental question of whether we should have a policy based, or largely based, on nuclear deterrence, rather than which particular sorts of weapon are necessary for such deterrence. In the view of Ken Booth, this has made it necessary to examine alternative policies very carefully. He admitted that any alternative policy would certainly have problems, but argued that there was no escape from ambivalence in defence policies.

In the United States, the discussions on the one hand of war-fighting aspects of Limited Nuclear Options and on the other hand of the President's Strategic Defence Initiative are interpreted by some as indicating that traditional views of deterrence are no longer considered adequate. The advocacy of 'no first use' of nuclear weapons by leading Democrats and statements by Henry Kissinger since 1979 on the US nuclear commitment to Europe raise doubts among many Europeans that extended deterrence still exists.

The fact that major opposition parties in many European countries do not accept the NATO 'dual-track' decision of December 1979 has already had its effects on the workings of Alliance institutions. Even relatively technical matters within NATO are now under much greater public scrutiny, and discussions such as those in the Defence

Planning Committee, which until 1979 were primarily technical, are now much more political.

In the discussion of a variety of possible changes to both British defence policy and that of the Alliance as a whole, there emerged three criteria against which change should be judged: (1) what the impact of the proposed change in defence policy would be on the United States, and on its security commitment to Europe; (2) how far such a change would discourage the Soviet Union from the use of force in Europe, or the Soviet political offensive in Western Europe; and (3) how far it would increase the sense of security of one's own people.

The most radical change proposed for NATO strategy would be the introduction of a 'no first use' of nuclear weapons doctrine. While there was general agreement that NATO was anxious to move to a situation in which there would be no need for an early first use of nuclear weapons, there was no agreement that it would be possible or desirable to move to 'no first use' on the Central Front. It was felt by many that the deterrent doctrine of flexible response remained valid and that NATO needed to preserve the deterrent threat that in the last resort it could use its nuclear weapons.

To move to 'no first use' would require a substantial strengthening of NATO's conventional forces. There was a wide measure of agreement that, given the current financial and demographic constraints, it was difficult to produce proposals for this that carried military conviction. It may be possible with new technology to undertake by conventional means military tasks that up till now could only be done by nuclear warheads, and to undertake with missiles what was previously done by manned aircraft. However, the introduction of such technology is unlikely to be carried out cheaply or quickly and will probably be countered by similar Soviet developments. Indeed, one participant stressed the considerable danger now posed to NATO by Soviet non-nuclear missile capabilities which, in the view of some American analysts, give them for the first time conventional options in Europe which would not be diminished in any way by the current discussions on nuclear arms control.

Conscription was suggested by Ken Booth as one method of enhancing Britain's conventional defence capabilities, and thus enabling Britain and NATO to move to a non-nuclear policy. It is discussed by both Ken Hunt and Ron Smith in their papers, in which they say that it would require a 15 per cent increase in defence spending even after allowing for the savings from the cancellation of Trident, and that there would not be a proportionate increase in defence effectiveness.

There was considerable discussion of the Trident programme. It was recognized that the case for maintaining a strategic nuclear deterrent is a political one and that it is not possible to find any quantifiable basis for assessing its strategic value as compared with conventional forces. This makes it difficult to have useful discussions about its cost in relation to the rest of the defence budget. Indeed, the view was expressed by some, but challenged by Leo Pliatzky among others, that money saved by the cancellation of Trident would not be available for other defence expenditure but would revert to the Treasury.

On the other hand, there can be discussion on whether Trident is in fact the most cost-effective strategic system. This would turn on the criteria used in judging the alternatives. If the two criteria referred to in government White Papers, the ability to inflict unacceptable damage on 'key aspects of Soviet state power' (the so-called 'Moscow criterion') and the requirement for a high degree of readiness and invulnerability to surprise attack, are absolute, then the choice is clearly limited. Some felt that these criteria could be relaxed, which would permit the consideration of various less expensive options. A further criterion which might be relevant in considering alternatives to Trident is the impact of different systems on arms control negotiations. It can be argued that this counts against the Trident programme, since it consists of only four submarines, each with sixteen missiles and a large number of warheads. It would be difficult to make any reductions in the number of submarines and maintain a credible deterrent. If the question of alternative systems were to be re-examined, then the advantages of commonality should not be over-looked. The cost overruns on Chevaline must serve as an awful warning to those wishing to propose a national solution. As Lawrence Freedman said, the choice can be seen as one between a production-line Rolls-Royce and a custom-built Mini.

Lawrence Freedman also suggested that one of the greatest successes of British nuclear defence policy is that it is perceived by Washington as being about sharing nuclear risks, whereas in fact it is about achieving nuclear sanctuary. The same point was made in a different way by Peter Stratmann, who said that Britain and France should think carefully about which political/strategic rationale they wished to use for their strategic nuclear forces. These forces can be justified as a national insurance policy against a US withdrawal of its nuclear guarantee to Europe, or alternatively as being held in trust for other non-nuclear countries in Europe. The first rationale is one that might suggest to other countries in Europe the uncertainty of the American guarantee, and this might have a contagious effect upon those who also want to get insurance policies for their own national survival in the event of an American withdrawal. In some circumstances this could lead some countries to neutralism. The second approach would stress that British and French forces are a complementary European deterrent and it could therefore be reassuring to other Europeans.

The other aspect of national defence policy that was examined for possible savings was Britain's commitments outside the NATO area and its capabilities for such out-of-area activities. Although in the late 1960s and early 1970s it had been possible to make considerable savings by the run-down of these activities, there is no longer a great deal of opportunity for saving here. With the exception of the capital costs of the Falklands – the replacement costs of ships lost and the cost of the airstrip and other facilities in the islands – much of the other expenditure is incurred by forces which are dual-earmarked and would be spent wherever they were stationed. While much of British defence activity outside the NATO area is appreciated by the United States, which sees it as complementary to its own activities, it is criticized for exactly this reason by many in Britain who are critical of US involvement in the Third World. They see it as an outdated relic of the Empire.

Britain's relations with the United States and its allies in Western Europe were seen to be in a period of transition. The dissatisfaction that clearly exists in Congress and elsewhere in Washington with the Europeans in general, because of what is perceived as their failure to provide for their own defence, does not distinguish between the performance of different Europeans. At the same time, there is some evidence of declining public confidence in Britain about US policies and programmes. American weapon systems deployed in Britain are no longer as successful in reassuring the British public. The attitude of public opinion to the question of the possible dual-key control of cruise missiles was a recent illustration of this.

On the other hand, there is wide agreement among policy-makers on the growing importance of our security relations with Western Europe, although it is not clear that this has extended to the public at large. While the particular role that would be seen for European cooperation in defence matters clearly varies among the political parties, many share the view that if American–European relations are likely to come under stress, it is important for Britain to be closer to Europe. In the discussion, however, both Pierre Lellouche and Peter Stratmann stressed the adverse effects on Europe that the Labour Party's proposals could create. They could in Pierre Lellouche's view lead to a Balkanization of Europe in security matters with each country seeking its own national solution.

One area in which a good deal has been expected of European collaboration has been in joint programmes for procurement of defence equipment. This, it was seen, can conflict with national objectives for defence policy, and indeed one participant expressed horror at the thought that the renaissance of the WEU and the IEPG might mean that yet another Whitehall department – the Foreign Office – would get increasingly involved in trying to influence defence equipment decisions. Decisions on defence procurement are already made in a way which has to take multiple objectives into account. While the principle that public purchasing should be organized as cheaply and as cost-effectively as possible was constantly repeated, it was seen to be difficult to establish general rules for procurement decisions. This seems to mean falling back on a case-by-case approach which, according to the more cynical of those present, means in practice that the rules can be changed each time.

Defence procurement, it was argued, is different from other procurement, since in defence one is always having to match and better the threat. Second-class equipment would mean putting at risk the lives of one's servicemen and ultimately the safety of one's country. In these circumstances, if there is no tough budget constraint, the soldier and the scientist have a common interest in 'gold-plating' – pressing for the last 5 per cent of performance irrespective of the extra cost. The only force operating in the opposite direction is the commander in the field, who would rather have something now than something slightly better in five years' time.

There was some scepticism about the view the present government has expressed, that the introduction of a greater degree of competition and contracting-out will enable very considerable savings to be made. Although there are clear advantages in such a policy, it was pointed out that it would not necessarily save civil service manpower and there were some high-technology projects in which there would be only one UK supplier.

In a situation of rising unit costs and shorter production runs, there was general agreement on the need for increased international collaboration. The greatest need for such collaboration will arise in those items for which R&D costs are already very high in relation to production costs. Rising unit costs have already forced Britain out of the production of full-scale aircraft-carriers and strategic bombers. Chevaline and Nimrod both present warnings of the difficulties of trying to run projects on a purely national basis. It is by no means clear that it will be economically sensible for Britain to build a successor to the Type 42 Frigate or the present generation of main battle tank on its own, or for Europe to build a successor to the Tornado aircraft. Neither is it clear what the mechanism is for ensuring such collaboration. It will require both agreement between governments on operational requirements, and agreement between companies in many cases to establish international collaborative consortia. The wide variation in the patterns of relationships that exist between Ministries of Defence, service staffs, research establishments and defence contractors in different European countries means that the implementation in practice of the frequent ministerial expression of support for collaboration will continue to be difficult.

The conference tried to assess the impact of the switch to level funding on the defence budget. It was suggested that the decisions on the level of defence spending had to be seen against the government's intention that there should be no growth in public expenditure overall. In these circumstances, the level of defence expenditure will not be removed from controversy, and those with other public expenditure priorities will continue to cast covetous eyes at the £18,000 billion allocated to defence.

It was agreed that there will be growing pressure on the resources available for defence equipment in the coming decade, because of the shock of adjusting from an average real growth of equipment budgets of 5-6 per cent a year to zero growth, the growing demands of the Trident programme and the lack of adequate provision for inflation in the government's plans. This may not lead to a formal Defence Review of the kind known in the past, at least not before the next General Election, but there will have to be adjustments in the programme, and they could be achieved by the traditional means of stretching programmes over a longer period, and by making economies on logistics, training and readiness. This can have a significant impact on defence effectiveness, but it is considerably less visible than cutting a programme or abandoning a role or mission.

If this is not enough and the Services' roles and missions come up again for scrutiny, there will be the traditional political and diplomatic arguments that BAOR is sacrosanct. Indeed, Peter Stratmann told the conference that it would be virtually impossible for any British cuts to be compensated for by either the Federal Republic or the United States. Such cuts would instead be likely to have a snowballing effect which would result in a lowering of the nuclear threshold. On the other hand, it was argued that, if anything, there was now a stronger case for surface ships in view of the increased anti-submarine effectiveness of towed array sonar which has become apparent since John Nott's analysis in 1981.

The RAF, however, might once more be in the firing line, with the project for a Future European Combat Aircraft. There will no doubt be controversy about the need for another generation of manned aircraft in view of the growing capabilities of non-nuclear missiles. Such military arguments will probably be weighed against the industrial and political arguments about the necessity to maintain a high-technology European aerospace industry.

If the 1980s are going to find in the end a new consensus on defence policy in Britain, some suggestions of its form emerged from the papers and the discussion at the conference.

1. There would be greater emphasis on the effectiveness of conventional forces if the resources could be found to achieve this. This augmentation of the conventional component of deterrence would enable less emphasis to be placed on nuclear weapons, and NATO could move to an explicit policy of 'no early first use'.

2. There would be more emphasis on developing an effective European pillar of NATO. This would result in better European political and military analysis, including perhaps a European threat assessment, and also significantly increase the share of defence equipment which is procured on a European collaborative basis.

3. There would be a renewed attempt to re-establish the basis for political détente. This would probably involve both macro-détente between the superpowers and micro-détente between individual countries in Eastern and Western Europe. It should be linked with progress in arms control in the nuclear, conventional and confidence-building areas.

It will not be easy to re-establish consensus. There will be inevitable conflicts between policies that deter the Soviet Union and those that reassure one's own population. Any change in policy will take time, since allies must be persuaded and new equipment obtained to implement the new posture. It is possible to indicate the direction in which one wants to proceed, but change in defence policy is very slow in practice. Politicians tend to have a time horizon which is limited to four or five years – the period between elections – but they must remember that changes in defence policy are likely to take fifteen to twenty years to implement.

Annex to Chapter 6

Calculating expenditure in cost terms

The expenditure figures in all the main tables are expressed in 1983/4 cost terms, i.e., constant GDP prices. These were derived from the cash figures contained in the government's Expenditure Plans 1984/5 to 1986/7, Cmnd. 9143, by deflating by a market price GDP deflator constructed on a financial year basis. For the years 1978/9 to 1982/3, this deflator was constructed from data contained in Economic Trends Annual Supplement, 1984 edition. For the years 1983/4 and 1984/5, we have incorporated the assumption contained in the PEWP that the GDP deflator will rise by 5 per cent per annum. Up to 1985/6 and 1986/7, GDP prices are assumed to follow the projections contained in the Financial Statement and Budget Report 1984: namely, to grow by 4.25 per cent and 4 per cent per annum.

In connection with the GDP deflator, we have used the data and assumptions which seem to have underlain the cash plans in Cmnd. 9143. Since the PEWP was published there have been, of course, a number of data revisions to the past estimates of the GDP deflator, but these have not appreciably altered the picture of cost expenditure trends. From 1982/3 to 1983/4, the GDP deflator rose by 4.4 per cent,[1] slightly less than the assumption of Cmnd. 9143. To the extent that GDP inflation turns out to be less (or more) than forecast by the government, the cash plans of Cmnd. 9143 will clearly imply larger (or smaller) levels of expenditure in cost terms. This is important especially in variant A, in which it has been assumed for some programmes (see Sections 2, 3 and 4 below) that spending remains flat in cost terms at its 1986/87 planned level. This must be kept in mind when considering the implied expenditure projections.

Public expenditure projections: methodology and assumptions

1. Education and Science, Health and Personal Social Services, and Social Security

The education and science expenditure projections are derived by applying costs per pupil/student by educational institution to estimates of future pupil/student numbers. The main sources for future pupil and student numbers were respectively DES Report on Education No. 97, Pupils and School Leavers: Future Numbers (1982), and DES Report on Education No. 100, Demand for Higher Education in Great Britain 1984–2000 (1984). The original analysis was based on 1982/3 unit costs and focused on the years 1989/90 and 1994/5.[2] The figures for 1988/9 and 1993/4 are based on linear interpolations of these projections adjusted for earnings and a number of other factors. It was assumed that the science budget remains flat in cost terms and that capital expenditure remains a constant proportion of current spending. In order to derive expenditure projections for the UK as a whole, all expenditure on education and science in Scotland, Wales and Northern Ireland was assumed to grow in line with that of England.

The expenditure projections shown in variants A and B assume that pay remains a constant proportion of the education and science budget up to 1988/9; in other words, that pupil/teacher ratios remain constant and that pay remains flat in cost terms. From 1988/9 onwards, pay is assumed to grow in line with private earnings at 1.5 per cent per annum in cost terms. No allowance is made in these projections for any extra cost associated with contracting (and expanding) the workforce in line with pupil/student numbers; nor is there any allowance for any improvement in provision. In the case of variant C, pay is assumed to follow the private sector from 1983/4 onwards. Allowance is also made for an increase in the participation of the under fives from 40 to 50 per cent by 1993/4, and higher education numbers are assumed to be at the top end of the range given in the recent DES projections (see above).

Health and Personal Social Services
The HPSS expenditure projections are derived by applying age-related per capita health costs to OPCS population projections. Capital expenditure is assumed to grow in line with current spending, and in order to make expenditure projections for the UK as a whole, it has been assumed that expenditure in Scotland, Wales and Northern Ireland grows in line with spending in England. Adjustments have also been made to allow for earnings growth, relative price effects and efficiency savings.

The age-related unit costs used to allow for the effects of demography are a combination of NIESR estimates[3] and, for the Family Practitioner Service, those published by the DHSS. Since these costs are net of charges, it is implicitly assumed that there will be no significant change in the real level or composition of health charges for the next decade. In the case of non-pay current expenditure, it is assumed throughout that in the case of the Health and Community Health Service and the FPS, prices will rise by 1.3 and 2.5 per cent per annum ahead of the GDP deflator. This is the assumption which used to be made by the DHSS itself.[4] We also assume that efficiency savings of 0.2 per cent per annum will be made on the whole programme. No allowance has been made for a shift towards community care, which would be likely to produce additional expenditure, nor for the upward trend in Personal Social Services unit costs.[5]

The expenditure totals for HPSS differ according to assumptions made about earnings growth. Variants A and B assume that index-linked pay (assumed to be 70 per cent of the HCHS wage bill and all of the FPS wage bill) grows in line with private earnings by 1.5 per cent per annum from 1983/4 onwards. From 1988/9 all pay in the HPSS is assumed to rise in line with the private sector. In contrast, variant C assumes that all HPSS pay grows in line with private earnings over the next decade.

Social Security
The construction of the social security expenditure projections is best understood if the programme is divided into three main components: National Insurance expenditure (contributory benefits), other social security expenditure (non-contributory benefits) and expenditure on administration. In the case of the last component, we have assumed that it remains constant in

cost terms over the next decade (but see the adjustment for wages growth below); the construction of expenditure projections for the first two categories is explained below.

Projections of NI expenditure are estimates derived from those contained in the GAD Quinquennial Review.[6] It is assumed that unemployment remains flat and that the numbers contracting out of the state pension scheme remain constant.

Non-contributory benefits such as Child Benefit and Family Income Supplement have been assumed to grow in line with the demographic projections for children for all variants. Single-parent families are assumed to increase as a proportion of total families at half the rate of increase of the past ten years, and this is reflected in projected expenditure on the appropriate benefits. Since increases in earnings-related NI benefits will involve lower expenditure on means-tested benefits, an allowance has been made for this; we estimate that approximately 20–25 per cent of ERPS will be offset by reduced Supplementary Benefit.

In variants A and B, we have assumed that benefits are uprated in line with prices, and wage costs (of administration) are assumed to remain flat in cost terms until 1988/9 and then to grow by 1.5 per cent per annum. In variant C, benefits are uprated in line with earnings and wages grow in line with those in the private sector from 1983/4 onwards.

2. Defence
In variant A, we have assumed that expenditure on defence remains flat in cost terms at its planned 1986/7 level, as set out in Cmnd. 9143. Variant B assumes that the NATO commitment of real increases in defence spending of 3 per cent per annum is honoured up to 1985/6 but grows at 2 per cent on average over the decade as a whole. Variant C, our top end of the range, assumes that defence expenditure grows by 3 per cent per annum throughout the period.

3. Agriculture, Fisheries, Food and Forestry; Law, Order and Protective Services; and Employment
Variant A assumes that the level of spending on these programmes remains flat in cost terms at its planned 1986/7 level, calculated on the basis of Cmnd. 9143. In variant B, expenditure is assumed to be at the mid-point of a linear extrapolation based on past trends (1978/9 to 1983/4) and future plans (1983/4 to 1986/7). This calculation involved regressing deflated expenditure on a linear time trend and a constant for these two periods for each programme, and then projecting forward. Projections based on past trends and future plans are shown in full in Table 6.A. We have used the projections based on the past trends of 1978/9 to 1983/4 to provide totals for variant C.

4. Trade and Industry, etc; Energy; Transport; Housing and Other Programmes
In variant A, expenditure on these remaining programmes is assumed to remain flat in cost terms at the planned 1986/7 level, as derived from Cmnd. 9143. Variant B differs from A chiefly because real earnings growth from 1988/9 onwards (in line with the private sector) is not assumed to be contained within the 1986/7 level of planned expenditure. In the case of energy, it is assumed that the programme will break even; the expenditure projection for

Table 6.A.   Public expenditure projections by selected programme calculated by extrapolating forward from past trends or future plans expressed in cost terms^a

	£bn 1983/4 cost terms	
	1993/4	
Expenditure implied by:	past trends	future plans
Agriculture, Fisheries, Food & Forestry	3.4	0.7
Employment	5.0	2.9
Transport	4.5	3.3
Law, Order and Protective Services	7.0	4.6

Source: NIESR.
^{a} See section 3 for an explanation of the construction of these estimates.

transport is a mid-point between an extrapolation based on past trends and one based on future plans (see Section 3 above). For variant C, earnings in all these programmes, with the exception of energy, are assumed to grow in line with the private sector throughout the next decade. Energy is again assumed to break even.

Notes
1. *Economic Trends*, September 1984.
2. Details are contained in a forthcoming NIESR discussion paper, 'Public Expenditure: The Next Ten Years', by M.S. Levitt and M.A.S. Joyce.
3. NIESR estimates yield slightly lower costs for the elderly and the young than is implied by the Department's estimates.
4. See the Second Report from the Social Services Committee, Session 1981/82, 1982 White Paper: 'Public Expenditure on the Social Services, Minutes of Evidence Volume II', Cmnd. 306-v, p. 190.
5. See the Memorandum submitted by A. Webb and G. Wistow in Cmnd. 306-iv, pp. 168-182.
6. This presents projections at 1981/2 earnings levels, which we have converted to 1983/4 cost terms; we also assume real earnings growth of 1½ per cent per annum. (National Insurance Fund Long Term Financial Estimates, House of Commons, 19 July 1982.)

Index